PRESENT TENSE

The Canadian Novel

Edited and with Introductions by John Moss

Contents are indicates as **Author** (Works) *Critics*

Volume I. Here and Now

Introduction. **Margaret Atwood** (The Edible Woman, Sufacing, Lady Oracle) *John Lauber, Catherine McLay, Wilfred Cude.* **Robertson Davies** Fifth Business, The Manticore, World of Wonders) *Gordon Roper, Ellen D. Warwick.* **Margaret Laurence** (The Diviners, several earlier novels) *Frank Pesando, Cheryl Cooper, Clara Thomas.* **Alice Munro** (Lives of Girls and Women) *J.R. (Tim) Struthers, Miriam Packer.* **Mordecai Richler** (The Apprenticeship of Duddy Kravitz, St. Urbain's Horseman) *Tom Marshall, John Moss.* **Rudy Wiebe** (And Peace Shall Destroy Many, The Blue Mountains of China, The Temptations of Big Bear, The Scorched-Wood People) *Hildegard E. Tiessen, Allan Dueck.* (204 pp)

Volume II. Beginnings (Expanded)

Introduction. **Frances Brooke** (The History of Emily Montague) *Mary Jane Edwards, Linda Shohet.* **Thomas Chandler Haliburton** (The Clockmaker) *Thomas H. Raddall, Northrop Frye.* **Major John Richardson** (Wacousta) *Robert Lecker, Michael Hurley.* **Susanna Moodie** (Roughing It in the Bush) *Sherrill E. Grace, Marian Fowler.* **James De Mille** (A Strange Manuscript Found in a Copper Cylinder) *George Woodcock, Kenneth J. Hughes.* **Sara Jeannette Duncan** (The Imperialist) *Alfred G. Bailey, Joseph M. Zezulka.* **Stephen Leacock** (Sunshine Sketches of a Little Town) *Douglas Mantz, Tom Marshall.* **Charles G.D. Roberts** (The Heart that Knows, Barbara Ladd, The Heart of the Ancient Wood, In the Morning of Time) *John Moss.* **Major John Richardson** (Wacousta) **William Kirby** (The Golden Dog), **Gilbert Parker** (The Seats of the Mighty) *L.R. Early.* (216 pp)

Volume III. Modern Times

Introduction. **Frederick Philip Grove** (Settlers of the Marsh) *Lee Briscoe Thompson, Henry Makow.* **Martha Ostenso** (Wild Geese) *Stanley S. Atharton.* **Morley Callaghan** (Luke Baldwin's Vow, Close to the Sun Again, "Getting on in the World") *Wilfred Cude.* **Sinclair Ross** (As for Me and My House) *John Moss.* **Hugh MacLennan** (Barometer Rising, The Watch that Ends the Night) *David Arnason, Elspeth Cameron.* **Elizabeth Smart** (By Grand Central Station I Sat Down and Wept) *Lorraine McMullen, John Goddard.* **Ethel Wilson** (Swamp Angel, Hetty Dorval, The Innocent Travellers, Lilly's Story) *Donna E. Smyth, George Woodcock.* **Ernest Buckler** (The Mountain and the Valley) *Alan R. Young.* **Sheila Watson** (The Double Hook) *George Bowering.* **W.O. Mitchell** (Who Has Seen the Wind, The Vanishing Point) *Ken Mitchell, Catherine McLay.* (264 pp)

Each volume is 5 1/2" x 8 1/2", illustrated, $16.96 Cl. $8.95 Pa.

Order from: **NC Press**, 31 Portland St, Toronto, Ontario M5V 2V9

THE CANADIAN NOVEL
VOLUME IV

PRESENT TENSE

A Critical Anthology
Edited with an Introductory Essay by

JOHN MOSS

NC Press Limited
Toronto 1985

PHOTO CREDITS

Michael Ondaatje, Carl Schurer
Mavis Gallant, John Mastromonaco
Robert Kroetsch, Nick Yunge-Bateman
Matt Cohen, Don Summerhayes
Carol Shields, Keo Nishizeki
David Helwig, Nancy Helwig
Jack Hodgins, Wayne Hiebert
Timothy Findley, Graeme Gibson
Audrey Thomas, Vancouver Sun

Cover illustration: Alex Colville, *Target Pistol and Man*, 1980, used by permission.

Canadian Cataloguing in Publication Data
Main entry under title:
The Canadian novel: critical anthology
Includes bibliographical references.
Contents: v. 1. Here and now — v. 2. Beginnings — v. 3. Modern Times — v. 4. Present tense.
ISBN 0-919601-67-7 (v. 4, bound). — ISBN 0-919601-65-0 (v. 4, pbk.).
1. Canadian fiction (English) — 20th century — History and criticism — Addresses, essays, lectures.*
I. Moss, John, 1940-
PS8187.C35 1978   C813'.54'09   C781285-9
PR9192.2.C35 1978

Printed and bound in Canada

We would like to thank the Ontario Arts Council and the Canada Council for their assistance in the production of this book.

New Canada Publications, a division of NC Press Limited, Box 4010, Station A, Toronto, Ontario, Canada, M5W 1H8

CONTENTS

INTRODUCTION

Caroline Walker,
Publisher
NC Press Limited,

Dear Caroline,
You asked on the phone a couple of days ago for my response to the hesitation of the SSHRC (Social Sciences and Humanities Research Council) about funding PRESENT TENSE. The following is my introduction in progress, which is probably the clearest articulation of my ideas on the subject.

*   *   *

Present Tense is the culmination of a series intended to gather a variety of essays on significant phases in the development of the Canadian novel, from its beginnings to the contemporary and postmodern works represented by this fourth volume. The intention has always been to offer the best possible examples of criticism in the widest range of approaches, so that each book would contribute not only to a better understanding of fiction, but also a better understanding of the art of essay writing and literary criticism in Canada.

In order to meet these criteria, I discovered very quickly that previously published essays were not always exactly what the volume required and new works had to be commissioned/requested/inveigled from people working in the field. The first volume consisted of four originals and ten reprints, some in substantially modified form. The next two used increasingly more unpublished material — and of the sixteen essays in Present Tense, by some of the most interesting critics writing in Canada today, not a single one has been previously published. The series that began as a service has become an important original source — for other critics, for scholars, for writers and, most important of all, for students of literature, both teachers and their pupils at secondary, undergraduate and post-graduate levels.

The phases of the Canadian novel marked by each volume are matters of editorial convenience up to a point, but they also represent genuinely discrete stages in the novel's development. There were a number of very significant early works, culminating with the best of Stephen Leacock, which have little enough in common, except in historical retrospect. These are considered in *Beginnings* (due to the exigencies of publication, the volume numbers do not correspond to chronological sequence but rather to order of appearance). There were a number of writers such as Margaret Laurence and Robertson Davies who clearly represented the contemporary achievement of the Canadian novel; the essays in *Here and Now* are devoted to their works. There were also a number of important novels belonging to that historically ambiguous period known as "modern"; many of their authors, such as Callaghan, MacLennan and Mitchell, are still writing today, while others have retired from the scene or have, like Grove, Ostenso and Wilson, long since died. These are the subject of the middle volume, called *Modern Times*.

The scope of the first three volumes in *The Canadian Novel* series might best be grasped by a straightforward listing of writers' names:

Frances Brooke	Elizabeth Smart
Thomas Chandler Haliburton	Ethel Wilson
Major John Richardson	Ernest Buckler
Susanna Moodie	Sheila Watson
James De Mille	W. O. Mitchell
Sara Jeanette Duncan	Margaret Atwood
Stephen Leacock	Robertson Davies
Frederick Philip Grove	Margaret Laurence
Martha Ostenso	Alice Munro
Morley Callaghan	Mordecai Richler
Sinclair Ross	Rudy Wiebe
Hugh MacLennan	

In this list may be seen the mainstream of the Canadian tradition. If another list were compiled of the essayists who have contributed to this series (most writers are considered by two or more critics), a good cross-section of the best people working in the field of Canadian studies would be apparent, including some of our most distinguished writer-critics, a number of whom have won multiple Governor General's Awards, and most of whom have written numerous books (several hundred, altogether), and some for whom this was their first publication.

What is missing in the above list, apart from a few notables like Mavis Gallant and Norman Levine, is any sense of the prophetic, any indication of where we are going from here. While many of these writers may yet delight us with new works, none, with the probable exception of Margaret Atwood, is likely to surprise us. And that is where *Present Tense* comes in — to fill a need, to provide essays and insights about the contemporary and postmodern novelists working among us towards an unknown, unpredictable, but exciting future. These are the writers who live on the edge of the present, whose work fibrillates with the tensions of experimentation, nervous with the possibilities opened by risk and chance. These for the most part are novelists who understand much about the art of fiction, and whether minimalist or extravagant fabulist, write to fulfill their own expectations of what fiction should be and do.

There is an over-lap between the writers listed below, whose work is considered in *Present Tense*, and writers in two of the previous three volumes. In many ways Robertson Davies is a postmodern Victorian and Robert Kroetsch is a Victorian postmodernist. Alice Munro is quintessentially modern in theme and characterization, contemporary in her social vision and her exquisitely transparent prose, and postmodern in her marvellous dexterity with time and point of view.

These are the people whose work is discussed in *Present Tense*:

Timothy Findley	Hugh Hood
Jack Hodgins	Matt Cohen
Mavis Gallant	Marian Engel
Michael Ondaatje	Audrey Thomas
Norman Levine	George Bowering
Carol Shields	Robert Kroetsch
David Helwig	

What makes these writers a group? As much as anything, the way the Canadian tradition is presently perceived.

In part because they have until recently lived their working lives outside Canada, Gallant and Levine have seemed beyond the mainstream. Subject to different influences, perhaps, their work seems somehow separate, more at home with such younger writers as Jack Hodgins and Michael Ondaatje. It would be foolish, however, to generalize about any of these writers in order to contain them in some critical construct, to justify their inclusion together. It would be as easy to argue that Ondaatje belongs in the company of Sheila Watson (or of Salman Rushdie or of William Gass, for that matter), or that Bowering should better be aligned with Frances Brooke or with James De Mille or with Elizabeth Smart. As valid a series might possibly have been arranged according to genre, region, theme, gender or the like. For *The Canadian Novel*, the culmination of both series and subject is in this present volume, *Present Tense*.

I have been careful not to label all of these writers postmodern. Historically, that may be the period we live in, those of us who have come into consciousness of ourselves between two holocausts, the last which took seventy million lives, and the next. But critically, in terms of literature, the term "postmodern" carries with it certain criteria to which not all of these writers subscribe or conform. Gallant's *Green Water, Green Sky* is structurally postmodern, although published in 1959, while Marian Engel's *Lunatic Villas*, which appeared only a couple of years ago, is not. Matt Cohen, who is clearly one of our most "contemporary" writers, is not in any sense postmodern in his novels (the short stories are another matter), while Audrey Thomas, who writes of age-old conditions, especially as encountered by women, most certainly is. And so it goes: is Timothy Findley postmodern, or do his last two novels simply capitalize on the achievements of those, like Kroetsch, Bowering and Hodgins who are outrageously so? Are David Helwig and Carol Shields? Certainly they show the influences of postmodernism — in structure, in language, in what I would call narrative minimalism. Yet they equally display in their work a thorough grounding in the same nineteenth century traditions of plot and character that informs the writings of Margaret Laurence, and in the modernists' concern for psychological, rather than social, verisimilitude and the extinction of authorial personality which typify the work of Hugh MacLennan and Ernest Buckler. And is Hugh Hood postmodern? What about Norman Levine? Both incorporate self into their art, not only as voice but as context; both draw the reader's attention to the novel as process, to the reader reading. Yet in some respects, both are more conservative than even a Morley Callaghan or a Stephen Leacock, more "old-fashioned."

The point is, postmodernism, like any other literary rubric, is just that, a label, a critical convenience, and not an aesthetic. (Think of the words "romantic" and "classic" and "modern": all labels, for critical and academic convenience; derived, by necessity, against chaos.) As a label, "postmodern" can be applied with varying degrees of accuracy or authenticity to a wide variety of works. As a label, it may be taken to have certain referents. In this book, it is purposely twinned with the term "contemporary." All of the writers considered are contemporary, and to some degree reflect in their writing those aspects of postmodernism which are most forcefully promulgated in the works of such non-Canadians as Italo Calvino, Alain Robbe-Grillet and Gabriel Garcia Marquez. As contemporary writers, whose work shows clear evidence of familiarity with contemporary and/or postmodern aesthetic theory, these Canadian writers comfortably share the common critical context provided by *Present Tense*.

In an essay called "The Literature of Replenishment," published in 1980 by *The Atlantic Monthly*, the sometime-postmodern American novelist John Barth struggles towards a definition of literary postmodernism. His conclusion, that its best practitioners fold together premodernist and modernist ingredients into a democratically accessible synthesis, seems hardly satisfactory. Barth acknowledges the difficulty of differentiation in a sequence of quotations which does more to illuminate these three discretely separate modes of fiction than anything he can say about them.

It is quite one thing to compare a line of Verdi or Tennyson or Tolstoy with a line of Stravinsky or Eliot or Joyce to recognize that you have put the nineteenth century behind you:

> Happy families are all alike; every unhappy family is unhappy in its own way. (Leo Tolstoy, *Anna Karenina*, tr. Constance Garnett)

> riverrun, past Eve's and Adam's, from swerve of shore to bend of bay, brings us by a commodium vicus of recirculation back to Howth Castle and Environs. (James Joyce, *Finnegans Wake*)

It is quite another thing to characterize the difference between these two famous opening sentences, to itemize the aesthetic principles — premodernist and modernist — from which each issues, and then to pro ceed to a great postmodernist opening sentence and show where its its aesthetics resemble and differ from those of its parents, so to speak, and those of its grandparents, respectively:

> Many years later, as he faced the firing squad, Colonel Aureliano Buendia was to remember that distant afternoon when his father took him to discover ice. (Gabriel Garcia Marquez, *One Hundred Years of Solitude*, tr. Gregory Rabassa)

It is difficult to characterize the differences, yes, and yet these quotations are manifestly as different as the cultures which spawned them.

The first bespeaks a rational middle-class realism; the second, the virtues of discontinuous and esoteric eclecticism. The third is postmodern. In the passage from Marquez, the reader does not receive (premodernism), perceive (modernism), but rather completes the possibilities of text, indeterminant as they may be. Our pleasure in reading Marquez is in the manipulation of our expectations which his text affords as the basis of our literary experience: in one sentence, seemingly incompatible times and places are fused; realism and the irrational are entwined; death, continuity, whimsy, nostalgia, the prophetic and the absurd are all brought together by nothing more than syntax and the will of the reader for linear coherence. The various segments of the sentence demand different responses, some opposing and some complementary. It is in our capacity to hold these, simultaneous, in our minds that we derive pleasure — rather than in what we can reconstruct through imagination (premodernism) or construct, through a combination of imagination and educated guesswork (modernism).

If one is wary, the following aphoristic evasion by Malcolm Bradbury, quoted by George Bowering in "Modernism Could Not Last Forever," will serve as a preliminary definition — beyond which there is only elaboration or silence: in postmodernism, the "alliance of writer, character, plot and reader becomes part of the subject of the novel." In the sense that all writing is about writing, as all words are about words, this statement holds universally true as a definition of narrative art. But in the sense that the reader reading completes the narrative event, not passively, acted upon or within, but actively, as a participant inside the fiction, the statement accurately describes the most important element of the postmodern mode. The principal event in the Marquez sentence is neither execution nor memory, but an exhilarating breach of expectations which their syntactical and narrative fusion arouses within the reader's mind.

In postmodern writing, the mind of the reader completes the action which the text initiates: the reader reads the reader reading. Consider the following stanza from Earle Birney's 1948 poem, "From the Hazel Bough."

her legs swam by
 like lovely trout
eyes were trees
 where boys leant out

What a joyfully unrestrained and utterly improbable set of images! Here is no metaphysical conceit, waiting to be resolved on
some perfect and unlikely plane of equivalence; here is a pair
of metaphors which, if considered, yield not some special truth
through correspondence but only a curious delight. Why? Legs
and trout, eyes and trees with boys in them, simply do not correspond, are not equivalents, nor do trout and trees relate, nor
in this context do legs and eyes and boys — and yet the stanza
works. They are all there together in a relaxed association determined by syntax and the reader's apparently inbred need to
establish coherence.

The stanza works by making the postmodern demand (1948!)
upon the reader to participate: the reader completes the implied
analogues out of his or her personal experience of the world, and
then merges these responses in a complex and delightfully elusive
synthesis. There is no connection between legs and trout except
that the impact of "her" legs, perceived, is the same as we might
feel, or imagine we might feel or the poet might feel, on seeing
trout swim by — it is only within and through us that the two
connect. Similarly, the effect of seeing her eyes is comparable
to the delight we might feel or expect to feel or the poet to feel
on seeing a tree-full of boys. The connection is not in the things
themselves, not in any particular properties they have in common; nor is it in the text, in anything that is said about them,
but only in our imagined experiences of ourselves, experiencing
— which the syntax and line-structure demand we do.

Postmodernism allows opposing realities to be simultaneously
present and equally true. It embodies the purposeful breakdown
of those conventions of time, place and causality which we have
previously thought to be the common links between actual and
narrative worlds — which, even when being defied, were accepted as truths.

In the essays to follow, some critics address the elusive tenets of postmodernism directly, some take them for granted, and some ignore them entirely. There is a splendid diversity not only in the works considered, but in the approaches taken, all of which, I sincerely hope, is to the reader's benefit.

Having said this, all that is left is to wish you luck. With or without the support of the SSHRC I believe this is a valuable book in a very worthwhile series.

John Moss
Bellrock, 1985

Postscript: postmodern/post-modern. The spellings vary and at this stage it is probably best to let the variants stand — until time and convention resolve the minor discrepancies between the two. Most critics seem to prefer the collapsed form. Occasionally both are used, but with discretion.

TIMOTHY FINDLEY

HISTORY TO THE DEFEATED
NOTES ON SOME NOVELS BY TIMOTHY FINDLEY

George Woodcock

The stars are dead; the animals will not look:
We are left alone with our day and the time is
short, and
History to the defeated
May say Alas but cannot help or pardon.
— W. H. Auden ("Spain 1937")

History, as *The Wars* and *Famous Last Words* have shown, is Timothy Findley's favourite though not necessarily most tractable material. In all his later and more interesting writings, we look back into a past that in the minds of most of us is completed — finished business: the late 1930s in *The Butterfly Plague* and his remarkable play about madness, *Can You See Me Yet?;* the Great War (as it was once called) in *The Wars;* World War II with the apprehensive years leading up to it in *Famous Last Words.* He is not reviving those lost ages as they were. He is taking history into the world of the imagination and in the process is creating his own myths which are also his own history.

But to suggest that Findley is a mythographer is not to subscribe to the Frygian clichés by means of which some of his critics have interpreted *The Wars* as a re-enactment of archetypal myths that are to be regarded as lying somehow outside history. My use of the concept of myth in this context presupposes a relation between myth and history quite different from that proposed by Frye. I cannot accept that myth is autonomous and apart from history and our apprehension of the phenomenal world, nor do I believe primitive man saw or sees it in this way.

To give an example, even today anyone who discusses with the Nishka Indians of British Columbia the matter of their land rights comes up against an attitude that depends on the historicity of myths, for most of the advocates of Indian rights accept as *historical fact,* not as symbolic fantasy, the legends that make their ancestors the autochthonous inhabitants of the land, and reject, on these grounds of myths interpreted as literal history, the archaeologists' arguments that they too were immigrants, coming over the Bering Strait. In treating myth in this way, they are typical of primitive man, for whom it was intimately related to the phenomenal world and was indeed its true history.

Myth, in other words, is a product of the emergent historic imaginations, of the attempt to give the world we experience an origin and a meaning. Each culture develops its own myths to the same effect. It is a similar emergence of the historic imagination, giving our collective life an origin and a meaning, that has tended to shape Canadian writing during recent decades and to induce its formative myths. The upsurge of actual historical and biographical writing is one aspect of it. But more important than the quantity of historical works published in Canada has been the imaginative quality of the best of them. Historians like Donald Creighton have not been content to provide us with a well-documented account of what they believe actually happened. They remember that, for the ancients, history like poetry had its muse, and writers like Creighton recognized the extent to which they were servants of Clio, not merely by cultivating the art of writing so that the best of their books could rank as literary masterwork, but also by shaping their accounts to draw a grand pattern, a myth, out of the mass of heterogeneous facts. Such historians were important not only for the information they provided but also for what they led us to believe; in a way perhaps more literal than any of their heroes, they *made* history.

This creative element in the writing of history drew historians and other kinds of writers together. The myths Creighton created had their political importance in the extent to which they helped inspire the more intellectual types of Canadian nationalism during the 1960s and 1970s. But they went beyond politics, just as they went beyond history considered as a mere academic discipline, in offering the themes and images, even the historic personae, that would inspire novelists and poets. The tributes that Margaret Laurence has paid to A. L. Morton, perhaps the greatest historian of the Canadian West, and other writers to Donald Creighton, are not however merely statements of indebtedness. They are rather acknowledgements of affinity, indications that the poets and novelists themselves had developed an historic consciousness, almost an historic sensibility; that for them history had become not merely a rich source of imagery and subject matter but also, even in a purely formal sense, a shaping influence. An imaginative vision of the form of the past has given shape to Margaret Laurence's novels as certainly as it did to Stendhal's or Tolstoy's. An imaginative grasp of local traditions has dictated the very speech rhythm and therefore the prosodic form of Al Purdy's poetry. The dense vitality our brief history takes on, in the works of so many of our writers of fiction and poetry, is one of the distinguishing characteristics of modern Canadian writing.

In applying this generalization to Timothy Findley, I would go a step farther and say, not merely that he shares an historic consciousness widespread among Canadian writers of his generation, but also that he is, in a more specific sense, an historical novelist. I am aware that the historical novel, highly respected as a genre in the nineteenth century, has become in our age a somewhat derided form of fiction, largely practiced by popular novelists who write according to formulae for readers who see the past as a place of escape, and history as romance. But the best of historical novels were and still are works of elaborate and often very self-conscious literary art, and they tend to fall into two main categories.

The novelist takes what information he has of the past, and out of it creates an imaginary world that is certainly not identical with the past, but is complete and self-consistent within itself. Flaubert writing *Salammbo* out of the relatively few facts known in his time about Carthage is an example of this kind of historical fiction, which is not really very far removed from the product of an artist historian, like Gibbon in *The Decline and Fall of the Roman Empire*, who creates a vision of the past, which even when it has been superseded by later evidence and later interpretations, nevertheless remains as a literary artifact. The other type of serious historical novelist is the writer who gives history a fictional form in order to draw some moral or political implications. The grand example is, of course, *War and Peace*, in which Tolstoy made his major statements on the nature of war and on the illusory nature of political power. Here again there are analogues among historians, like Spengler using a cyclic interpretation of history to project a pessimistic philosophy.

Reshaping events to make moral or political points is only a step away from reshaping events for aesthetic purposes, as novelists like Robert Graves did in his Claudius series and Ford Madox Ford in *Parade's End*, both of them creating portraits of civilizations at critical turning points but at the same time writing with a high consciousness of form and of style, so that their novels stand as literary artifacts outside any question of their historical authenticity or of the thoughts about human societies that, almost incidentally, they induce. Timothy Findley's best and most recent books, *The Wars* and *Famous Last Words*, fall — I suggest — into this last category. Indeed, I am somewhat surprised that none of the critics has yet studied the resemblances between *The Wars* and *Parade's End* — not only between their respective visions of the horror and waste of trench warfare in World War I, but between Ford's Tietjens (that noble, outraged man) and Findley's Ross as characters, and between the visions of sexual relations as brutally rapacious that both novelists offer. However, such a comparison is not the aim of this essay, and I make it mainly to suggest how clearly *The Wars* rests within the tradition of historical fiction.

In both the novels I am discussing, Findley uses formal frameworks based on historical methods even when, as in *Famous Last Words*, he combines them with a boldly fictional device, making the author of the memoirs about real persons, that Lieutenant Quinn so laboriously transcribes, that invention of Ezra Pound's early poetic fancy, Hugh Selwyn Mauberley. "You begin at the archives with photographs," says Findley two pages into *The Wars*.[1] Whether the shaping intelligence of the book is actually addressing the researcher, or the researcher addressing the reader, or whether "you" is meant in the more neutral sense of "one," is not at all clear, and perhaps the ambiguity is intentional.

The fact is that the novel is presented as a kind of secondary record, derived from rummagings among archival relics — "Boxes and boxes of snapshots and portraits; maps and letters; cablegrams and clippings from the papers" — and from taped interviews given by a couple of survivors from the events that fill the book (p. 6). The illusion of authenticity is quite deliberately created, and that illusion is part of the fiction. Somehow or other, we are expected to assume, all the scenes that are described directly in the third person have been created out of the debris of fragmentary records and surviving memories. There have been hints, in accounts of conversations with Findley, that some at least of the incidents in *The Wars* are based on the Great War experiences of members of Findley's own family. Be that as it may, we are faced with fiction as historical pastiche, and with a consequent problem in the relationship between style and moralism in fiction.

On the surface, indeed, *The Wars*, with its neo-Naturalist determinism that makes its characters appear the victims of both heredity and circumstance, and even more *Famous Last Words*, with its cavalier blending of historical and fictional personages and its concentration on people who are devoid of the pride of principle, seem divorced entirely of fictional moralism. In a recent brilliant essay on Timothy Findley as novelist ("Look! Listen, Mark My Words!" *Canadian Literature* 91), John F. Hulcoop has related Findley's practice to Oscar Wilde's theories on the importance of style, in literature and in life alike. And a cluster of Wildean phrases — part of the series of epigrams that prefaced the first edition of *The Picture of Dorian Gray* — can very appropriately be applied *on one level* to the type of fiction Findley has developed. "All art is at once surface and symbol. Those who go beneath the surface do so at their peril."

All this is true, of Wilde's work as well as of Findley's. Yet in Wilde's case those who have risked going below the surface, who have dared to read the symbols, have discovered the ultimate Wildean contradictions: that, as I showed long ago in *The Paradox of Oscar Wilde* (1949) and Joyce Carol Oates more recently in *Contraries* (1981), the dandy's emphasis on surface and style is often the thin ice concealing a moralism of almost Dostoyevskian intensity.

The case is rather similar with Findley. Discussing any of his novels, one inevitably says much about style and surface, and by doing so acknowledges not merely his special literary dexterity, but also the growing sophistication of a Canadian fictional tradition that has come to the point where forms and artifices, parodies and pastiches, are the serious concerns of serious writers. Yet they are not their only concerns, and one would lose a great deal of Findley's two most recent novels if one's understanding of them ended with the aesthetic, or if one assumed, given they have such a strong vein of determinism, that they were ultimately pessimistic.

One can indeed apply Auden's lines which I use as the epigraph for this essay to both Robert Ross of *The Wars* and Mauberley of *Famous Last Words*, each in his own way irrevocably on the wrong side, Mauberley for his involvement in a quasi-Fascist cabal, Ross for his defiance of the British army in a Quixotic attempt to rescue horses from the insane carnage that was eating up men by the thousands on the Flanders front. Mauberley is in the end horribly murdered, and Ross lives the last years of his truncated life a prisoner in mutilated inactivity. Both, by any normal standards, are utterly defeated. And history, indeed, can neither help nor pardon, for there is no possible reversing of their destinies.

But there is a difference here between literature and history, considered merely as the sequence of events. For the imagination may not be able to help or pardon, but it can offer understanding and compassion. When Clive, the soldier poet in *The Wars,* is asked, "Do you think we will ever be forgiven for what we've done?" ("we" meaning his generation), he answers: "I doubt we'll ever be forgiven. All I hope is — they'll remember we were human beings" (p. 185).

It is the retention of his humanity, the power, after all he has endured from the inhuman forces of war, to make a gesture in favour of life, that is Robert's final triumph at the moment of his apparent defeat. Having shot his senior officer and deserted, he rescues a hundred and thirty horses from almost certain death, only to be trapped and surrounded by pursuing soldiers. The barn in which he and fifty of the horses are sheltering is set on fire.

> But just as the walls began to fall in on top of the fifty horses — all of them standing in their places while they burned — Robert turned the mare and she leapt through the flames — already falling — with Robert on her back on fire. (p. 221)

The burning hero: it is a kind of apotheosis as well as a destruction. And Robert's triumph comes in his strange tenacity, in his clinging to life, through pain and hopeless mutilation, so that when the nurse Marian Turner in her pity offers him an overdose of morphine, his answer is "Not yet."

> "Do you see?" He might have said: "No." He might've said: "Never." He might've said: "Yes." But he said: "Not yet." There, in those two words, in a nutshell — you have the essence of Robert Ross. And perhaps the essence of what it is to be alive. *Not yet* has been my motto ever since — and here I am. (p. 224)

A few moments before she tells this incident Marian Turner — that ancient lady who still says "Not yet" — had described the bombing of the field hospital at Bois de Madeleine, and had evoked an image that was not only related to Robert's holding on to life, but also potently evoked one of the dominant structural as well as symbolic relationships of the book, that between men and animals.

> We nurses lived in tents, you understand, and these were all destroyed as well as the damage done to the hospital which was in someone's house. I remember the strangest sight when the raid was over. I'd been hiding under a bed and when I crawled out and stood up I

> looked down the rows of platforms where the tents had
> been and there, at the edge of the step, sat a pure white
> cat we'd had as mascot. It was cleaning its paws!
> Serenely cleaning its paws. Well . . . life goes on and a
> cat will clean its paws no matter what. (p. 222)

The cat is clearly, at this point, being introduced as a fabulist exemplar, offering man a model of conduct. There are other similar exemplary uses of animals in the novel: the toad who survives a gas attack because he is able to survive under water and control his breathing; the coyote behind whom Robert runs on the prairie and who leads him to a secret water hole, showing the combination of intelligence and instinct by which the animal takes advantage of his environment but does not, like man, attempt to dominate it and — by dominating — to destroy.

But animals are not used merely in a fabulist manner. They become extensions of the human characters, or perhaps rather their reflections in a different realm of consciousness, where culpability is replaced by innocence. Robert, running with the coyote, running later with the horses in an English paddock, is declaring a kinship, just as his friend Harris does when he lies dying in an English hospital and remembers how he would swim with shoals of mackerel, as if theirs were his element, and hear the music of the whales. One of the most appealing and elusive characters of *The Wars* is Robert's fellow officer, Rodwell, who keeps in his dugout a small menagerie of animals whom he had rescued when they were injured in artillery bombardments. Only the toad survives, and when Rodwell is sent to a part of the front that has been subjected to a terrible attack by flame throwers, he confides the animal to Robert, who eventually liberates it in its native mud. Rodwell — who shortly afterwards commits suicide because he cannot prevent shell-shocked soldiers from torturing rats and cats to death — also leaves with Robert the books of sketches on which, as an artist, he has spent his spare time in the trenches. Later, in a train on the way to "Blighty," Robert dips into the sketchbooks:

> There was the toad. Quite, as Rodwell had promised,
> realistic — lacking entirely any sentimental nuance. Just
> a plain, bad-tempered grumpy toad. Robert smiled. He
> leafed through the pages. There were birds and
> mice. The rabbit and the hedgehog. More toads. A
> frog and some insects. Then, towards the back of the
> book, he found himself. *"Robert."* He was lying asleep

by the candlelight in the dugout. His mouth was slightly open. One hand reposed on his breast. He was
wearing Harris's bitten gloves. The other hand hung
down towards the earth. The likeness was good. Un-
nerving. But the shading was not quite human. There
was another quality — speckled and fading into
brightness where his clothes touched his neck and
cheek. Robert could not decipher what that quality was
— until he'd finished leafing through the book and
glanced through the others (there were five, all told.) In
all of them — on every page, the drawings were of
animals. Of maybe a hundred sketches, Robert's was
the only human form. Modified and mutated — he was
one with the others. (p. 158)

What had Rodwell meant by this? Or was it just the way he
drew?

Whether or not Rodwell meant anything at all, his insight
prefigured Robert's subsequent action — his first unsuccessful
attempt to liberate horses he sees as doomed by artillery bombardment, and later, after he becomes a deserter, his more successful liberation, this time of the trainload of a hundred and thirty
horses he finds shunted into a siding. When he is finally cor-
nered, he identifies himself completely with the horses; his pur-
suer, Major Mickle, calls on him to surrender and he answers —
though there is no other human being with him — "We shall not
be taken."

It was the *"we"* that doomed him. To Mickle, it
signified that Robert had an accomplice. (p. 220)

The motives that underlie Robert's acts are left deliberately
unclear; we have, like the researcher who comes sixty years after
the event, to piece them together from the given fragments. But
it is clear that his anger at the death of the first batch of horses,
and his killing of Captain Leathers, are merely the climax of a
long process in which he has come to the point when he must
make some manifestation for life against the mindless carnage
and destruction that he has so far passed through undestroyed,
and there seems no better way of doing so than to attempt the
rescue of those innocent beings, the animals, and especially of
the horses, which are regarded as the utterly dispensable material
of war. In their subjection to the destructive elements that war
imposes on them, men and animals are together, though it is only
man that is culpable, and in half-conscious ways both Rodwell
and Robert offer themselves as sacrifices to redeem man's

culpability, which gives a final point to the poet Clive Stourbridge's hope that the humanity still existing in his generation
may be remembered.

Like the relationship between men and animals, which provides
one of the great balancing factors in the structure of *The Wars*,
the elements also play a significant symbolic and formal role in
the novel, and here again the implications are dualistic. "Earth
and Air and Fire and Water" are the words that Juliet d'Orsay
has written on Robert's tombstone, and their presence is more
than the revival of ancient science. Throughout the novel they
are present destructively — in the water of the great shell holes
where Robert almost drowns, in the earth that almost smothers
him when his dugout collapses, in the air that is made blue and
deadly by the presence of poison gas, and above all in the fire
that rages during the artillery bombardments, and especially in
the *ersatz* apocalypse of the terrible flame thrower attacks which
the Germans release as "Operation *Gericht.*"

> Fire storms raged along the front. Men were exploded
> where they stood — blown apart by the combus-
> tion. Winds with the velocity of cyclones tore the guns
> from their emplacements and flung them about like
> toys. Horses fell with their bones on fire. Men went
> blind in the heat. Blood ran out of noses, ears and
> mouths. Wells and springs of water were plugged and
> stopped by the bodies of men and mules and dogs who
> had gone there for safety. The storms might last for
> hours — until the clay was baked and the earth was
> seared and sealed with fire. (p. 151)

And it is fire that in the end destroys Robert.[2]

There is a doubtless intended irony in recording the German
name for their flame throwing operation, since the result is in
its own way a *Gericht*, a judgement, on those who let loose such
destructiveness on the earth. For all the elements have also, in
the novel, their regenerative side. Water is another home for Harris. The earth on which he runs with coyotes and horses gives
strength to Robert. The novel ends with breath, which is air —
a photograph of Robert with his dead sister Rowena.

On the back is written: "Look! you can see our breath!"(p.
225). And you can. Even fire mirrors the rage and the spirit
within Robert, so that the image of him at the end "on fire" is
a tragic but also a triumphant one. This dual aspect of the
elements reinforces one's impression of *The Wars* as, in some in-
explicit way, the product of a quasi-Zoroasterian vision; it is there

in the determinism one uneasily feels to be such a dominant factor, and in the sense of a perpetual conflict of opposing forces for which fire is the uniting image, Ormuzd and Ahriham its double faces. It is this ambivalent vision that gives the book not merely its meaning but also its form.

Famous Last Words is in appearance a very different novel from *The Wars*, more cynical, more blackly comic, more stylized. Yet in the way Findley goes to work there is much in common between the two books, for in the later one also he is mingling the literary genres and turning the actual world — the world of history — into the raw material, to be manipulated at will, of an art that acknowledges no myths but its own, no models but preceding artifacts. Findley's concerns with literature as the offspring of literature leads him, in *Famous Last Words*, to seek characters of two kinds; those who actually come out of literature, and those who come out of life and may even be famous but whose roles have been so artificial and so lacking in consequence that history can through them be manipulated easily into a writer's artifact.

As his narrator, Findley takes a character entirely out of literature: Hugh Selwyn Mauberley, the aesthete who Ezra Pound conceived and thought out of existence in 1920. A verse from *Hugh Selwyn Mauberley* seems to set the tone for the world of *Famous Last Words:*

> There died a myriad,
> And of the best, among them,
> For an old bitch gone in the teeth,
> For a botched civilization . . . .

It is the botched civilization that we encounter at the novel's first point in time, 1924, when Mauberley meets Wallis Simpson in Shanghai, and remarks: "It was a dreadful time; there was so much dissolution of the past and fear of the future. Nothing to stand for, nothing to reach for."[3]

Findley's Mauberley defies the fate Pound laid out for him, for he does not pass "from man's memory in *l'an trentenièsme/De son age* . . . ."[4] but lives on to become, like his creator in real life, an apologist for fascism, and to die at the hands of Nazi agents during the chaotic aftermath of World War II. In the intervening period he has become deeply involved in a reactionary cabal, of which Ciano, von Ribbentrop, Lindbergh and Mrs. Simpson are members, plotting to supersede the reigns of Hitler and Mussolini by a new European order of which the figurehead will become that pathetic shell of a princeling, the briefly reigning King Edward VIII. As world events show, the plot fails; it may not have existed at all in actuality. It exists for the purposes of the novel, which is sufficient, since it provides Mauberley with the material for the memoir that is his posthumously discovered masterpiece.

There are two verses in *Hugh Selwyn Mauberley* that seem to have given Findley the clues on which to base the circumstances of Mauberley's composing the masterpiece Pound had denied him. The first:

> The 'age demanded' chiefly a mould in plaster,
> Made with no loss of time,
> A prose kinema, not, not assuredly, alabaster
> Or the 'sculpture' of rhyme. (II, 29-32)

And the second:

> 'His true Penelope
> Was Flaubert.'
> And his tool
> The engraver's. (I, 250-253)

Fleeing from Italy, Mauberley finds refuge not only from the allies but also from Himmler's agents, in a deserted luxury hotel high in the Alps. There, awaiting his pursuers, he takes a silver pencil, which becomes his "engraver's tool," and scores on the walls and ceilings of four of the rooms the contents of the notebooks he had brought with him — the record of the barren conspiracy in which peripherally he was involved. His enemies eventually track him down, murder him, and burn his compromising notebooks, but before they arrive he has completed his work and added on the ceiling the sign of his own hand outlined by candle soot. Mauberley's record is read and recorded by a young American lieutenant, Quinn, who is part of the bizarre reconnaissance unit which provides a kind of low comic chorus to the mock heroic drama that is, as "the age demanded," written "in plaster," with "no loss of time" and is in its own way a "prose kinema, not, not assuredly, . . . / . . . the 'sculpture' of rhyme."

In Mauberley, as the script unfolds, we become aware of a dual persona. He is — on one aspect — the weak and neutral man, scared by the physical contacts that may entrap him, so that he lives all his affairs in the mind, but led by his very lack of will into the associations that eventually must destroy him. In the

other aspect, Mauberley is the artist who feels a complete power
over what he creates, and who writes on the wall, for Lieutenant
Quinn to read with troubled delight: ''All I have written here
is true; except the lies'' (p. 59). Quinn is justifiably puzzled
when he tries to understand ''how Mauberley, whose greatest
gift had been an emphatic belief in the value of imagination, could
have been so misguided as to join with people whose whole ambition was to render the race incapable of thinking'' (p. 48).

And when we read what Lieutenant Quinn — with the help
of many candles and cigarettes — gleans from the scored walls,
we realize that Mauberley has in fact claimed his privilege as an
artist to chronicle but also to imagine and invent. And so the
story he tells is not merely what he has seen, for there are whole
incidents narrated in which he does not appear; it is also what
he invents when his imagination plays over the actions of people he has known.

On the way Findley, rather like Tolstoy, presents us with views
(perhaps not his own) on the nature and effects of war and the
real character of history. ''A war,'' Mauberley tells us, ''is just
a place where we have been in exile from our better dreams'' (p.
176). And, describing an occasion when he sat with Wallis and
von Ribbentrop, he remarks:

> So this is history as she is never writ, I thought. Some
> day far in the future, some dread academic, much too
> careful of his research, looking back through the blessed
> glasses of a dozen other ''historians,'' will get this mo-
> ment down on paper. And will get it wrong. Because
> he will not acknowledge that history is made in the elec-
> tric moment, and its flowering is all in chance. At the
> heart of everything that shakes the world, there may be
> nothing more than a casual remark that has been
> overheard and acted on. There is more in history of im-
> pulse than we dare to know. (p. 180)

Yet, in the ironic event, it is history as process rather than accident that sweeps Mauberley to his destiny.

For all its inconsistencies, Mauberley's account goes far beyond
what Pound attributed to his original: ''Nothing, in brief, but
maudlin confession'' (p. 308). It is, uncompromisingly, literature
as style, with Wallis Simpson as its ultimate example in life.

> The face she saw in her private mirror was a face no
> other human being had seen. It was her midnight face,
> and mostly in her mind. The true face — lifted and lac-

quered — was the one she showed to others and the
world. (p. 191)

Which is nothing more than Wilde's doctrine of the truth of
masks.

But just as in Wilde, that kindest of men, a moral being underlay
the dandy, so in *Famous Last Words*, we are never free from the
moralism that goes with the territory of fiction. It is there, at the
beginning, in raging Ezra, whose morals may be upended, but
whose rage is nevertheless against a world lost in corruption. And certainly it is there in the two eventual commentators: Quinn, who believes in the understanding that forgives,
and his superior officer, Captain Freyberg, who believes that to
understand the enemy is to betray one's cause — which is Quinn's
truth inverted. And finally, as a manifestation of the urge to live
on that lies at the heart of even the most extreme aestheticism,
there is Mauberley's own remark, as he remembers the caves of
Altamira and reproduced their smoke-ringed handprint above his
own engraved messages:

> Some there are who never disappear. And I know I was
> sitting at the heart of the human race — which is its will
> to say *I am*. (p. 173)

In such a statement — which echoes that of Clive Stourbridge
in *The Wars* — style becomes its own morality, and understanding becomes more important than help or pardon.

Notes

1   Timothy Findley, *The Wars* (Toronto: Clarke, Irwin & Co., 1977), p. 5. All
further references to this edition will appear in the text.
2   One is reminded at this point of the part that destructive fires play in so many
of Findley's works — e.g. the fires of *The Butterfly Plague* ("Real fires, symbolic fires. All burning — all eating — most of them conjuring death"), and
the fire that turns Wallis Simpson's great fete in *Famous Last Words* into a black
comic disaster.
3   Timothy Findley, *Famous Last Words* (Toronto: Clarke, Irwin & Co., 1981), p.
67. All further references to this edition will appear in the text.
4   Ezra Pound, *Hugh Selwyn Mauberley (Life & Contacts)* in *Personae*, copyright 1926
by Ezra Pound, I, 19-20. All further references will appear in the text.

JACK HODGINS

DISBELIEVING STORY:
A READING OF *THE INVENTION OF THE WORLD*

Frank Davey

1. don't ask questions

Hodgins' novel begins with a prologue that focuses on Strabo Becker (beckoner), a ferryman from the British Columbia Ferry Authority "who waves his arms to direct traffic" toward the island where most of the action of *The Invention of the World* will occur. A Charon figure, surely, signalling the epic nature of the pages to follow, but a Charon with a twist: "Becker wants to be God." As he works he mutters the words of a popular song — "he'd rather be a sparrow than a snail," "rather be a forest . . . than a street,"[1] "rather sail a-wa-a-ay" — apparently wanting each time to be larger, to occupy the larger space. Yet paradoxically he is committed to the inside of his small cabin, to his hoard of documents of a single story. Facing this collection of documents of the brawling career of the Irish con-man/religious leader Donal Keneally, Becker has resolved to be a god on a small scale.

> He has chosen to nest on a certain piece of this world and to make a few years of its history his own. The debris of that history is around him and he will reel it all in, he will store it in his head, he will control it; there will be no need, eventually, for anything else to exist; all of it will be inside, all of it will belong only to him.

Strabo Becker, in fact, would be our narrator — not only a beckoner but, through his sharing his other name with the 1st century B.C. Greek geographer, be also our historian, geographer, and mapmaker. "Sometimes this god-man almost believes that he owns this island, that he has perhaps invented it" (p. x). Yet Hodgins lets Becker tell only the second major section of the book, "The Eden Swindle," a section characterized by Becker's skeptical rendering of fantastic event, and the last section, "Second Growth," marked by an ebullient epic viewpoint. The fourth section, "Scrapbook," consists of documents Becker has assembled toward a narrative; the sixth, "The Wolves of Lycaon," is a reminiscence by Keneally's widow Lily that has been tape-

recorded by Becker. The actual narrator of the novel is an unnamed genial voice that addresses the reader in the prologue, that
introduces Becker's two sections, his documents, and his tape-
recording, and that relates four other sections mostly through the
viewpoints of single characters. When Becker does begin to nar-
rate he is not god-like at all, has given up all hope of "invention." "Trust me or not, believe what you want, by now the
story exists without us in the air," he begins "The Eden
Swindle."

> I am not its creator, nor is any one man; I did not in-
> vent it, only gathered its shreds and fragments together
> from the half-aware conversations of people around me,
> from the tales and hints and gossip and whispered
> threats and elaborate curses that float in the air like
> dust. (p. 69)

In Strabo Becker are foreshadowed the polarities of the
novel: walled space versus the unwalled, control versus vision,
chaos versus imagination and invention. Becker encompasses
these, longing "to be God" yet essentially humble before his
materials,

> . . . don't ask Becker to answer questions. He's a shy
> man, who knows only this much: that the tale which
> exists somewhere at the centre of his gathered hoard, in
> the confusion of tales and lies and protests and legends
> and exaggerations, has a certain agreed-upon begin-
> ning: . . . . (p. xi)

longing to "invent" and, in fact, leaving the stamp of his skep-
ticism on "The Eden Swindle" and of his zest for life on "Second Growth," yet declining credit for his invention. At a critical
moment in the novel he will interpret the action in terms of an
authoritarian image from the past,

> "Pilgrims to the valley of Jehosaphat," he said, "reserv-
> ed stones for themselves to sit on at the last judge-
> ment." (p. 313)

yet a moment later declare the novel's most resonant idea, that
when you begin to "disbelieve" in myth "you can begin to believe
in yourself" (p. 314). Like several characters in the novel, he confuses imagination and domination, feeling vaguely ashamed of
his artist's wish to give shape to what he has gathered.

He will absorb all, this chaos, he will confront it and absorb it, and eventually he will begin to tell, and by telling release it, make it finally his own. Becker, on this day that you've met him, is singing, though broodingly, that he'd rather be a sparrow than a snail.

2. *to make it his own*

In the opening chapter that follows we see two characters who have very much not made something their own: Danny Holland and his latest girlfriend, "the Zulu." They are having a lovers' quarrel.

> From around the curve beneath the highrise the Zulu's sedan soon reappeared. And from somewhere down beyond the customs house Danny Holland's pickup returned, roaring and bouncing up the slope. They rushed towards each other from the end of the street. In front of the coffee-shop windows of the Coal-Tyee Hotel their brakes squealed, both vehicles slid sideways and whipped back again; their noses met with a harsh, grinding crash. Headlights shattered and fell in pieces to the pavement, grills collapsed, fenders folded back. In the terrible silence that followed, both drivers' heads were wooden-rigid; from behind the glass they glared at one another.

The something they have not made their own is the medieval joust, armoured by their two vehicles, Danny Holland's "upright exhaust pipe" throwing up "plumes of challenge." The story here controls them; they submit to the necessities of its form, linear violence, a winner and loser, the male sexual metaphor. The male metaphor means that a woman who submits to this story necessarily loses, as the Zulu does.

> Engines stalled. Something heavy dropped from under the sedan and the back end settled like a tired bull. A moment before the quiet impact the woman's door had opened and she leapt free, rolled over twice towards the hotel, and righted herself in a sitting position against a light pole. She held an arm hugged close against her waist, nursing it, rocking. A small stream of blood glistened on her cheek. (p. 5)

With her losing, the story transforms itself into another metaphor of male violence, the bullfight, as Danny victoriously takes out "a red and white" handkerchief to blow his nose while the Zulu's sedan settles "like a tired bull."

In *The Invention of the World* history and mythology can tyrannize — particularly those patterns inherited from classical and feudal Europe, armoured combat, castles, forts, duels, legends of divine intervention. Above all, these myths tyrannize because they are male myths created by a patriarchal culture, and limit male and female action to paths characteristic of that culture but not necessarily relevant to our own. A second time in the opening chapter the characters re-enter those paths. When Danny Holland appropriates Madmother Thomas' donkey, she attacks him with a peavey, holding it "in front of her like a lance." But although she overwhelms him, she cannot bring herself to injure him and "defeated, she stood back and drove the point of the peavey into the ground between her feet."

Holland's head leapt back, laughing, laughing (p. 32). In the patriarchal story the woman cannot win, the peavey, the lance, the phallus here are the necessary weapons but they are not her weapons. What she needs is a new story, perhaps without weapons, perhaps even without enmity. What she needs is to make a story her own, or possibly to make her own story. Invention.

3. in or out

There are two major narratives in *The Invention of the World*, that of the Irish messiah Donal Keneally's strange birth and early life and of his eventual founding early this century on Vancouver Island of "The Revelations Colony of Truth," and that of Maggie Kyle's childhood much later in a logging camp on Vancouver Island and of her eventual restoration of Keneally's abandoned "House of Revelations."

The Keneally story comes first to us in Becker's "The Eden Swindle" as a parody of the birth of the half-divine hero; Keneally is conceived in a half-witted peasant girl by "a monstrous black bull with eyes that shone like red lanterns and a scrotum that hung like a sack of turnips." The bull symbol of patriarchally organized cultures — Siva's black bull Nandi, the Mithraic bull of Assur, the Cretan bull, king Minos's double, who begat the minotaur on Pasiphae — here combines with stories of Zeus's rapes of Europa and Leda. Later the girl gives birth within a circle of ostensibly Druidic stones on a mountaintop, to which she appears to have been led by instinct. At the moment of birth "the

earth had reached up to swallow her. Layers of soil were closing together to form a narrow crease across the circle of
stones. Mouth of earth or whatever, it had disgorged a
child." The girl here merges with earth. Her life is enclosed by
another patriarchal myth, Mother Earth, — "mouth of earth"
Becker/Hodgins echoes for us — reducing her to the punning
metonymy of a mountaintop *mons veneris.*

Keneally's childhood in Becker's narration follows the whim-
sical fantasy patterns of the tales of the Mabinogion. He is the
comically miraculous child, precocious, great-limbed, his guar-
dians are appointed in unbelievable dreams. His acts of magic,
however, originally appearing to tap occult powers, become as
he grows older mere parlour tricks. His control over people
grows less subtle, achieved more by deceit, and brutality, than
by awe or belief. His central achievement, the transporting of
his entire Irish village of Carrigdhoun to Vancouver Island to
found The Revelations Colony, is done by his exploiting the
villagers' fear of violence and change and their hatred of their
English landlord. His efforts to run it as a feudal fief, a patriarchy, result in desertion, rebellion, and murder.

We are told nothing of Maggie Kyle's birth. We first see her
in the crawl space under her parents' tarpaper shack, close to the
condition of Keneally's mother, swallowed by earth. As she
grows she becomes the other side of Keneally's aggressive sex-
uality, its passive recipient. With a "series" of departing lovers
she becomes the series of women over whom he once had
power. Her desire becomes to break the patriarchal drama which
demands she play this role; she would make her life "her own."

Although the literal destination of Maggie Kyle is the same as
that of Donal Keneally — the main house, the "House of Revelations," of The Revelations Colony — the narrative shapes of their
lives become almost opposites. Rather than being born on a
mountain, Maggie first appears under a house behind, to the west
of, Vancouver Island's mountains. Her wish is to go up. "Take
me climbing up, rising up to the very centre of whatever there
is behind us. So that I can see" (p. 19). His is to go down and
in. In to Nora O'Sullivan, Brigid Moriarity, Eileen of Kerry, the
wife of the mayor of a nameless Vancouver Island city, into Nell
Maguire and finally into the fantastic network of tunnels he digs
in his old age under the House of Revelations. He begins life

on a mountaintop and ends dead under his house within a collapsed tunnel. Maggie begins under her parents' house, climbs
out to the east coast of the island, out to Ireland, up Keneally's
mountain, up to freedom from the masculine myth of suppress-
ing physical power.

4. re-enactment or re-invention

> The loggers were younger than they used to be, of
> course, but they quickly took on the shapes and at-
> titudes of the older men. Boys a year out of high school
> had already got themselves sagging beer bellies and
> sway backs and sunburnt throats. They swaggered in
> their work clothes like kids who'd just discovered a
> basement dress-up trunk: hard hat, torn T-shirt or
> undershirt, jeans too large and held up by the regulation
> wide braces, caulk boots. (p. 21)

Hodgins' title says "invention" but the most vivid images of the
novel are of enactment, of opening the dress-up trunk and "taking on the shapes" therein. Theatrical images which echo scenes
in another Hodgins book, of the rituals of sumo wrestling, of the
Barclay family theatre.[2] Keneally desires the role of "Father," of
"conjuror-leader." He begins to seek Irish to accompany him
by putting on "a display of levitation, hypnotism, illusion, and
preaching, intended to knock their eyes out" (p. 97); he would
replace their vision with ritual. When this enactment fails, he
finds in some Irish dress-up trunk the robes of a sultan who performs the assembly and destruction of a "God-machine." What
he offers his listeners is a set-piece story, "The Promised Land,"
a journey out of a "land of repression and poverty into a brand
new land of opportunity" (p. 97).

Wade Powers uses books as his dress-up trunk, building an imitation nineteenth-century fur-trading fort to be his tourist
business. Like Keneally, copying.

> Copying a sketch he'd found in a history book, he built
> it out of rough timbers the thickness of railway ties, and
> put a high stockade fence around the whole thing so no
> one could get a close look without paying. (p. 129)

He too seeks to enact a promised land, a patriarchal form, ideal,
unchanging. He rents a cabin on his land to Virginia Kerr, a
painting-instructor from the city, and casually becomes her

lover; "This was close, he thought, this was close to the ideal existence" (p. 136). His business prospers; "Things were perfect" (p. 151).

Within his fort he had built a prison, into which one day the stranger who is Wade's mysterious double steps.

> When Wade stood in the prison doorway, the man was leaning up against the curved rock wall, looking back at him. "I wonder how many people have died in here," he said. "I heard once about a man who was locked up in one of these, down-island, a hundred years ago. After three years they let him out but within the day he was back begging to be let in again."
> "I never head of him," Wade said.
> "I can't remember which bastion it was in. I guess it couldn't have been this one."
> Wade put one hand on the clammy stones. "No. It couldn't have been this one. Nothing like that happened here."
> "But still," the man said. "It would feel like a pretty small world. There'd be nothing in it but yourself. Or what you thought was yourself."
> "They love this prison," Wade said. "The tourists. They all go in there and imagine themselves locked up." (p. 159)

For Wade the fort is a stage for his own self-absorption, a stage for the "locked-up" selves of the tourists who visit, offering them all an enactment of their private despairs. Like the "Promised Land" it is patriarchal, authoritarian, military. It is a closed, repetitive drama, a succession of duplicate performances. When he impulsively locks the stranger in the dungeon it is his own self-image he is creating: locked in an endlessly repeating dramatic role. When he discovers that the stranger has escaped, has *invented* his escape from a prison that has "no way to unlock it from the inside," Wade himself feels liberated, recommitted to the world of "sunlight" outside himself.

> For a moment he stood in the doorway to the prison and contemplated the possibilities of silence. Then he ducked out, chose sunlight, and heard the beginnings of life again. Tires whined by on the highway; a jet streaked eastward ahead of its own sound; seagulls screeched. He heaved across the yard toward his car. (p. 163)

5. Prophecy or Truth

There are three prophetic communities in *The Invention of the World*, the Second Coming community from which Maggie's housemaid Anna has fled, the Jimmy Jimmy Arts & Crafts in Maggie's old home of Hed, and Keneally's The Revelations Colony of Truth. Interestingly, each implies an authoritarian opposite; Anna has initially run from a paediatrician/father who had "nagged" her "all her life . . . to stand up straight" (p. 50). Jimmy Jimmy is attacked and killed by the middle-class father of one of his followers, Keneally's colony is in part a consequence of the exorbitant rents charged the Irish villagers by their English landlords, "the whole British Empire" (p. 87), specifically here one Robert Horgan who enforces his demands through an armed bailiff and a pair of snarling dogs" (p. 86). Yet each also embraces its own kind of patriarchal authority, its own structures of isolation — like Wade's fort — and closure. Anna's commune leader moved his community to an abandoned coppermine; Jimmy Jimmy located his commune in a nearly abandoned logging town and self-absorbedly named himself twice in naming his people; Keneally located his colony "on a high precipice above the sea," like the Irish bailiff walked with a "huge ugly dog," and designed the colony settlement "in the shape of a perfect circle."

> The well was the centre, he explained, because it was
> the source of light for them all. The log houses for the
> colony families were built surrounding this centre just as
> the ancient men had placed the stones in circles high in
> the mountains of Ireland. (p. 121)

Closure and re-enactment — re-enactment of the mountain circle of stone within which Keneally believed himself to have been born. A bid also for the perfection to which Wade aspired through his fort and indefinite liaison with Virginia.

Two of the prophetic communities openly seek "truth"; the coppermine commune awaits the perfection of the second coming, "but when the second coming was postponed for some reason or other . . . came down out of the mountain." Keneally names his colony "The Revelations Colony of Truth." For each, truth is re-enactment of past models — the duplication of a Celtic stone circle, the *second* coming. For Wade, however, truth comes in passing through the doorway from the structure into sunlight; for Maggie and Becker it comes not in looking into a closed form but in looking out over the world, as when they gaze at the hidden life of Vancouver Island from a Twin Otter and their pilot says to them, "That's what real is, that's what true is, it can be hid but it can't be changed."

6. House or Home

> But Anna never came inside the house if she could help it, except to eat or do specific jobs that Maggie lined up for her. She stayed outside as much as she could, she liked to work in the garden, or skittered in the back door and up the staircase to her bedroom when she was driven in by dark or the weather. Houses seemed to hold some kind of threat in them for her, she'd pull you out of them if she could, or stand on the verandah for any talking that needed to be done. (p. 49)

Wade's fort, Keneally's circular colony, the crawl space under Maggie's childhood cabin, Maggie's cabin near Hed, the Celtic circle near Carrigdhoun — throughout *The Invention of the World* Hodgins strews images of defined space. The first of these images is young Maggie's crawl space, where she retreats from her drunken parents "among the rusted cans and broken toys and brood hens and dry lifeless dirt." The cabin is on the west coast of Vancouver Island; Maggie feels enclosed, not only by the repetitiveness of her parents' quarrels and the crawl space but by the village's geography, "water on three sides and mountains behind" (p. 18).

One of the last of these spatial images is Maggie's own cabin in Hed, another logging village, where over approximately fifteen years, at the base of a mountain, in a dying orchard, in a "little gray shack right up at the end" of "a narrow gravel road" (p. 34), she bore four children to a "whole series of men" who lived with her. Again it is the repetitiveness of life in this shack that Maggie is most aware of, the "series" of men, the babies she "hardly noticed," left "inside her . . . like thank-you notes."

Contrasted with such images of enclosed space is the mountaintop, with its potential for unobstructed vision. On first meeting the itinerant Madmother Thomas in her home village, young Maggie wants to ask to be taken out and up. "I want to get out of this place, I want to see more" (p. 19). The Irish mountain near Carrigdhoun, with its Druidic stone circle, offers both the opening and the closing image. For Keneally, for his foster mother Grania Flynn, it is an earthen vagina that "has opened up to swallow" his mother during his birth. Simultaneously it is the maternal vagina which "disgorged" him (p. 83), the vagina he is still attempting to re-enter when he dies within the network of tunnels he has dug beneath The Revelations Colony. For Maggie, this Irish mountaintop is a place of vision: "if there was magic here," she reflects, "it wasn't in the stones, it was in the command they had of the earth" (p. 313). Both experiences of the mountain are qualified, however, by the waving occupants of a small black car who interrupt Maggie by hurling a bottle into the stone circle as they careen past, mocking both its mythic power and the illusion of "command" and "dominion" the altitude has given Maggie. One may need a mountaintop perspective to gain insight into one's life — as Maggie gains here into her feelings toward Wade Powers, and as Wade gains into his fears about his "buried twin" (p. 315) — but most of life is lived at lower levels, "beneath the bush, hardly mattering" (p. 322).

Closure itself does not always require closed space — as we saw in the closed dramatic pattern followed by the duel between Danny and the Zulu. Madmother Thomas' half-century of wanderings across Vancouver Island in a donkey-drawn manure spreader in search of her birthplace is as repetitive and barren as any walled-in life. Answers in Hodgins' novels are not simple, or the same for all characters. While the "open" road draws Maggie toward growth, for the Madmother, as the emptily turning tines of her manure spreader (in proper use a deliverer of fertility) attest, it is an overwhelmingly sterile way. In fact insight for the Madmother comes when she enters within walls and realizes that "it wouldn't hurt me, now and then, to move inside for a while . . . and be comfortable . . . . There's no law says crazy people aren't allowed to be pampered a little, now and then" (p. 334).

The essence of closure, we see here, is not the building — the stone circle, the fake bastion, the crawl space — but the life-drama that one feels compelled to live out: Wade's compulsion to live free of risk; Keneally's compulsion to enter and re-enter the womb; the Madmother's compulsion to find her place of birth; Maggie's compulsion to be drawn into antagonistic dead-end relationships with men like Danny Holland.

When Danny promises to come to their son's wedding she feels trapped by him into their old violent drama: "if that man showed his face she was liable to scratch his eyes out, or worse; . . . panic uncoiled in her chest . . . . " (pp. 54-55). She feels compelled by him into a head-on duel of their trucks: "he'd made her, . . . he'd caused her to do that" (p. 62). Only when she looks up and sees the other people in her life, Wade, Becker, Anna, Julius, looking at her with concern, and sees that she has a life other than that defined by her violent relationship with Holland, and that within this larger context Holland "doesn't matter" (p. 63), can she begin to escape the closure.

A particular building in *The Invention of the World* can be either confining or liberating depending on who lives in it and how he or she "invents" it. For Maggie, the gray house in Hed is a prison of memory. She visits it near the end of the novel to discover a boy and a girl have taken it over; "Maggie had forgotten how small the place was . . . she'd bang into walls here every time she turned around" (p. 328). The young couple, on the other hand, have re-invented the house, have enlarged the space of its imagination into a garden behind which has "wonderful soil" and from which "some day he could haul . . . produce into town to sell, or to a farmer's market . . . . " (p. 330). Similarly, the House of Revelations is a place of obsession and confinement for Keneally, the place where in his tunnels he ultimately "screws" himself into mother earth. But for Maggie, one of whose first acts on taking possession had been to burn its old furniture, it is a place of hope — "the flames reminded her of a slash fire, burning off the nuisance debris to make room for newer growth." She too — with an Adamic imagination paradoxically free of the retrospectively-focussing Eden myth — re-invents.

> And it was her house now, to grow in. When Maggie Kyle took possession of a house she absorbed it, it entered her bloodstream and was fed from the same sources as her legs were, or her hands. It breathed with her, and reflected her state of mind. Bedrooms, she said, you'll be restful places; and every room on the second floor became a place of quiet and softness, where even the crazy angles of the ceiling-roof leaned in as if to offer comfort. When she had the huge kitchen remodelled it was for convenience and speed: this is a service-center, she said, things go out from here to keep the rest alive. (p. 43)

7. mock epic or new epic

The concluding scene of the novel, Maggie and Wade's wedding feast, gives us yet another image of space transcended.

> The visiting loggers, who discovered themselves left out of the battle, went mad and turned their weapons (chainsaws) against the hall. They sawed tables into pieces, they cut up benches, they cut holes in the walls and carved designs on the floor, they reshaped toilet doors into deer and store-room doors into bear, they sawed the steps away from the building and cut elaborate air-holes in the roof. (p. 349)

Throughout this scene we recognize the epic conventions, the epic dinner, the epic catalogue of wedding gifts, the epic battle in which the chainsaw performance occurs, the epic speeches that follow by the "government man," by Danny Holland, and (for one and one-half hours) by Wade himself. But these conventions are not part of a mock epic that reduces the contemporary by contrasting it to an heroic past. Becker's tone in narrating this section is joyous rather than ironic; his narrative of the feast ends in the happy death from over-eating of Miss Anna Muldance, his battle is concluded by Maggie and Wade's lovemaking; his catalogue of gifts expands from blenders and cheese cutters to become the tragicomic inheritance of Canadian humanity.

> Junk mail. Thirty acres. Twin grandchildren. American oil tankers. Bad television programmes. Tax notices. Insurance premiums. Advertising. The French language. Surprises. Suspicions. Celebrations. Revelations. Meditations. Weddings. Funerals. Elections. Rising prices. Hollow promises. Special deliveries. Television commercials. Disapproval. Free samples. Hope. The bomb. Crime. Ecology. Faith. Charity. Life. Truth. Grief. Despair. Tantrums. Psychology. Biology. Lethargy. Jealousy. Reconciliation. Inspiration. Sentiment. Rage. Patience. Joy. Torment. Excitement. Serenity. Criticism. Regret. Relief. Rejoicing. Complaining. Tedium. Beauty. Grace. Forgiveness. Fashions. Laughter. Courage. Cowardice. Danger. Desire. Wonder. Worship. Pride. Immortality. Humility. Friendship. The right to vote. The right to complain. Speeches. Overpopulation. Food shortage. Restless youth. Badly-treated Indians. Disappointed immigrants. Passion. Retirement. Neglect. Loneliness. Love. (pp. 352-353)

Epic expansiveness, a bursting generosity of images and words, connects here with the shattered walls of the building to argue a richness and vitality of life that cannot be contained — at least on earth — by walls or circles, a richness that can be sampled only by adventure, risk, by the willingness to invent one's life and make it, like Becker makes the wedding or Maggie makes the House of Revelations, one's own. Here too we get the final word of the novel on circles, when at the end of his speech Wade recites Lily's poem,

> What was good shall be good with, for evil so much good more: on the earth the broken arcs; in heaven a perfect round.

and recalls "a pilot who told him once that a rainbow, from up in the sky was a full circle" (p. 351). The broken arcs (arks?) of our world are the circles of heaven? Earthly perfection lies in the fragment rather than the whole, or hole?

8. to disbelieve in Keneally

> "Myth," he said, "like all things past, real or imaginary, must be acknowledged . . . . Even if it's not believed. In fact especially if it's not believed. When you begin to disbelieve in Keneally you can begin to believe in yourself."

So argues Strabo Becker as he helps Maggie scatter Keneally's ashes within the stone circle of his birth. What is Keneally? He is the stone circle, the circle of cabins, Cuchulain circling back to rebirth. He is the Promised Land returning upon itself, the second coming, Madmother Thomas visiting and revisiting Vancouver Island towns hoping to circle back on her place of birth. He is patriarchy, the Mosaic leader, the man who would be God, believing he will control history, that there will be one story, his story, that will become all his people's stories. He is Danny Holland, expecting the story of himself and Maggie will always be the same story and looking "confused" when Maggie realizes he "doesn't matter" (p. 63) to her, that she is free to depart from the script. Keneally is the past compelling the present, overcome when the Madmother decides "What does it matter if I look for the place or not?" (p. 333). He is Europe shaping North America in its own closed patterns, the epic, the pastoral, the quest romance, the *return* to the garden.

Keneally is the bearer of archetypes, the critic who argues that stories are made of other stories. He is the story-teller who offers an old story, one "the priest had been offering . . . for centuries" (p. 97), "a glimpse of . . . Eden" (p. 98). As story-teller he stands as a warning to all who would tell stories, to Strabo Becker who is also tempted to tell a closed authoritarian tale, to act as "God." For as Becker indicates, there is another way, to acknowledge that stories exist "without us in the air" (p. 69), that there is no single story, only "tales and lies and protests and legends and exaggerations" (p. xi) and the myriad inventions men and women make therefrom. No story, but stories, as there are also myriad lives that need conform to no single story.

Strabo Becker's problems as historian — how to speak of a man who enclosed his life within an assumed pattern without creating a narrative that is similarly enclosed, how to honour the fragmentariness and confusion and subjectivity of one's records, how to "tell" while disbelieving in story — are also Hodgins' problems here as novelist. Thus his declining to allow Becker to be our only narrator, his inclusion of "Scrapbook" and "The Wolves of Lycaon" as materials ostensibly filtered through neither narrator. Thus too his third-person narrator's adoption of Maggie, Wade, and Julius in turn as point-of-view characters, reminding us again of the subjectivity of human perception.

The Invention of the World denies Frye's theory of the source of literature. It sees myth and archetype as prisons which require life to be lived reflexively, compulsively, within closed dramatic patterns. It shows character deconstructing the myths which dispossess them of their lives. In the context that Hodgins builds of Europe versus North America, these characters become metaphors for Canadian culture, a culture here that should seek vision rather than shelter within inherited forms. Hodgins disperses the novel's narrative viewpoint, making each of its eight sections in some way relative to the others, framing them so that they each become "inventions" rather than the "world." Fictions among fictions. It is finally us as readers who have to assemble the fragments, the broken arcs, and invent the rainbow.

Notes

1   *The Invention of the World,* (Toronto: Macmillan, 1977), p. ix. All further quotations are from this edition.
2   *The Barclay Family Theatre,* (Toronto: Macmillan, 1981).

MAVIS GALLANT

MAVIS GALLANT AND THE CREATION OF CONSCIOUSNESS

Ronald Hatch

In 1950 Mavis Gallant packed her belongings and flew eastwards across the Atlantic. Young and with very little money, she might have taken a holiday exploring post-war Europe before returning to her interesting job as a reporter with the *Montreal Standard*. She had, however, resigned the security of a monthly paycheque determined to search for the freedom to write as she wished. She began with the short story because she was attracted to the possibilities of the form and also because she was able to sell stories to magazines.

As readers of *The New Yorker* are aware, Gallant has been publishing with them for over thirty years; a fruitful association allowing her to live entirely off her writing, she has also written two novels and a number of longer fictions which her editors have called novellas, at least one of which, *The Pegnitz Junction*, has the scope and weight of a short novel. These novels are all experimental in form: *Green Water, Green Sky* (1959) is composed of interlocking short stories, each of which portrays a core situation from a different point of view; *A Fairly Good Time* (1970) is the closest to the traditional form of the novel, building on a coupling of past and present events, the one reflecting the other; *The Pegnitz Junction* (1973) is partially a dream voyage with all the dissociations of the dream state.

As a writer, Gallant was strongly influenced by her experience of the 30's and 40's, with the Depression leading to the growth of fascism and finally World War II. Her work reflects not only the individual's need to create new forms of consciousness, but also the political perception that for the western nations the post-war period was going to be "business as usual." As a result, many of her characters convey a sense of dis-ease, living amidst the wreckage of great civilizations, the ruins of which are unable to supply the materials for a new culture. Her fiction also projects a strongly social and political flavour even when most personal, since her characters reveal the distance between individual desire and sustaining social patterns. Consequently, her novels read like poems, rarely presenting an obvious narrative line on which the reader can ride easily and comfortably to the last word of the plot. While her characters inhabit a world of tangible reality, we encounter them not as whole human beings, but in the silences of narrative breaks, the babble of different voices, the illogic of nursery rhymes, and the sudden flash of a revealing image. Language, for Gallant, shadows the imprint of the past with all its hidden wrongs.

Given her fascination with the processes by which the past comes to inhabit the present, it is hardly surprising to find that Gallant has written a great deal about the family wherein the patterns of the past are handed on to the next generation. *Green Water, Green Sky*, Gallant's first novel, describes the relationship between a daughter and her mother, Florence and Bonnie, in which the two become so dependent upon one another that the child never develops a sense of herself, and eventually goes mad, a scene which is among the most brilliant and haunting in contemporary fiction.[1] The point of the novel is not, however, to affirm that parents must give their children freedom, but to explore the effect of family relations upon childhood consciousness. By introducing other characters who have undergone similar experiences although not as extreme as those of Florence, Gallant makes us aware of the "pathology" or deadening influences inherent in all such relationships.

Florence's cousin George comes to realize that parental love, even at its most positive, creates bonds and obligations, a "structure" or cage for the individual. Normally when one refers to the influence of the family, the argument runs that certain "traits" are passed on as a consequence of family style, or that the parents give commands, suggestions or models, which the child either accepts or rebels against. *Green Water, Green Sky* plunges well below such commonplaces to create a situation in which we observe children developing at a stage before they are completely formed individuals. Gallant portrays children as free flowing and opposing psychic forces which are eventually "bound" into a force or direction which constitutes the individual. This binding of energy gives the individual a sense of freedom, but since he is "bound," his choices contain all the early oppositions, ready at any moment to subvert his intended purposes.

Chapter one of *Green Water, Green Sky* first establishes an atmosphere of childhood. With the child immersed in the watery stuff of existence, conscious linear thought has not yet been developed. Gallant's opening presents in fact a modern creation myth, similar to Milton's epic, but owing more to the Blakeian sense that creation is, paradoxically, the fall, since creation will force the multivalent powers into one Urizenic pattern. What Blake gave in cosmology, Gallant renders in psychology. Indeed, Gallant's use of recurring images and her sense of being under water evokes a psychotic condition remarkably like that of Freud's unconscious, a state unencumbered by a syntax of formal logic and grammar but finding expression through connecting images.[2]

The story takes place largely in Venice, witnessed through the eyes of seven-year-old George, a cousin of Florence. Although the basic scenes emerge through the eyes of a child, there is also the figure of an older George, about seventeen, who is piecing together his memories. While the situation contains Freudian parallels, Gallant develops her characters through a mirroring of the self-image: George does not "tell" the story, since we slip from past to present and into the past again with so little obstruction that time itself disappears, a basic factor for an effective representation of childhood. The events take place during a hot summer day in Venice where the effect of the heat on this city of reflections turns everything liquid and green. The green of the Venice water is the green of Florence's eyes. A glass bead turned in the hand or held up to the eye fills the air with "pigeons and bells" (GWGS p. 19). Memories are placed "one on the other, glass over glass" (GWGS p. 7). Metaphor replaces the temporal frame: people and things *are* one another, the entire world being connected through the agency of image.

In this liquid atmosphere, Gallant effects a sleight of hand by making it appear as though the patterns of the adult are superimposed on those of the child. She reveals with startling clarity the fundamental difference in the two ways of thinking. As a child, George lives amidst opposites with no need to reconcile them into a more systematic structure. In the opening, for example, George discovers that his parents, wanting a day's sight-seeing on their own, have gone off, leaving him with his aunt and Florence. Filled with resentment, he shows desire for his parents by raging at them. At the same time, George learns that his Aunt Bonnie "loves" him, not because he is George, but because he is a Fairlie, and she desperately wants to retain her links to her family. Florence, on the other hand, "hates" him and wishes him dead, not because he is George, but because he is a Fairlie. As a child, he accepts all of these oppositions with no difficulty, but as a young man of seventeen, he finds himself an individual with one set of acceptable attitudes, the others being repressed. The transition from one stage to the other has always puzzled psychologists, and they have found it difficult to explain how it occurs without a major upheaval. As an adult George seems to have come through unscathed. Even his parents regard him as a complete success: "At seventeen, he was a triumphant vindication for his parents of years of hell" (GWGS p. 3). Yet he stammers, and in moments of crisis, turns with alarming regularity to God: "God, help me this once, and I'll never bother you again" (GWGS p. 5). With George, Gallant makes us aware of the two different states, showing us George as a child and adult — one image over the other — and leaving us to ponder how it happened that free-flowing childhood experience was converted into the "bound" ego of the adult. Gallant can afford to leave us in limbo with George because she will return to him.

As in most novels about consciousness and psychic forces, Gallant relies on the principle of doubling and it is in her portrait of Florence that we see the actual transition from child to adult taking place. At fourteen, Florence is at the age when the conflicting claims of love and hate need final resolution. With all the heightened perception of a child who senses the image of meaning but cannot yet explain the development, George sees that his presence as a beloved child in the nest of a loving family is triggering a response in Florence. She hates him for belonging to a family and threatens to kill him, to push him into the water and let him drown. One senses Florence's own thrashing in the watery element; she feels exposed without the protection of a family. Instead of giving us a narrative explanation, Gallant introduces a single image of rejection: Florence breaking a cheap string of glass beads and throwing them across the piazza in an action that George senses as wildly feverish and almost mad. It is of course an impulse of utter abandon, an impulse that so frightens George that it drives him to the opposite extreme. He runs wildly about collecting the beads for Florence, "anxious about what strangers might think." Many years later George still has one of these beads, token of the need to avoid the frightening abandon exhibited in Florence. Indeed, as we recognize later, this is George's route to "sanity." He will never break the string or chain of childhood connections; he will save appearances.

Yet as Gallant knows full well, the transition from child to adult is not effected through the power of any one emotion, but through a marriage of opposites. Florence's violent breaking of the string is matched a few minutes later by an equally violent act of cleaving to her mother. Florence says to George:

> "She'll never do anything any more. I'll always keep
> her with me." That wasn't affected. There was no toss
> of hair, but the same queer pushing attitude of hands he
> had seen after the necklace broke. She meant these
> words, they weren't intended for George. It was a
> solemn promise, a cry of despair, love and resentment
> so woven together that even Flor couldn't tell them
> apart.   (GWGS p. 11)

Love and resentment fuse together here into a life choice in which the "queer pushing attitude" is incorporated but not given visible expression. Unlike George, Florence commits herself entirely to an action of love which is also hate. Indeed, the moment of fusion is over so quickly that in normal circumstances it would go unnoticed. Florence's family, in fact, notices nothing, and even the reader is lulled for a time when he sees that Florence appears later to be living the usual life of a young woman. Marriage to Bob Harris is imminent, and the earlier period in Venice has been forgotten. Yet George cannot forget the terrifying moment when "breaking" became "embracing," when death became life. Curious and also anxious to help, he offers Florence her Venetian glass bead, an image of the past which might bring her good luck, which might remind her of what she has done. Yet Florence cannot remember the scene in Venice, and claims she does not need luck, that she never was a person who broke things. Such *hubris,* such repression of the instinct to break free, obviously bodes no good, and prepares us for future developments.

As has been mentioned, Gallant composed *Green Water, Green Sky* as separate stories. In fact the first three were published in *The New Yorker* early in 1959, the same year as the novel appeared. Unlike other novels composed of short stories, such as Margaret Laurence's *A Bird in the House* and Alice Munro's *Lives of Girls and Women, Green Water, Green Sky* does not simply follow the life trajectory of one character from childhood to maturity. Indeed, it would have been impossible for Gallant to work in this mode, since she begins with the assumption that children are born into a web of family relations. The individual does not grow out of the web but repeats the primal relation over and over again in new ways. A second reason why separate stories proved so attractive to Gallant is that she can present various individuals in different situations, while repeating the same underlying patterns.

Gallant begins Chapter two, not with George or Florence, but with Bonnie about a year after Florence's marriage. We move from what was essentially a child's preconscious experience of multiplicity to the adult's sense of himself, which also comprises several people in one. As Gallant comments about Bonnie: "After years of struggling to remain adult in a grown-up world, she had found it unrewarding, and, in her private moments, allowed herself the blissful luxury of being someone else" (GWGS p. 21). Still partly the child of her earlier years, Bonnie also resembles a character out of Kipling, a "Mrs. Hauksbee, witty and thin, with those great rolling violet blue eyes." And yet she is neither of these exactly, for she "had left off being tender Bonnie without achieving the safety of Mrs. Hauksbee" (GWGS p. 23). With several masks, none fitting exactly, Bonnie is no one in particular, a negative, yet as we know only too well, much can come from nothing. The same sense of dislocation holds true for the other adults in the story. For example, Florence's husband, Bob Harris, is a successful modern wine merchant, but he lives in old Parisian rooms because of a nostalgic fondness for the past. Unable to understand the past, he collects it in "good" and "important" pieces of furniture.

If a dissociation of sensibility controls the normal state of adult life, weakening purpose but preserving "sanity," then the reader wonders how Florence will deal with her fusing of love and hate into a single emotion. Our first meeting with her comes as a shock because Gallant drops her description of people existing more or less happily in a compromise of their own devising and suddenly shows the compromise for what it is, a dislocation of reality capable of turning against the individual at any moment:

> It was three o'clock in the afternoon. Florence was
> walking with cautious steps along the Boulevard des

Capucines when the sidewalk came up before
her. (GWGS p. 27)

Florence's earlier fusion of love and hate breaks apart when she
can no longer exist as an entity in control of the world. Gallant's
evocation of madness is by no means a whirl of atoms, a return
to chaos; Florence undergoes an attempt by the world to reassert
its potential for unlimited variation, that state which exists before
the will bends the psyche into a particular form and direction. Florence experiences "the effort of lines to change their
form" (GWGS p. 30), a sense that the world rightfully exists as
free-flowing undetermined forces.

Since language provides one of the main means by which the
mind controls the world, objects in flux being condensed into solid
nouns, one of the first things that happens to Florence is that she
loses her ability to fit language into coherent patterns. She can
recall scraps of poetry, but can no longer use the language of the
past to inform the present. As with T. S. Eliot, such scraps are
fragments shoring against ruin; Florence, however, perceives
such ruin as her desired primeval state. Gallant creates a similar
situation when Florence's new friend Doris comes to visit and
struggles with "memories and impulse she could neither relate
nor control" (GWGS p. 72). As these people use it, language
repeats but does not elucidate the central primal childhood
experience.

Yet the language of the novel itself, because it works obliquely, allows us to see that Florence's approaching madness, while
appearing on the surface as a fall into chaos, means for her a
return to the primary authority of childhood experience. When
Florence disappears from this world into madness, she reappears
in her mind as a child on her pony, riding into the all-welcoming,
all-embracing arms of her father. We have never seen this
man; he has been repressed even from the story. But in
Florence's subconscious he has always existed as a living
presence. Her love for him, which she disavowed consciously,
finally reasserts itself. What society sees as a loss of control,
Florence experiences as the regaining of protection, the return
to the all-loving, all-knowing father. In a Romantic interpretation, Florence's madness might be seen as the loss of herself, a
form of suicide, but in fact Florence experiences the opposite. She
finds her self.

Whereas the first two chapters evoke the inner world of the mind, in which the clear light of reason gives way to transparency and watery reflections, Chapter three moves into the social sphere, supposedly the domain of hard facts. Gallant shifts the time frame as well, so that Chapter three, in which Florence meets Bob Harris, actually takes place before the events in Chapter two. In part, of course, Chapter three explains how Florence came to marry Bob. More than that, it evokes the sense of the public world as a forced flight. The setting shifts to the beach at Cannes in the last two years of the Fourth Republic with the sense of corruption everywhere. Cannes is reduced to "sand, and cigarette butts, and smears of oil" (GWGS p. 113). The heat reminds one of the stay in Venice, but with a new quality of senseless routine suggesting the inferno of Hell in which Sisyphus performs his unending task.

Gallant also introduces a new character, the schoolmaster Wishart, an Englishman in America and an American in England, an "insect" who lives on the invitations of women like Bonnie whom he admires for her elegance, her family and what he takes to be her money. Wishart embodies the worst of the post-war vanities, making his living in America, but taking his pleasure in Europe. It is the presence of Wishart, the would-be social climber, which eventually sends Florence in flight from the world of Cannes, straight into the arms of Bob Harris.

Ultimately, then, the endless monotony of the social world resulting from its repetitions creates the need for flight. Not surprisingly, personal relations appear to provide a solution. Florence flies from the sense of the repeated moment, the corruption of the late 1950s, but what she seeks refuge in — the newness of Bob Harris — is hardly better, for he represents the "monster" of modern business without attachments to the past, and altogether lacking in taste. Yet to Florence "newness" liberates, since it reproduces the childhood feeling of "a watery world of perceptions, where impulses, doubts, intentions, detached from their roots, rise to the surface and expand" (GWGS p. 111). Because Bob lives in a continuous present of ongoing relationships, Florence sees him as a release from a past which condemns her to endless repetition, a form of life Wishart embodies in his succession of hostesses whom he despises but lives from parasitically. As Gallant indicates, Florence's turn to Bob involves the most dangerous of ideas — "only you can save me" (GWGS p. 112). Once again she gives up the multiplicity of self for the blinding passion of love which releases the individual into the safety of her lover's arms, the lover being a surrogate for the father. The chapter ends in a superb succession of falling dominoes, falling masks: Wishart reveals himself as an insect, Bonnie as an old woman, and Florence as a "poseuse." It is one of those moments of revelation which could open the individual to his real self, but which is so frightening that flight appears the only answer. Florence catapults into Bob's arms, clearly another move in the direction of complete security which will help to unleash the forces of the unconscious already witnessed in Chapter two.

In a novel so entirely given over to expression through overlapping images of the past subverting the present, the ending obviously presented Gallant with a difficulty. She needed to leave her readers with a sense of the action coming to a close, and yet also with the sense of the present never being free of the past. In other words she cannot have any of her characters standing completely free of the past. The final chapter, seen through the eyes of George, takes place in a Paris restaurant soon after Florence's hospitalization. Since George is the one character capable of understanding enough of the past to use it to free himself, we watch with eagerness as he fights to circumvent Bonnie's self-serving memories of Florence.

In the end, however, Gallant shows how, even with the best intentions, the individual distorts the past to make room for the present. When Bob suggests that George visit Florence, feeling that George knew Florence well and that the sight of a friendly face might help her, George replies with "the most considerate thing he could think of" (GWGS p. 154), that he had seen his cousin only six times, that they hardly knew one another. George tells half the truth, and has been "considerate" from his point of view. He leaves Florence entirely to Bob, thereby relinquishing "all claim" from the family. He sets her free. But in giving up family claims to Florence, he also denies Florence and his own past. His victory becomes his defeat, or his defeat his victory, depending on the point of view.

Gallant concludes pessimistically that individuals can rarely discover the ground of their being, and even when they do so in moments of memory, dreams and hallucinations, it proves impossible to use the insights to free the individual entirely from the past. And yet for all the pessimism of its conclusion, the novel daringly enacts the web, illustrating that although man cannot know truth he can embody it.

After publishing *Green Water, Green Sky* in 1959, eleven years passed before Gallant's second novel *A Fairly Good Time* appeared in 1970.[3] This gap in time is somewhat deceptive, however, since Gallant began writing the new novel only a year or two after the publication of *Green Water, Green Sky* and worked on it throughout much of the sixties. Living entirely from her royalties, Gallant has found it easier to complete shorter works. Finding the necessary time to complete long projects has always proved difficult. Only after the publication in *The New Yorker* of her extended eye-witness account of the 1968 student revolution in France (for which she received a lump-sum payment) was she able to put aside sufficient time to finish the new novel. The longest of Gallant's fictional works, *A Fairly Good Time* comes closest to the traditional novel: a long prose work possessing a central character within a social context, mediated by a unified point of view. Yet within this conventional form, Gallant combines social satire with an investigation of how the world, accustomed to perceiving life as a struggle for victory, repulses a free act of love.

A Fairly Good Time belongs to a long tradition of novels which describe the meeting of North American innocence with European sophistication, a tradition going back at least as far as the novels of Henry James, Edith Wharton and Sara Jeanette Duncan. As Gallant's title page indicates, the novel's title comes from Edith Wharton's story "The Last Asset." In Gallant's rendering, Shirley assumes the role of the innocent-abroad, a young Canadian of twenty-six, one of the many young people in the sixties who married "a week after graduation," and then set out on the grand tour of Europe for a honeymoon, with little in their heads and just enough money to travel around the warmer climes in dirty clothes. Unlike most of the people who returned to Canada with rolls of undeveloped film and touristic experiences, Shirley suffers an irrevocable alteration of character when her husband Pete is killed in Italy in a fluke bicycle accident. Subsequently she moves to Paris where she learns sufficient French for a bohemian life-style. She has a wide circle of friends almost all of whom are "foreigners" like herself.

Shirley recounts a familiar story of the sixties: young people imitating vaguely the life-stories of twenties-writers such as Hemingway, Stein and Callaghan. In Shirley's case, however, fate again takes an unusual turn: she marries a Frenchman, Philippe Perrigny, a journalist for Le Miroir, Who sees in Shirley a refuge for his bourgeois family. Unlike most of the members of the "lost generation" who never learned French and were always outsiders, Shirley suddenly finds herself within la vie francaise. The problems which result when French decorum and logic confront Canadian casualness and impulse are a sheer delight, creating some superbly comic scenes. The humour, moreover, by no means develops always at the expense of Canadian innocence; Gallant offers a satiric account of French life remarkable for its exposure of the deadening conventions beneath the surface of style and wit.

Gallant has remarked that the impulse for the novel came when she saw a young woman, obviously American, on the Paris Metro returning home early in the morning after a night out. The young woman was wearing a raincoat, had her hair cut in a peculiar fashion, and seemed somewhat at a loss. She was also wearing a wedding ring, and Gallant recalls thinking that she would have some explaining to do.[4] As she develops in the novels, Shirley combines both impulse and caprice resulting in a zany, impetuous attitude to life which would drive anyone to distraction. She cannot remember where things are kept, rarely manages to clean, forgets appointments, and seems virtually to live in a continuous present. Yet she is also extravagantly warm-hearted, concerned with suffering, and as free of duplicity as it is possible to be — the embodiment of North American innocence, with all its ingenuousness.

While the reader inevitably finds himself laughing at Shirley's erratic behaviour, he cannot help admiring the way she deals with the complexities of organized French life. Her solution to the laundry problem, for example, is simple: she lets it accumulate and then once or twice a month takes it by taxi to the cleaners. Since she has noted that taxi-drivers become surly when asked to go only a short distance, she has fallen into the habit of taking the laundry to a cleaners across town. Bizarre though the system is, it works. Once married to Philippe, Shirley discovers that the French method requires one to list each item of the laundry in advance so that on a given day it is ready for a delivery boy who collects the clothes in a cart, and then returns them a week later, tightly folded, full of pins, highly starched, and missing buttons. The clothes have to be unpacked, checked off against the original list, unfolded, the pins taken out, and then everything put away. To Philippe it all seems sensible and logical, and he cannot understand why his wife seems incapable of doing such a simple task. The point, of course, is that it is not simple. Shirley's method, although unorthodox, is vastly simpler.

As a comedy of manners and a satire on national types, *A Fairly Good Time* succeeds enormously. Yet as one reads further in the novel, it becomes evident that Shirley becomes more than a satiric device: she offers a challenge to attitudes which others confidently assume are natural and inevitable. One of the axioms of social comedy is that we are not required, as in tragedy, to sympathize with any of the characters to understand their psychological processes. Yet in *A Fairly Good Time* we observe Shirley closely from the inside; indeed we are allowed to see the world, almost without exception, only through Shirley's perceptions. As the unformed North American free in Europe, Shirley embodies consciousness before it has been schooled to see the world through social lenses.

This may seem a contradiction in terms after what has been observed in *Green Water, Green Sky* of Gallant's depiction of the growth of the children's personality. Needless to say, a completely "natural" consciousness would be contradictory, since all individuals are born into some kind of social conditioning. Yet as a Canadian living in France, Shirley is something of a babe in the woods, a foreigner whose social rules do not apply, and who is therefore free to make her own. Or, of more interest still, not to live by rules at all, but to respond creatively to situations as they arise. Earlier in *Green Water, Green Sky* we observed how a person who finds herself completely walled in, without a sense of self, can float away from the world. Now in *A Fairly Good Time*, we watch Shirley refusing to acknowledge the reality of such walls, and walking straight into them. The surprise is that although she sometimes ends up bruised, she often walks straight through.

Gallant creates this sensation of a reality with only imaginary walls by beginning the novel at the point where Philippe has walked out, leaving Shirley to reflect on past events, attempting to understand why her husband has left her. The unusual feature of the novel is that there rarely seems a present moment, for the past always becomes the future, and what should be the present, the ground on which the character "stands," dissolves into consciousness. In other words the past becomes the future by means of the agency of consciousness. Indeed, the story calls the very nature of clock time into question, and for most of the novel we move in what might be called "subjective" time.

When Mrs. Castle visits Shirley in Paris, for example, Shirley thinks about calling for a telephone, and even though she knows there are no table phones in Paris, the phone seems to appear. As a result, the reader's experience of the novel confirms Shirley's own feelings about the openness and fluidity of existence. Unlike traditional novels which tend to assume a given "realistic" present in which individuals with their first-person points of view are situated, *A Fairly Good Time* reverses the ordering and begins with the notion that consciousness itself helps, through its processes to order reality.

In this respect, Shirley's sense of reality differs dramatically from that of others. Philippe, for example, assumes a world already formed, something which exists apart from him. Since Shirley is his wife, he expects that she will behave exactly as his mother and all other Frenchwomen are supposed to behave. For Philippe, things are what they are, always the same and necessarily so; for Shirley, however, the world rises into being, at least partially, through her responses and actions. While all of this may sound terribly solemn and conjure up a notion of existence as perception, in fact Shirley's misadventures are not solemn at all, but both comic and painful.

Shirley is not some Heideggerian existentialist who thinks about *Geworfenheit*, about being thrown into the chaos of the world. She wants contact with others, wants love; that other people seem to want order and precision thoroughly confuses her. At times the sense of being an exile in a strange land where she can understand every word in a sentence and still not understand the sentence becomes so absurdist that she can mistake her own reflection in a mirror for a friend, and end up walking into herself.

Put another way, Shirley embodies the comic principle of anarchy. Indeed *A Fairly Good Time* displays some obvious parallels with Kingsley Amis' *Lucky Jim*, a novel which Shirley, ironically, has been reading. The arbitrary conventions of order frustrate both characters, but Shirley experiences a far more radical situation, since she does not even appear to see the world as others see it. Where Jim acts cunningly, Shirley is oblivious to realities, a female cousin of the great Don himself, forcing us to rethink our conventional views of man's place in the universe.

The reader's experience of Shirley as a walking catastrophe, always responding to situations as she-is-at-the-moment, not as some created *persona* who stands beside her, reveals the arbitrary nature of social attitudes and the hollowness of those who live their lives for and within such attitudes. Before long, Shirley's impulsiveness becomes genuinely attractive, and as this occurs, we recognize Gallant's extension of the question posed implicitly at the end of *Green Water, Green Sky:* is it possible to break out of duality into singleness of spirit without doing damage to the multiplicity of experience?

Gallant's larger aims become apparent if we step back from the novel's teeming surface to examine its structure. *A Fairly Good Time* opens with a god-like fiat, a letter from Shirley's mother, Mrs. Norrington, which she hurtles at her daughter like a missile. The letter's frigid rationalistic style — it begins "Dearest Girl" — reveals that Mrs. Norrington is about as distant from her daughter as Jahweh was from his chosen people. Only later do we learn that Shirely has sent her mother a *cri de coeur*, which her mother has chosen to ignore by talking learnedly about the bluebell Shirley enclosed in a previous letter. With its abstract diction and its certainty of expression, the opening letter sets the stage for everything we have come to associate with man since the Renaissance: his pride, his individuality, his knowledge, and his certainty that his purpose is to offer rational explanations of an object world set over against himself.

Mrs. Norrington even implies that Shirley's problems arise from having never learned to ask questions about the nature of time, questions which Mrs. Norrington believes she could easily have answered. The rest of the novel develops an active response to this opening letter, an answer, not in the sense of an explanation of events unfolding in time, but a confrontation with time itself as Shirley continually crashes into being, with the outcome a spontaneously created world, not known from the outside, but experienced from the inside.[5]

That Gallant is developing a sense of cultural background which goes well beyond any simple sense of family is shown when Mrs. Cat Castle, a friend of the Norrington family, turns up in Paris to visit Shirley and presents her with a book, saying that it is all Shirley will likely receive from her family. It turns out to be an old children's book entitled *The Peep of Day*, a series of questions and answers intended to teach children the Christian message.

The book surfaces periodically throughout the novel, with Shirley dipping into it, child-like, for words of wisdom to sort out the chaos of experience. Each time, she finds the mournful lesson that children should not trust themselves. The author relishes situations where the child's friends and relatives suddenly die. From the Christian point of view, the individual should draw back from himself and the world so as to put his faith in God. Consequently children learn early to keep their own bodies and the world at a distance. They come to "understand" the world rather than submit themselves to it, and they therefore objectify the world against themselves.

Against this dolorous view, Shirley can proffer nothing easily optimistic: *"We have been abandoned* was all she knew about the universe"* (AFGT p. 49). Yet the vertigo inherent in this nihilism turns out to be far more liberating than the cautionary attitudes endorsed and created by the author of *The Peep of Day*. Shirley's sense of dizziness corresponds to that found in true children's literature such as *Alice in Wonderland*, which accepts from the outset that the conventional rules of the world do not apply. People like Philippe and Mrs. Norrington pride themselves on having escaped the darkness of previous generations, but they remain as divorced from the world in their intellectual premises as the author of *The Peep of Day*.

Shirley's mother may be "one of a family of militant, university-trained prairie women" (AFGT p. 46), may have published a thesis on Ruskin, and may even be enlightened enough to sympathize with Ruskin's long-suffering wife Effie Gray, but she has not herself broken down her Cartesian dualism to live passionately in the world. She understands ideas, but her own life has been one of idealistic isolation, an isolation that in the end renders even her rationality eccentric. Had Gallant chosen to write only about Shirley's past — her memories of Philippe — the novel would have left her as a woman without a present, drowning in the past. As it stands, however, Shirley meets a young French girl, Claudie Maurel, who at first sight seems to be another Shirley. Claudie will eat a meal in a restaurant, without any money, simply assuming that someone will take pity on her youth and beauty and pay for the meal. That someone turns out to be Shirley, who can sympathize with Claudie's plight because she knows that it could easily have happened to her.

But where Claudie is merely cunning, Shirley proves thoughtfully concerned. Thus Gallant uses the *doppelganger* to show us the difference between uncaring random behaviour and a truly warm-hearted responsiveness which becomes ultimately authentic and psychologically rewarding. This may seem paradoxical at first, since what has been stressed in the first part of the novel is Shirley's impulsiveness, but throughout the second half, we recognize the difference between action based on gifts of love which take the individual inside experience and the mere manipulation of experience through carelessness or cunning. Claudie, moreover, introduces us to the authoritarian French family structure. The unspoken rules and obligations of such families are of so violent a nature that in the end they reduce Claudie to a state of childlike submission corresponding to what we saw earlier in Florence's insanity.

As was the case in *Green Water, Green Sky* language acts once again as one of the most subtly pervasive traps for the individual. Yet as a "foreigner," Shirley possesses a certain degree of freedom. Her French is good but not perfect, and therefore she never trusts entirely what other people are saying. She overhears language and can treat it as something neutral, not something which simply takes her over, as so often happens when one uses automatically one's mother tongue. In her friendship with James, a Greek living in the flat above her, she perceives how he uses her and his other women to live out an ancient dream of the satyr surrounded by wood nymphs. Over his bed, she writes in lipstick — "CORO DI NINFE E PASTORI" (AFGT p. 112) — or, "chorus of nymphs and shepherds," the foreign language forcing us to effect the translation from Italian to English just as Shirley has translated James' actions into their mythic form.

Shirley's major realization is that "Language is Situation" (AFGT p. 22). This does not mean simply that different situations require different languages, but that the language itself creates situation. For example, Philippe's friend Geneviève is writing an interminable novel about her disastrous love life with her husband and her desire to make love to a man who very much resembles Philippe. When Philippe talks about Geneviève, he uses the language of her novel. Shirley notes: "It was a form of expression the two roused in each other, as if some third, gassy, invisible presence — a substitute for passion — occupied each of them in turn" (AFGT p. 22). The language possesses them; they do not possess it.

The whole question of language has of course almost become a cliché in modern literature. Realizing this, but also recognizing that it remains the central problem, Gallant introduces the issue through Philippe as a cliché in his article on the imaginary dramatist Tofolu Groupe. Like all of Philippe's articles, it is entitled "The Soundless Cry," and goes on at some length describing how we are seized by "vertigo" of "both mind and body" (AFGT p. 213). The irony is that Philippe himself never feels gripped by such vertigo. Moreover, the interview is a complete sham, because Groupe was so drunk at the time he could not say anything. In fact Shirley finds an earlier draft of Philippe's interview in which he had given his real sense of the situation, that man suffers not from too little comprehension of others but from "the complete comprehension" of others, a state created by Philippe's belief that he understands Shirley and everyone else comprehensively. For Philippe, his intelligence provides a perfect image of the world's structure. For Shirley, both versions of the interview, both views of language, lack validity because they are both concerned with "knowing"; neither makes the leap to sympathetic involvement.

If *A Fairly Good Time* presents a comic but forlorn view of man as an alien amidst his man-made concepts, it also presents the world opening up at one or two places. Gallant shows how a person like Shirley involved creatively in the world is permitted moments when the outside world breaks through the human barriers of consciousness. The most important incident — one neither psychological, sociological nor philosophical but perhaps close to religious — occurs late in the novel and portrays Shirley's finding of the bluebell. This flower has haunted the novel as one of its unifying images. Shirley recalls how she found the bluebell while on a Sunday visit with Philippe to his friend Hervé in the Parisian suburb of Orsay. Since Philippe served with Hervé in the Algerian war, the visit should be a special time. But it is a horror from beginning to end. There is a snarl of traffic to leave the city, and Shirley notes how the lights hang "over the road like dead animals." What is supposed to be the country turns out to be a "fungus extension of Paris" (AFGT p. 246). In their new flat, Hervé and his wife show them all their modern conveniences; they eat lunch "on a chrome-legged formica table dragged out of the kitchen" (AFGT p. 247). Proud of not being "bourgeois," Hervé claims to live like a student, although the furniture screams the opposite. When they go out for a walk, Shirley sees "what remained of a grove of trees," and the places where bulldozers have "backed and turned" destroying all the paths.

In the midst of this desolate landscape, without warning, Shirley and Hervé's wife see "a lake of blue" and for a moment "the new, sweet fragrance that rose from the blue lake was a secret between (them)" (AFGT p. 249). The lake of bluebells, so beautiful and fragrant, breaks through the torn landscape like a visitant from another world. Until this point "the low color tone of the suburb, the washed out sandiness of the afternoon" (AFGT p. 249) had made Shirley feel as though there were a "filter" in her mind as well as a weakening in her eyes. But the combination of colour and fragrance penetrates the numbing afternoon, and allows her to feel again intensely and brightly.

Hervé and his wife experience nothing of the piercing beauty, only a chance to collect free wild flowers. Hervé says: "Get all you can, for once." And Shirley reflects: "So that was what their life was about" (AFGT p. 249). Shirley is now judged incompetent because she collects only one flower for herself. Indeed from this point on she realizes that others regard her husband as "poor Philippe," because she has no ability to collect and consume. Yet for Shirley, such experiences are a validation, breathing significance into the story of her life. Her near annihilation occurs because other people around her, even her husband, seem to have no awareness of the experience. For them life means collecting as much as you can before someone else takes it first.

Gallant also goes on to suggest that what appears to be merely an aesthetic experience for Shirley may well have moral and social ramifications. A clear connection exists between the individual's ability to open himself to existence and the kind of social and political world he develops. Gallant has mentioned that when she began the novel, she thought that it would be about the Algerian conflict, but as the novel progressed the conflict became the background. As setting, however, the conflict supplies the larger dimension to the individual struggle to claim victory over life, always to obtain more.

While Shirley tries to live her life in the present, France engages in a bitter war with its colony, Algeria, attempting to prevent the people there from taking control of their own political destiny. When the people of Algeria took up arms, France went to war (undeclared though it was) and split the nation in two, creating a virtual civil war in France. The novel reflects all of this: Shirley remarks several times about the bombed apartment in her building; she witnesses the police beating up people in a restaurant; her friend Renata collects newspaper pictures of the police violently breaking up demonstrations. The political violence takes root in the violence people do to themselves when they abstract consciousness from individuality, an abstraction which effectively turns the individual-society dialectic into a "me-it" situation. The individual no longer takes part in existence, but stands outside, attempting to murder existence.

At the same time as she was working on *A Fairly Good Time*, Gallant began a series of stories about Germany and the Germans. These stories began appearing in *The New Yorker* in 1963, and in 1973 she collected five and added to them the recently completed novella or short novel, *The Pegnitz Junction* which gives the book its title.[6] Gallant had been concerned with the German situation ever since the war when, as a young reporter on *The Montreal Standard* she had been given the task of writing about the first pictures taken of the concentration camps after the British and Americans arrived. She had remarked several times in interviews that these pictures were a turning point in her life, that she felt she must try and understand how such an unparalleled atrocity could have occurred.[7]

Of course Gallant was by no means alone in her horror at the millions of dead in the concentration camps. The entire western world continues to react to the holocaust. What distinguished her response was that she saw the need to ask questions about the Germans, whose pre-war culture was regarded as one of the high points of Western civilization. She wanted desperately to understand why civilization had proved no barrier to barbarism. She tells of writing in her diary, "I wrote, then, that the victims, the survivors that is, would probably not be able to tell us anything, except for the description of life at point zero. If we wanted to find out how and why this happened it was the Germans we had to question."[8] Gallant's German stories constitute her own questioning of the German people. As she has commented: "It is not a book about fascism, but a book about where fascism came from."[9]

Such a statement can be misleading if one imagines that Gallant was attempting to recreate the 1930s and 1940s. Indeed, George Woodcock, enormously well-read in German history, has even disagreed with Gallant about the main thrust of the stories, saying that they are not so much about "where fascism came from" but about "the emerging world of modern Germany" after the war.[10] While Woodcock is correct about the setting being postwar Germany, he overlooks the point that for all the de-Nazification that took place after the war, many of the earlier habits of thought in the actions of everyday life persisted. Gallant reproduces, not the politics of Nazi Germany, but the possibilities of fascism as grounded in the personal attitudes of ordinary people. As she says: "I had the feeling that in every day living I would find the origin of the wars — the worm that had destroyed the structure."[11]

As a result, Gallant finds the stories in *The Pegnitz Junction* "intensely political," not because they deal with politicians or political treaties, but because they explore fascism's "small possibilities in people."[12] In her earlier novels, Gallant had shown how her characters lived and moved in a present which was very much conditioned by the past; in *The Pegnitz Junction* her characters attempt to create new lives in the postdiluvian period, but they must contend with similar attitudes to those which enabled Hitler's National Socialists to become the dominant political party in the 1930s. One should not forget that Hitler was elected by the German people, and even though he never received an absolute majority, his party won the largest number of votes.

Gallant has remarked that she likes *The Pegnitz Junction* "better than anything else" she has done because she believes that here she finally succeeded in giving at least a partial answer to her own questioning of why civilization collapsed into fascist atrocity.[13] *The Pegnitz Junction* bears witness to the breakdown in personal responsibility leading to social breakdown. This sense of disintegration makes the storyline somewhat difficult to describe, and for a newcomer to Gallant's writing the novel may at first appear difficult and obscure.

On the surface it describes a train journey, taken by Christine, her older lover Herbert, and his son, called little Bert, from Paris to their home in southern Germany. They never reach their destination, but along the way we gradually become aware that nothing is right or normal about the journey or the people. What appears a united family, the holy family of Christian tradition — father, mother and child — reveals itself as fractured. Moreover, by the end of the novel, so many stories have been introduced that everything appears about to fly apart. The storyline resembles the course of Germany itself: the young couple eventually board a train continually rerouted all over the map, the train itself acting as a metaphor for Germany's political journey, a journey hopelessly out of the people's control. The mixture of real-unreal introduced by the lack of a central plot line helps to convey the nightmare quality of life in Germany during the war years.

For all its surrealism, *The Pegnitz Junction* clearly develops from Gallant's exploration in her two earlier novels of the role of consciousness in the creation of the world. Only now Gallant's characters wander through history and literature as well as geography, with the novel building discontinuities by the introduction of other stories which often take us back in time. Not simply a stylistic trick, Gallant's flashbacks demonstrate that her characters inhabit the past as well as the present, the world of ideas as well as the world of objects. In the old adage, those who ignore the past are condemned to repeat it; modern Germany is notorious for the way it attempted to forget the horrors of the war or push them aside in the somewhat cynical materialism of the economic miracle, Germany's *Wirtschaftswunder*.

Yet to speak of "Germany" in this abstract manner does the novel an injustice. As always, Gallant begins not with abstractions but with characters and their problems. Indeed, her aim in writing *The Pegnitz Junction* requires that she avoid abstractions because she wants to show that large scale political attitudes have their basis in individual attitudes to experience. Gallant's crucial insight into her characters in *The Pegnitz Junction* is that they suffer from a lack of genuine self-will. Having no quality of self-determination, they take their identities, their cues to action, from alternatives which are presented, so to speak, prepackaged. These alternatives derive from other characters, from a communal past or from literature; although the individual believes himself to be free, outside of time, he remains caught within a web or dialectic from which no possibility of escape exists.

The sense of a larger world-will finds representation in the image of the train which has control of the characters for most of the novel. How to break the train of events so as to initiate one's own actions becomes the central question. The question remains veiled, however, for openness here would presuppose an understanding of the problem that in itself would create at least a partial solution. Nevertheless, the novel ends with Christine, Herbert and little Bert at a junction where a decision is finally in the process of being made.

The dilemma of the individual caught in the past is reminiscent of what was seen in both the earlier novels. In *The Pegnitz Junction*, however, the sense of the past as an atmosphere of memory in which individuals flounder helplessly develops much more strongly. Christine sits passively for much of the journey absorbing "information" telepathically from the minds of her fellow passengers and from what she sees in the surrounding countryside. The novel also abounds in half-submerged references to German history and literature. At various points we meet Kafka's Castle, Wilhelm Busch's Julchen Knopf, refugees from behind the wall and commandoes disguised as children. In fact the train trip enacts a catastrophic journey through Germany's past in which the central protagonist cringes before the continual bombardment of information through which she can never find a clear channel for her own self, if such a thing should exist.

When individuals in the novel attempt to escape the forces of the past and their society, they find themselves contradicting themselves through their actions because their impulses do not stem from a unified sense of self. Christine, for example, has allowed herself to become engaged to a theological student, but finds that he uses his endless discussions and analyses of their situation as a means of circumventing any real intimacy. To off-set this, she takes an older lover in Herbert to whom she has a strong sexual attachment, but with whom discussion is impossi-ble. Yet her motives are even more complex, for while she needs Herbert sexually, she wants to escape her feminine dependence on the body and the emotions to gain a greater development of her mind. She has in fact been a model but has recently given this up and is trying to "be less conscious of her body" (PJ p. 4). To develop her intellect, she reads a book of essays by Dietrich Bonhoeffer, on the examination reading list for her fiance. However, she reads Bonhoeffer while on a lovers' holi-day in Paris with Herbert. In the midst of all these mind-body contradictions, we hear the voice of the child, little Bert, asking for attention, for love. The larger contradictions press so adamantly, however, that the child is alternately ignored and spoiled. The whole situation gives the impression of a person frantically running inside a wheel, making no real progress because the meaning of any particular action is subverted always by its context.

In the German situation this lack of individual will takes on a horrifying character when we realize that Christine is reliving the journey to the concentration camps. What with the fires along the track, the order to seal the windows, the continual changes in direction and the friendly conductor who becomes a threaten-ing guard, Christine's modern-day trip forms a palimpsest of the trip to the camps. This idea gains even greater authority in three separate incidents. The first occurs in Paris when the hotel porter swears at them and locks them out of their room. The second takes place in Strasbourg where Christine takes her ritual shower in conditions which suggest the camp showers. The third hap-pens at Pegnitz itself when Christine and Herbert become separated and Christine must wait with little Bert for the arrival of their train. In the waiting room the other women are sitting in groups by nationality — Polish, French, Greek, Russian, Dutch — waiting fearfully and passively for something to happen. So strongly does the situation recreate the atmosphere of the camps that Christine finds herself preparing to "inform" on

Herbert. Moreover, the conductor has now turned into an SS officer, and has completely cowed the other women with his charade, thereby creating Christine's moment of crisis when she either throws in her lot with the events of the past or decides to pursue her own future. Gallant suggests that just as the Jews, Slavs and Gypsies were led passively to their deaths, so the Germans allowed themselves to become passive victims to a greater will, that of fascism.

Yet fascism was never simply an abstraction: not only did it have its political embodiment in the figure of Hitler, but countless millions of people gave up their wills to shadowy ideals suddenly made concrete. Herbert, for example, is an engineer who can never confront a threatening situation openly. He retreats, and then writes letters, taking refuge in the printed word. Similarly Christine takes refuge in the idea of being in love, just as Florence does in *Green Water, Green Sky*. At the crucial moment in the waiting room at Pegnitz, Christine turns to her book by Bonhoeffer for advice. At first such a move might seem promising, but we have see the same pattern in *A Fairly Good Time* with Shirley's *The Peep of Day*, and it has become clear that intellectual answers are never adequate responses to personal dilemmas. They simply distance the individual even further from his own sense of self.

Still, Bonhoeffer's *Ethics* are in a different category from *The Peep of Day*. Since Bonhoeffer himself has become a symbol of the Germans who resisted, who were murdered for their beliefs, his theology might well offer an avenue of escape for Christine. On opening the book she sees the words, "The knowledge of good and evil is therefore separation from God. Only against God can man know good and evil" (PJ p. 87). She reads no further, but rejects Bonhoeffer's concept of morality, saying to little Bert: "No use going on with that."

The puzzle is that when one reads in its entirety the essay from which Christine quotes, one discovers that it attempts to deal with the very dilemma facing Christine.[14] Bonhoeffer wants to release the individual from the state of human confusion about good and evil, about what is to be done, by offering a transpersonal vision where action comes about from doing God's will, not merely man's will. Bonhoeffer describes the situation which occurs when the individual loses his own personality to become the spontaneous instrument of God's will.[15] Why, then, does Christine turn down this advice?

Although Bonhoeffer's theology may have worked for him in his own day, in the post-war period it looks surprisingly like a variant of fascism. Both Bonhoeffer and National Socialism urge the individual to give up his will for a greater will. Yet as was seen in *A Fairly Good Time*, Gallant suggests that the individual may find himself, not when he gives himself over to something or someone else, but when he actively participates with his whole being in the situation before him. The individual must throw himself, not into God, but into the world.

Gallant couches Christine's final quandary in terms reminiscent of the last decision made by the millions of people who were forced into the camps. She is in her usual state "wondering and weighing, as reluctant as ever to make up her mind," when suddenly "a great stir started up in the grey and wintry-looking freight yards and they could see from the window. Lights blazed, voices bawled in dialect, a dog barked" (PJ p. 87).

Clearly the scene describes the moment seen in countless films when the prisoners are marched from the train to the camps. The other women around Christine stand up and leave, and little Bert rises to follow. The call to the slaughter given, the entire waiting room empties. Yet at the crucial moment, Christine finds the energy to act: she holds back little Bert, and the two of them remain alone in the waiting room while all sounds of life disappear outside.

The will to live has triumphed, and clearly the reason it triumphs in Christine has nothing to do with rational understanding or Christian dogma. On the contrary, it triumphs because the individual finds her whole self in the moment when she enters the present, thereby bringing the present into being as she brings herself into being. Moreover, it is important to observe that having done this, Christine is now free to begin telling little Bert the story he has been asking for throughout the novel. She has mentioned this story earlier, a story about five brothers all with the name of George but each pronouncing the name differently. Herbert had claimed that such a story would only confuse the boy. Yet Christine disagrees.

At the end as the boy and young woman sit next to each other for comfort, Christine begins for the first time in her own voice to tell the story. The novel ends with her beginning to name the five different names all of which mean the same, but designate different people. Although *The Pegnitz Junction* ends with Christine still at Pegnitz, still not home, story-telling offers the means to complete a voyage begun many years earlier by Florence and Shirley. Only now, there is no confusion, no wild searching for meaning: story-telling has allowed the heroine to find herself at home everywhere, with the journey still continuing.

Notes

1   Mavis Gallant, *Green Water, Green Sky* (Boston: Houghton Mifflin, 1959). All further references are to this edition, with page numbers in parentheses.
2   Gallant's characterization may well have its basis in Freudian ideas of the mind. She has mentioned that in her youth, most of the intellectuals and writers in Canada were reading Freud. While finishing her schooling in New York, Gallant lived with a psychiatrist's family and had the run of his library.
3   Mavis Gallant, *A Fairly Good Time* (New York: Random House, 1970). All further references are to this edition, with page numbers in parentheses.
4   Interview with Geoff Hancock in the special issue devoted to Mavis Gallant of *Canadian Fiction Magazine*, No. 28 (1978), p. 58.
5   For an interesting discussion of catastrophe as creation, see Harold Bloom, *Agon: Towards a Theory of Revisionism* (Oxford: Oxford University Press, 1982), pp. 91-118.
6   Mavis Gallant, *The Pegnitz Junction* (New York: Random House, 1973). All further references are to this edition, with page numbers in parentheses.
7   *CFM*, p. 39.
8   *CFM*, pp. 39-40.
9   *CFM*, p. 41.
10 George Woodcock, "Memory, Imagination, Artifice: the late short fiction of Mavis Gallant," in *CFM*, p. 83.
11 *CFM*, p. 40.
12 *CFM*, p. 41.
13 *CFM*, p. 37.
14 Christine actually quotes two passages from Bonhoeffer. See Dietrich Bonhoeffer's *Ethics*, ed. Eberhard Bethge (London: Collins, 1964) pp. 18, 20.
15 See especially Bonhoeffer's short section entitled "The World of Recovered Unity," in his *Ethics*, p. 26.

MICHAEL ONDAATJE

MICHAEL ONDAATJE AND THE TURN TO NARRATIVE

Ina Ferris

When Michael Ondaatje published *The Collected Works of Billy the Kid* in 1970, he signalled a crucial generic shift in his writing — the shift from lyric to narrative. In making this shift, Ondaatje placed himself in exemplary relation to contemporary literature, for his individual move reflects the move of the literary culture as a whole. Increasingly, narrative has become the privileged form for serious literary inquiry and experimentation, challenging the centrality that Romanticism granted to lyric and that lyric continued to assume until well into this century. For Ondaatje the shift to narrative has been neither simple nor unilateral (lyric enters significantly into his narratives), and the narratives he creates are of a peculiarly hybrid kind, prompting one recent reviewer to note that Ondaatje's work is ''continually slipping through the net of categories.''[1]

But it is precisely for these reasons that Ondaatje presents so illuminating a case of the postmodern writer who characteristically searches for but distrusts narrative structures, who seeks to connect words and world but remains unsure of either term or of whether they are in fact two terms at all. As the current authority of Jacques Derrida (making his slippery way from signifier to signifier) suggests, the problem of language has come to absorb our attention. What is it that words do? And for a literary inquiry into such matters, narrative with its claim to referentiality presents itself as the mode that focuses most clearly the currently pressing questions about reality and language.

Ondaatje's own narratives provide a particularly sharp focus, for their insistence on historical reference moves into the foreground the whole problem of the relationship between words and world. *Billy the Kid* is based on the life of William Bonney; *Coming Through Slaughter* (1976) draws upon the career of the New Orleans jazz pioneer Buddy Bolden; *Running in the Family* (1982) grows out of the history of Ondaatje's own family.[2] The historical grounding points to Ondaatje's allegiance to the traditional mimetic role of fiction, but the deliberately problematic nature of the grounding simultaneously places in question the possibility of fulfilling that role. Central to his inquiry into fiction is the problem of the function and power of the literary imagination, and as Ondaatje struggles with this question, his understanding of the imagination alters significantly from the earlier to the later narratives.

All of the narratives play with the possibility of the imagination's recovery of history, aligning themselves with the fictional tradition whose classic modern instance is Robert Browning's *The Ring and the Book* and whose contemporary consequence we see in works like Norman Mailer's *The Executioner's Song*. Browning sets up the problem of the relationship between "fancy" and "fact": can the imagination somehow pierce through to the truth of historical fact? Can its words achieve an authentic recovery of a moment in the past? Browning's answer is (cautiously) affirmative: through the "spark-like" power of the imagination, he asserts, "something dead may get to live again."[3]

More sceptical than Browning, the Ondaatje of *Billy the Kid* nevertheless shares the Victorian poet's view of the function of the imagination and implies a similar confidence in its power to (on Browning's word) "resuscitate" the past. But Ondaatje's latest work, *Running in the Family*, assumes an unbridgeable distance between then and now, replacing the earlier model of the imagination as penetration with a model of the imagination as construction.

This shift is illustrated concisely in the pages of Credits and Acknowledgements appended to each of Ondaatje's narratives. Ondaatje is, of course, obliged to include such pages, but he also exploits directly the disruptive potential of including this non-fiction convention in an apparent fiction, its inherent power to unsettle reading by making the reader wonder what in the book is fiction, what is fact, and what difference does it make. In *Billy the Kid*, Ondaatje notes that "I have edited, rephrased, and slightly reworked the originals. But the emotions belong to their authors." In *Coming Through Slaughter*, the Acknowledgements section concludes: "There have been some date changes, some characters brought together, and some facts have been expanded or polished to suit the truth of fiction."

Running in the Family follows the list of individuals consulted in the course of writing the book with the statement: "If those listed above disapprove of the fictional air I apologize and can only say that in Sri Lanka a well-told lie is worth a thousand facts." The sequence is highly suggestive. From an initial insistence on the substantial convergence of fictional construct and historical source (despite editing, the "emotions belong to their authors"), Ondaatje moves to an emphasis on their divergence in *Coming Through Slaughter*, setting up a hierarchical opposition that asserts the priority of the "truth of fiction" into a "well-told lie."

Somewhere between *Billy the Kid* and *Running in the Family*, it would seem Ondaatje has abandoned the correspondence theory of truth that has traditionally sustained mimetic theories of art for a coherence theory with its neo-Kantian separation of artistic form and empirical reality. There is no transcription, only inscription. But this is too sharp and misleading a distinction, and it would be a mistake to assume that Ondaatje has exchanged his concern with the referentiality of fiction for the delights of fabulation. What has altered is less Ondaatje's sense that art must somehow correspond to reality than his sense of what constitutes the reality to which art corresponds.

Initially Ondaatje works out of the definition of reality implicit in the romantic tradition of lyric which his own poetry enters. Romantic lyric makes reality a matter of consciousness and locates the "I" of the poet as its formal principle, as in the Wordsworthian lyric. But from Wordsworth's visionary "spots of time" to the solipsistic "moments" in Walter Pater's notorious Conclusion to *The Renaissance* is only a short step, and Ondaatje's poetry is continually haunted by the threat of solipsism.

In the troubled musing of "Spider Blues," he creates his most memorable image of that threat, drawing on the Swiftian image of modern man as a spider in order to brood over "spider poets" and their "vanity of making." The spider "making lines out of the juice of his own abdomen" is identified as a "kind of writer" who "thinks a path and travels/the emptiness that was there/leaves his bridge behind."[4] Ondaatje's ambivalence is apparent here: the spider's making is self-centred and tenuous (doubly vain), yet the spider does make something in the void. At once attracted to and repelled by such making, Ondaatje seeks through narratives that derive from something outside the self to affirm a creativity that is not "vanity" and to escape the claustrophobia and precariousness of the "I" travelling its self-spun paths in air.

But his first effort at a narrative work, *Billy the Kid*, merely reinforces the lyric trap, for despite its cultural reference to the history
and legend of William Bonney, the entire work depends on an
internal, psychological definition of experience and on an intense
identification of writer and subject. While such identification
lingers in his next narrative, *Coming Through Slaughter*, the world
of this fiction no longer dissolves so completely into the ego of
its hero, and a more explicit narrative frame distances narrating
voice and fictional subject. Sam Solecki sees this frame as only
"ostensibly historical," and he is certainly correct in emphasiz-
ing that Ondaatje grounds his story less in time and history than
in psychology and myth.[5]

Ondaatje translates the historical question of what happened
to Buddy Bolden into a psychological search for the inner
Bolden. But at the same time his narrative strategy continually
reminds the reader that this book represents a self-conscious effort at recovery from a distance. Where *Billy the Kid* plunged immediately into the fictional recreation of the past, *Coming Through
Slaughter* begins by establishing its distance: "Float by in a car
today and see the corner shops." And when toward the end of
the narrative the narrator dissolves into the authorial "I" and
identifies itself with Bolden ("When he went mad he was the
same age as I am now," p. 133), the moment works not so much
to fuse subject and object as to emphasize the irrecoverability of
the object. The deliberate intrusiveness of the authorial self addressing the lost Bolden and yearning to "think in your brain and
body" serves but to underline the instance and difference from
which it speaks. Bolden cannot be penetrated, reanimated, but
only constructed in the light of the present, perceiving "I." This
does not mean — though it verges on doing so — that history
is only the self in another key; what it does mean (as *Running
in the Family* confirms) is that Ondaatje has sought of the imagination something it cannot do, has asked the wrong question.

Accordingly, in his latest work Ondaatje asks not "what happened?" but "how is it remembered?" His interest, in other
words, has now shifted from history as event to history as the
narration of event. *Running in the Family* assumes the inevitability
of mediation, listening to and recording stories, musing over
memories, recognizing that it must itself remain "incomplete." The book defines itself not as an effort at some kind

of authentic recovery of the presence of the past but as an act or (to use Ondaatje's own term in the Acknowledgements) a "gesture" of continuity. Early in the work Ondaatje records a vivid dream in which he recognizes himself as "part of a human pyramid" made up of his family, and the image underlines the partial nature of his own book. *Running in the Family* enters into a continually renewed tradition of story-telling: "No story is ever told just once. Whether a memory or funny hideous scandal, we will return to it an hour later and retell the story with additions and this time a few judgements thrown in. In this way history is organized" (p. 26).

The participants in both the making and telling of this history elude essential knowledge, and as the narrative nears its end, it returns repeatedly to the enigma of Ondaatje's dead father. "There is so much to know," Ondaatje comments about his father, "and we can only guess" (p. 200). Gestures of penetration — the desire to know a moment fully and authentically — are deceptive, but gestures of continuity are possible and valuable, speaking to something central and enduring in the human condition. So *Running in the Family* takes as its subject the mediations that constitute human reality as what we remember and transmit, and in this way making reality itself secondary, derivative. If this reality is indeed the reality that matters, then the spider poet no longer "thinks a path" but listens a path, commemorating rather than creating.

This shift in the role of art and artist is a difficult one for a romantic writer like Ondaatje to make, for it means surrendering the dream of originality. The aesthetic doctrine of originality (an eighteenth-century idea developed by the Romantics) transfers the origin of art from outside (nature or tradition) to inside (the artist's own imagination). Truth in art becomes equated with what the late eighteenth century termed "genius," no longer a common property but a unique perception. Aside from placing extraordinary pressure on the individual artist, the notion of originality also tends to define art in general as transgression — a rupturing of common bonds and laws — and so it generates the still potent Byronic figure of artist as outlaw. But transgression exacts punishment; the outlaw is marked by suffering.

In the complex of ideas that constitutes the doctrine of originality, suffering stands as at once the price and the sign of originali-

ty. The self can authenticate what it originates only by total commitment, the commitment that we identify as seriousness. And
in our culture, as Susan Sontag reminds us, "the supreme token
of seriousness" is suffering. Applied to art, this equation means,
as Sontag further notes, that we "measure truth in terms of the
cost to the writer in suffering."[6] *Coming Through Slaughter*
demonstrates Ondaatje's powerful attraction to this metonymy
of suffering-seriousness-originality, but at the same time the novel
exorcizes that attraction in its brooding over the self-destructive
career of the jazz pioneer Buddy Bolden, who went mad in his
early 30s and spent the remaining twenty-four years of his life
in an insane asylum.

Jazz is an art built on improvisation — hence, an art that ac-
cords supreme value to novelty — and its temporal reference is
the moment. Taken to its logical extreme, as in the playing of
Buddy Bolden, it is an art premised on its own evanescence: a
continuous act of self-cancelling originality. Bolden's music
(never recorded) exists only in and through the moment. "If you
never heard him play some place where the weather for instance
could change the next series of notes," a character comments,
"— then you *should* never have heard him at all" (p. 37).

Almost obsessively, the novel reiterates that Bolden's search
for originality involves a surrender of his art and of Bolden himself
to the pressure of the moment. His mind, we are told, is
"helpless against every moment's headline"; his music is coarse
and rough, immediate, dated in half an hour" (pp. 15, 43). Life
and music intertwine, doubles for one another: "his music was
immediately on top of his own life" (p. 37). For Buddy Bolden
life is flux, and — in a kind of literal realism — art must enter
into and become flux itself. So any structure (as stasis) is a lie
and an illegitimate assumption of control. Bolden himself refuses
to control his music because, he says, "I had no power over
anything else that went on around me" (p. 99). He attacks all
gestures of structuration, from the windows and doors that intrude their order into the "magic of air" that is his medium to
the "clear forms" of John Robichaux's waltzes that make every
note "part of the large curve, so carefully patterned" (p. 93).

The note, not the phrase, is Bolden's basic unity, and he seeks
— paradoxically — the "right accidental notes." His characteristic
form of performance is the street parade where he plays in bursts,

moving in and out of the crowd, in and out of silence, and where "at each intersection people would hear just the fragment I happened to be playing" (p. 94). Listening to his music, his friend Webb describes it as "showing all the possibilities in the middle of the story" (p. 43). But in order for it to do so, the music (and Bolden himself) must be always in the middle, always in the present tense. Significantly, Bolden simply appears one day in the middle of a New Orleans parade ("Born at the age of twenty-two"); he never speaks of the past and a later disappearance from the city prompts Webb to consider that Bolden may be "wiping out his past again in a casual gesture, contemptuous. Landscape suicide" (p. 22). Bolden's music, intense and compelling, wipes itself out at each moment, the notes "forgotten in the body because they were swallowed by the next one" (p. 14). Committed to newness, to innovation, his music is committed to forgetfulness: "Every note new and raw and chance. Never repeated" (p. 95). Tormented by what lies outside order, avoiding repetition and closure, Bolden's discontinuous art refuses memory, continuity, and meaning. His aesthetic is a kind of mimesis, positing the identity of the temporality of life and art and seeking a moment of absolute fusion where all differentiation between person and artist, between art and life, between audience, art, and artist will dissolve. One day in the middle of a parade, going "round and round in the centre of the Liberty-Iberville connect," Buddy Bolden achieves that fusion — and goes mad "into silence."

Like Bolden, Ondaatje distrusts closure, affirming in a recent interview his preference for a fiction that (rather like his own) has "lots of spaces and inquiries but never fully rounded off and framed."[7] In contrast to Bolden, however, Ondaatje works with language, with written words, and so with a medium steeped in memory, affirming connectedness, and depending on iterability. Even as he creates Bolden's story, Ondaatje sets himself apart from his musician hero by the mere fact of writing. But *Coming Through Slaughter*, aware of the difference, is yet oddly reluctant to admit it fully, remaining in some way hostile to itself as writing.

In *Running in the Family* the hostility has disappeared. The book opens with a writerly prologue ("Half a page — and the morning is already ancient") and is unusually full of allusions to the literary tradition, invoking figures as diverse as Goethe and Austen and Shakespeare. Throughout it is marked by an awareness of and interest in its own status as writing. Ondaatje has said of *Running in the Family* in relation to his earlier narratives that "it's not so much an act of war. The others were."[8] His reference here is to the gentleness of this book in contrast to the violence of *Billy the Kid* and *Coming Through Slaughter*, and that very gentleness is at least in part a consequence of his abandoning the internal war waged in the earlier narratives; the war against their own medium, against the constraints, the opacity, and the inevitably mediate nature of written language. *Running in the Family* is — emphatically — a piece of writing.

Ondaatje's acceptance of writing does not signal a move into abstraction and away from the concreteness of the world that has always engaged his imagination. On the contrary, Ondaatje now stresses that writing is itself a concrete thing and that its value lies precisely in this fact. As signifiers (in Saussure's sense) words are sense objects (sounds and marks) and so participate in the material world. For Ondaatje their materiality must not be ignored or repressed on behalf of an ideal of language as a transparency on the world. So he alerts us early to words as things-in-themselves by lingering over *Asia:* "The word sprawled. It had none of the clipped sound of Europe, America, Canada. The vowels took over, slept on the map with the S" (p. 22). One of the most memorable passages in the book is devoted to a celebration (and visual illustration) of the "curling" alphabet of the Sinhalese. In this "most beautiful alphabet," the letters are "washed blunt glass which betray no jaggedness." Even as the shapes stimulate Ondaatje's imagination to metaphoric play, he reminds us of the prosaic material circumstance that accounts for their origin. The vertical letters of Sanskrit were not possible in Ceylon where the Ola leaves used for writing were too brittle: "A straight line would cut apart the leaf and so a curling alphabet was derived from its Indian cousin. Moon coconut. The bones of a lover's spine" (p. 83).

Nor does the insistence on words as words mean that Ondaatje has embraced the notion (bruited about in Paris and New Haven) that words are *only* words, unstable signifiers generating more signifiers in endless self-enclosed play. In *Running in the Family* writing is meaningful inscription, a marking that asserts human significance, desire, and community. Two historical anecdotes make Ondaatje's point. In the 5th Century B.C., he tells us, "graffiti poems were scratched onto the rock face of Sigiriya — the rock fortress of a despot king."

In 1971 during the Insurgency, the government of Sri Lanka turned a campus into a prison. When the students were allowed to return, they discovered — and transcribed — hundreds of poems "written on walls, ceilings, and in hidden corners" (p. 84). Anonymous writers, centuries apart, turned to writing to record and assert their presence and their freedom despite imprisonment. By doing so they also signalled their faith in a future — in readers to read and to remember. Ondaatje affirms such faith in the continuity of language as significance when he joins his words to those of the anonymous poets who produced the early Sigiri Graffiti.

These poets, he notes, wrote conventional love poems, impersonal lyrics to "mythological women" that draw consistently on stock metaphors: breasts are "perfect swans," eyes are "long and clean as horizons" (p. 84). Paying tribute and linking himself to their tradition, Ondaatje writes "Women Like You," a poem combining the contemporary rhythms and images of his own language with the formulaic metaphors of the ancient poets:

> you long eyed women
> the golden
> drunk swan breasts
> lips
> the long long eyes (p. 94)

Rejecting the drive for originality and for an authentic expression of individual consciousness, lyric now takes its place as part of the larger narrative effort to transmit and commemorate cultural memories. Ondaatje here encounters the past in a personal way, but the personal is itself no longer defined by uniqueness.

Though writing is as susceptible to destruction as any other form of human making, it assumed the possibility and value of preservation. Unlike Buddy Bolden's music, it counters rather than submits to the moment, seeing time not as a series of always present moments but as historical duration. Writing is a marking (as opposed to a performance), and as such it alters the material, temporal world of which it is a part. When Ondaatje speaks of his desire "to touch . . . into words" the members of his family, he is speaking of making them part of the physical world, adding them to its vocabulary. But "into words," as he well knows, is not "into being." In this book Ondaatje has accepted the mediate nature of his own activity, recognized that he cannot penetrate to essence and somehow reanimate the past. What he can do is record and preserve the memories of the past and so ensure that it remains inside the realm of present meaning.

This is not to suggest that Ondaatje now sees writing as simply a matter of notation or as a fully controlled and conscious activity. He presents it as a mysterious and mysteriously generative process, bringing to articulation what the writer himself does not foresee: "Watch the hand move. Waiting for it to say something, to stumble casually on perception, the shape of an unknown thing" (p. 190). Writing demands as much a passive waiting in the self as an active shaping by the self. The crucial point is that in *Running in the Family* (in contrast to his earlier narratives), Ondaatje identifies himself fully with the act of writing — and with the art of narrative. As the genre of telling, narrative assumes that there is something to be told (one "tells a story," for instance). In other words, it assigns priority to something that exists outside language, even as it is expressed in it, and so defines the words of the narrative as secondary and as different from the something they tell. Words are inevitable but words are also inevitably mediate, and narrative finally denies the possibility of any absolute, unique convergence of telling and what is told.[9]

For Ondaatje, *Running in the Family* suggests, the turn to narrative is at once reassuring and dispiriting, an opening up and a closing off of possibilities. In the "gesture" of fidelity to a communal past enacted by this text, there is wisdom and humility, but there is also a sense of loss and a troubling kind of resignation. Near the end of his excursus into family memories, Ondaatje writes:

> During certain hours, at certain years in our lives, we see ourselves as remnants from the earlier generations that were destroyed. So our job becomes to keep peace with enemy camps, eliminate the chaos at the end of Jacobean tragedies, and with "the mercy of distance" write the histories. (p. 179)

Inevitable as such a response may be in the context of recollection and hedged as it is with the qualification of "certain hours," there is something disturbing about this passage. And its source is the allusion to Jacobean tragedy, an almost Prufrockian moment of "No. I am not Prince Hamlet, nor was meant to be;/Am an attendant lord."[10] Free of Prufrock's particular neuroses, Ondaatje's own literary metaphor nevertheless implies a similar cultural condition: a giving up on the possibilities of significance in contemporary culture, a sense of the present as somehow marginal — mere "remnants." If the metaphor itself suggests a pleasure in linguistic play, the elegiac rhythm counteracts that energy, carrying with it that enervating sense of being a "latecomer" diagnosed by Harold Bloom in The Anxiety of Influence. For all its humour, beauty, and tenderness, Running in the Family betrays a tiredness, a lassitude that such a passage uncovers, raising the possibility that beneath its genuine and positive commitment to continuity and community lies a potentially corrosive despair.

Notes

1 Gary Draper, "Stranger Than Fiction," Books in Canada, 11, (Dec. 1982), 19.
2 The Collected Works of Billy the Kid (Toronto: Anansi, 1970); Coming Through Slaughter (Toronto: Anansi, 1976); Running in the Family (Toronto: McClelland & Stewart, 1982). All references are to these editions and will hereafter be included in the text.
3 The Ring and the Book (New York: Norton, 1961), Bk. 1, 11. 748, 722, p. 17.
4 There's a Trick with a Knife I'm Learning to Do (Toronto: McClelland & Stewart, 1979), pp. 62-63.
5 "Making and Destroying: Michael Ondaatje's Coming Through Slaughter and Extremist Art," ECW, 12, (Fall 1978), 34. See also Stephen Scobie, "Coming Through Slaughter: Fictional Magnets and Spider's Webbs," ECW, 12, (Fall 1978), 5-22.
6 Against Interpretation (New York: Dell, 1966), pp. 47, 49-50. Sam Solecki's article (see previous note) is especially helpful on the role of suffering in art.
7 Quoted in Alice Klein, "Ondaatje Writes Home," NOW, (Oct 7-13, 1982), 7.
8 Ibid.
9 My remarks on narrative here draw generally on contemporary narrative theory and reflect, more particularly, its typical reliance on dualistic models of narrative. The dualism of narrative seems to me crucial to Ondaatje but for a critique (and summary) of the most influential dualist models, see David Carroll, The Subject in Question (Chicago: University of Chicago Press, 1982), pp. 14-26.
10 T. S. Eliot, Selected Poems (London: Faber, 1954), p. 15.

NORMAN LEVINE

NORMAN LEVINE'S NOVELS: HOME AND AWAY FROM HOME

Robin Mathews

A writer of prose fiction, Norman Levine fashions short stories about small but revealing incidents that often involve a male narrator in a finely crafted moment of revelation. The longer works deal more with social milieu and more trenchantly with an alienated narrator in embarrassed financial circumstances. Levine is best known for his short stories which have appeared in many countries and in seven languages over the more than thirty-five years he has been publishing. For most of that time he has been an expatriate writer strongly connected in consciousness and reference to his native country and producing, besides his short stories, three larger works: *The Angled Road* (the U.K., 1952, Canada, 1953), *From a Seaside Town* (1970) and *Canada Made Me* (1958). The last title, *Canada Made Me*, unlike the first two, is usually considered a travelogue and not a novel, but because of its place in Canadian literary genre and because of Norman Levine's fictional method, I intend to claim it as a novel and to show the significant place it has in the development of his idea of fiction.

Albert Norman Levine was born in Ottawa in 1923 and attended York Street School and the High School of Commerce in that city. His parents lived in the part of Ottawa known as Lower Town, among rag collectors and pedlars who were immigrants from Europe and who formed a milieu of mostly poor people slightly separated from the rest of the community because of their newness to the country. Levine's own father was a pedlar of fresh fruit and vegetables.

The Ottawa days have provided the writer with some of his most touching stories: "A Canadian Upbringing," "A Father," "In Lower Town," "A Memory of Ottawa." Those days, too, led him, often, to suggest that the Canadian offspring of those (mostly Jewish) immigrants moved into crude commercialism, vulgar social behaviour, and cultural barbarity. Levine's apparent lack of generosity — at least in his fiction — to his youthful contemporaries is matched at times by his harsh judgement of Canada and Canadians in general.

Like many of his generation who had little chance to travel or pursue advanced education, Levine was significantly affected by the Second World War. He was trained as an officer, during which time he was actually rehearsed in the social graces. As his narrator describes the experience in the short story, "In Quebec City," the new officers "were instructed how to use knives and forks. How to make a toast. How to eat and drink properly. It was like going to a finishing school."[1]

Levine went to England, to a world that strongly affected many young Canadians of the time and marked them deeply for life. England provided a unique atmosphere of cooperation, good cheer, and heroic unity arising out of the war effort. Norman Levine has spoken of that atmosphere, its excitement, the attraction it afforded to those who were young and discovering, as he was at the time. But England provided more: its historic beauty, its sense of a deeply rooted culture, and — what is probably very important — its willingness to accept the young, adventuring Canadians without erecting social barriers against them.

At the end of the war Levine came back to Canada and was able — partly as a result of the educational assistance made available to veterans — to attend McGill University. (His first novel is dedicated to the McGill Chairman of English of the time.) After three years at McGill he received a fellowship at King's College, London, where he returned in 1949 to begin more than thirty years of expatriation mostly in St. Ives, Cornwall, and only recently ended that period, in 1980, after the death of his wife in England. He presently lives in Toronto where he has taken up his writing life and has been welcomed with increasing sympathy into the literary and the larger cultural community of Canada.

His reception in his home country may signal a softening of attitude because exiles and expatriates have not been strongly approved in the last decades. The reason for animosity towards them — whether the emotion has been just or unjust — is not hard to find. The people who left — say those who stayed at home — didn't want to shoulder the work of fighting for a reasonable cultural life and a reasonable place for artists in it. The expatriates, say the stay-at-homes, "ran away" from a hard and thankless, but necessary task. The people who exiled themselves developed a reputation, moreover, for turning upon Canada and Canadians and aspersing them in harsh language. Those who went away — on the other hand — have seen the picture differently.

Mordecai Richler, one of the most obnoxious of exiles, has written: "young writers who found Canada too bland and parochial for their taste left because they were bored and there were no more than farm-club opportunities for them at home."[2] Richler's searing attacks upon Canada and Canadians coloured more than a decade of his expatriate commentary. He first left Canada in his teens and later became a major commentator abroad on Canadian identity and character — having never been West of the Ontario border.

Richler reports that in Montreal during the late forties, "we actually had a course on Canadian writing at Sir George Williams University: it was a standing joke among those of us who cared about literature."[3] That attitude did not arise from the astonishing sophistication of a set of backwater eighteen-year-olds — as Richler might like to think — who could see the burning relevance of foreign literature and the triviality of our own. The attitude arose, rather, from forces more profound and disturbing than Richler has ever been willing to admit.

Norman Levine has never attacked Canada with the savagery characteristic of Richler. He was a gentler exile, and he gives a number of more personal reasons for leaving his homeland. Indeed, in his short story "A Canadian Upbringing," his narrator says the reasons he gives for leaving change with the character of the questioner.

> When people ask me why did I leave Canada to go over to England, the answer I give depends on the kind of person who is doing the asking.
>   If it is someone of my own generation, at some party, I tell them it was because of the attractive English girl who sat beside me at college and took the same courses as I did, and who was going back when she graduated. If it is someone like my bank manager, I say it was because of the five-thousand-dollar fellowship I got for postgraduate study. The only condition being that I had to do it at some British University. And if the question comes from an editor, I tell him that at that time I had just written a first novel and my Canadian publisher (to be) having read the manuscript said that I would have to go to New York or London to get it published, then he would look after the Canadian market.[4]

The quotation is presented at some length, for those are all reasons Levine gave for his own decision to leave Canada when he gave an Ottawa reading on April 7, 1983 in the Lord Elgin Hotel. He gave other reasons that evening, too. England was cheaper to live in. He had a bank manager in England who would let him overdraw in a way no Canadian bank manager would, he told his audience. And, in relation to the advice given by the Canadian publisher, who he named that evening as Jack McClelland of McClelland and Stewart, Levine inferred that the country had little basis upon which to support people seriously committed to the literary arts. Some in the audience may have remembered the more intense statement written in the "Author's Note" of *Canada Made Me*, where Levine writes he had "run away from the country . . . in that freighter . . . in 1949 . . . . "

Whatever the reasons, Norman Levine's own expatriation, his use of Canadian narrators in fictions set outside of Canada, the persona of the angry and anguished narrator in *Canada Made Me*, the tensions Levine expresses about Canada and Canadians in much of his work, and the familiar tone of his characteristic narrator as a stranger who is never fully at home form the largest part of the impression readers have of Levine's public identity.

Expatriation, then, and the image of the stranger observing contribute significantly to the perception of Levine's writing. He hasn't attacked Canada with the severity Mordecai Richler has used, possibly because Levine grew up through the Depression and fought as a Canadian officer in the Second World War. Richler did neither. But both men seem to have been propelled by forces that they may have been quite unconscious of when they were making what seemed to them to be their entirely personal decisions to leave.

Canada after the Second World War presented the artist with more choice and more reason to accept or reject association than, perhaps, at any other time in its history. The war effort had marked the first major national activity since 1931, the year in which the nation cut the last, large colonial ties with Britain by means of the Westminster Act which gave Canada full control, finally, of its own treaty-making powers. Canada was not, until 1931, a fully independent, sovereign nation. The country came out of the Second World War proud and economically strong, having an efficient industrial complex and the third largest mer-

chant fleet in the world. Clearly a Canada existed against which
the sensitive and critical could react; the nation was in a general
boom period and — despite legitimate criticism about the lack of
support for artists — mobility was increasing and the standard
of living was rising demonstrably.

The country was, in fact, moving towards a new attitude to the
arts and culture, but not fast enough for some. At the very time
the members of the Massey Commission — the Royal Commission on National Development in the Arts, Letters and Sciences
— were conducting their investigations and dealing with the aftermath of the *Report*, Norman Levine, Mavis Gallant, Mordecai
Richler, Joe Plaskett and others in the artistic community were
beginning their long expatriations. The new materialistic vitality in the country may have offended some of them, though Levine
believes the basis of rejection was deeper than that. At any rate,
Great Britain for Levine and Richler, France for Gallant and
Plaskett seem to have provided the milieu the artists required.
And they were joined by writers and artists from all over the Com-
monwealth who seemed to believe the cultures of their own countries were — to quote Richler again — "a standing joke among
those of us who cared . . . . "

Ironically, anti-colonialist battles were beginning all over the
world, and in Canada a move towards an insistence upon
legitimacy of home culture was about to explode. And so, at the
present time, Norman Levine, Mordecai Richler, and Mavis
Gallant are all living in Canada, are recognized here for their
literary achievement, and command appreciative and informed
audiences they probably wouldn't have believed possible when
they forsook Canadian shores many years ago.

Norman Levine's first novel, *The Angled Road*, obviously the
work of a young writer, depicts the growth of a young man in
Ottawa and his attempt to find a satisfactory place in life. The
work shows signs of experimentation with form and
language. Levine, himself, has written that he doesn't "think
much of the novel" because of the uncertainty he detects in it. A
reader who is not as concerned as Levine is with the goal of a
developed and fixed fictional voice may well judge the author is
being too harsh with his own early work. Levine argues that *The
Angled Road*

became fiction because I couldn't tackle the life around
me. The characters in the novel are really like the
characters in a story like "In Lower Town," or "A
Father." To have shown them as I did, in *The Angled
Road* is to have made them smaller than they are as
human beings.[5]

He goes on to say that it was only with *Canada Made Me* "that
I began to understand what writing was about."[6]

That statement is important. For Levine has developed a style
that normally involves a first person narrator. It uses a spare
prose, often marked by simple sentences and a texture of surface observation. It seems to be the result of a philosophy that
demands attention to the visible and a compulsion to house
perception in a source that cannot be questioned. Most of his
early prose, as he says himself, was written in the third person,
and he later lost interest in it. The first person narrator, a very
strong aspect of *Canada Made Me,* provided him with the control,
the sense of immediacy, and the fictional assurance he was looking for. Indeed, many readers believe he creates only slightly
rearranged autobiography. Anna Collins, for instance, writing
in *Books in Canada,* declares that, for Levine

writing is telling the truth about the one certain thing —
what has happened, or not happened, to him.[7]

The statement is probably an oversimplification of Levine's, or
anyone's creative processes, even though Levine's method in-
vites comments of the kind. Writing of the work he developed
after his early period, Levine says:

I used the first person as a device — to get quickly into
my material — to bring something quickly across to the
reader — and to make him think that what he is reading
is true. I also feel more at ease, in writing, when I use
it. Perhaps because it allows me to be more detached.[8]

As a device, as a stylistic technique, the first person permits
Levine to catch the reader's ear, to convey an air of verisimilitude
(to the extent, even, that some readers are led to believe he is
writing autobiography). Normally, one would believe that the
use of the first person would *prevent* a sense of detachment, but,
for Levine, the first person allows him to occupy the being of the
character he is creating and to develop that character with confidence. The factual similarities between his fiction and his own

life can cause difficulties. But he isn't simply writing about himself and, indeed, his sense that the depiction of Lower Town characters in *The Angled Road* "made them smaller than they were as human beings" is an argument for that claim. When he says, elsewhere in an interview, regarding *The Angled Road*, "My narrator there I didn't think was me at all,"[9] he is, paradoxically, making the same point. By writing in the first person, by placing himself imaginatively in the situation of the story, Levine is able to remove the heavy-handed judge, the disapprover, the social censor, and is able to experience *among* the characters created, letting their legitimacies make their own statements.

The Angled Road. lively, youthful, somewhat uncertain stylistically, deals with a milieu of poverty, depressed times, and domestic unhappiness in which David Wrixon, the sensitive protagonist, grows up, begins to work for a living, and aches to get away.

> He wanted to be free from the pettiness and the stuffiness of this environment, from the hopeless resignation and tragedy.[10]

He studies at night, joins the air force, and goes to the war in Europe, lives a life of chance acquaintances, is responsible for a pregnancy that he insists be terminated. He falls in love with an English girl, and as the war ends he finds himself in conflict about his future, his connection to his Lower Town, Ottawa past, his relation with his English lover. He turns away from her, returns to Canada, to study, manual work, and finally departure for university — and, apparently, freedom.

The basis of *The Angled Road* is the story of a young man who must shake himself free from oedipal compulsions in order to be truly free in the world. The theme is treated lightly, but it is present throughout. David stands, the evening before he leaves his home in Ottawa, under a "warped print of a nude Echo and Narcissus" (p. 9). When he begins a liaison in England, he is temporarily unable to engage sexually, until his companion explains:

> The trouble with you darling is that you still like your mother, not that there is anything wrong, but don't you see . . . that could explain a lot of things. Stop thinking of her, at least when you're with me. (p. 63)

Later when he leaves the woman whom he has believed he was
in love with, he does so as if he fears any kind of definite engage-
ment, as if he fears ceasing to be a traveller and a spectator. He
thinks of Ottawa.

> Dorset Street lives, but I am not a spectator there. I am
> part of it, and being part of it, I feel submerged. The
> qualities are there, but I shall only be able to see them
> once I never have to return. (p. 121)

He admits that his "first love, and his longest, was his mother,"
who is part of what Dorset Street means.

But he returns to Canada, studies to achieve freedom again,
and goes to work in the Northern mines before returning to
university where he wishes to destroy his old self and begin anew.

The novel, quite clearly, is episodic. It mixes point of view in
a way that is more interesting, perhaps, than successful. It moves
from event to event and from one level of insight to another
without a sense of organic unity. And yet the novel has a vitality and an integrity of feeling that makes it a better than average
first novel.

Five years after *The Angled Road* Levine published a different
kind of book, *Canada Made Me*. It has been called "this strange
travelogue,"[11] "his autobiography,"[12] and it is treated in the
Literary History of Canada under travel books.[13] Elizabeth
Waterston reports that the book "reflects the shock, stimulus,
elation, and despair roused in a sensitive observer by this nation."[14] Waterston conveys the taste and the mood of the book,
too, in her description of the narrator's experience:

> In Halifax, after a fantastic trip out he meets a burlesque
> reception: rudeness in customs, official boredom and
> petty corruption, and a hearty reception only from a
> Kellogg's representative, passing out boxes of Corn
> Flakes "from the Canadian wheat field . . . and cheap
> too . . . . " Certainly the Canada he travels is vulgar
> and careless, a shoddy world of dingy restaurants filled
> with blank-eyed girls and leather-jacketed youths. Blobs
> of chewing-gum stuck underneath the table signal the
> return to Canadian life.[15]

Levine has already been quoted as saying that he only began
to "understand what writing was about" with the writing of
Canada Made Me. Concerning that book, he continues:

> There is the visible world. And I like to record
> it. When people appear, I brought them in whenever I
> felt that they were needed. Sometimes they didn't quite
> happen the way I have them. Sometimes I moved
> things around. Sometimes I made-up characters and
> what they did in order to bring something across.
> As I say, it was with this book that I began to under-
> stand what was involved in writing and developed a
> method which I have gone on using.[16]

That method, using the first person narrator involved with apparent actuality as well as memory and the past, permits the
author to establish a legitimacy and an emotional conviction, to
"set" his action, and to prepare an apparently objective picture
of experience. Levine says:

> I start with some emotion, some feeling, something that
> has happened to me or something I have observed. And
> I want to trap this emotion. Sometimes I can do it in a
> short story. Sometimes it takes a novel to do it.[17]

Levine doesn't claim that *Canada Made Me* is fundamentally a
travelogue or that it's an autobiography. The work is, perhaps,
one of those literary kinds we call the semi-autobiographical
novel, a genre well tested in Canadian literature and related to
the documentary which has a special place in Canadian creative
consciousness. The semi-autobiographical novel permits the
writer to make extraordinary claims of factual truth: it allows an
"I was there" quality to the events; it assists the documentary
purpose by suggesting that the internal responses of the narrator
to external facts are the kind the reader would have in like
circumstances.

Since *Canada Made Me* was written as much for the English audience as for the Canadian one it falls neatly into the Canadian
genre of documentary primarily intended for a distant audience,
to bring the reality of Canada to them in factual detail so that they
might judge its suitability as a place of settlement or immigra-
tion. Levine denies that aspect, saying he has "never written
for an audience. I write for myself."[18] That may be true at the
same time as he published the book first in England and presented
the "Author's Note" as if addressing English readers. Such a
phrase as "whenever I came up to London" could hardly be intended for other than English readers.

The first major work of the kind that I have described is, of course, Susanna Moodie's *Roughing It In the Bush*. In that work a sensitive immigrant faces many of the same experiences Levine's protagonist does: the customs experience, landing in Canada, travelling and experiencing a segment of the population, comparing Old World and New World values and commenting upon the society that appears to be formed and forming. The other famous representation of the genre is F. P. Grove's *In Search of America*. Grove takes the continent for his canvas, but — in a longer work than *Canada Made Me* — he goes more deeply into the philosophical determinants of the societies he experiences and in a famous footnote opts for life in Canada rather than in the United States.

The peculiarity of *Canada Made Me* in the genre is that it is not the story of a narrator coming to Canada for the first time and deciding, all things weighed, to remain and identify with the country. It is, rather, the tale of an expatriate, fascinated by the country and possessing an idea of it as an emotional condition almost, returning to confirm the validity of his previously-made judgement. In the "Author's Note" Levine declares he felt a need to make the physical journey back, to make a reconciliation, not to run away from the country as he had previously done. As he says: "I wanted to have a last look at my country and leave it with a good taste in my mouth." There is no suggestion in that statement that he wants to reconsider his idea of the country.

Turning the genre inside out, Levine writes of the failure of the Canadian experiment. Perhaps that is the emotional sense he had of the country when something insistently drove him to return and make the physical journey over its surface. Perhaps, too, as he says: "There were a lot of young people who seemed to be drifting at the moment. Also, I liked the visual. I realized in *Canada Made Me* that the visible world has a right to its own experience."[19] At the end of the journey, back in London, the narrator walks out of a pub:

> I wondered why I felt so bitter about Canada. After all,
> it was part of a dream, an experiment that couldn't
> come off. It was foolish to believe that you can take the
> throwouts, the rejects, the human kickabouts from
> Europe and tell them: Here you have a second
> chance. Here you can start a new life. But no one ever
> mentioned the price one had to pay; how much of
> oneself you had to betray.[20]

Levine loads the dice, selects, arranges, philosophizes, and creates character just as Susanna Moodie and F. P. Grove do before him. *Canada Made Me* is informed with a sense of chance and accident, a philosophy of pointlessness, a search for values in a world where the soil upon which values grow has been eroded and undercut. It is a world of fallen aspiration, of vulgar social responses, of ephemeral relations and a vagrant sense of social order and achievement. The narrator often concentrates on himself, on his own poverty, and on his need to beg and borrow his way through the adventure. Indeed, the fact of his own poverty forces him, according to the terms of the book, to the run-down ends of town amid alienated and impecunious characters. When the narrator does present educated and reasonably content people, they are revealed for the most part as empty, or hypocritical, or opportunistic.

To the reader who gives himself or herself to the novel, it gives back a sense that Canada is culturally barren, a wasteland of alienated, crippled, or hollow people. The conclusion Levine comes to — the conclusion quoted earlier — is consistent with the body of the text, that Canada "is an experiment that could not come off."

Levine's "anti-settlement" novel, like his own original expatriation struck a note that was central to the intellectual history of the time. Canada was in a phase of "junior partnership" with the United States; surges of nationalistic feeling ran through the body politic, and cries for self-determination were raised in the country. The infamous Pipeline Debate of May 1956 eventuated in the defeat of the Liberals in the election of 1957. John Diefenbaker, with a vision of the Canadian North in development, won the largest majority ever obtained just a year later. But uncertainty about Canadian culture and identity was a constant characteristic of the time as foreign ownership grew and "continentalism" increased apace. The famous defeated Walter Gordon protectionist budget of 1963 was representative both of the attempted resistance to U.S. takeover of the Canadian economy and culture and of the failure of that resistance to gain power and effect change.   Norman Levine's book, published in England in 1958, avoids all comment on political events and barely touches on the question of foreign ownership. But if the semi-autobiographical settlement novels of earlier days declared the possibility of a dynamic, unified nation with noble aspirations, *Canada Made Me* presents the failed possibility and writes the story down in the person of an impecunious Canadian traveller, revisiting his homeland and finding alienation, disorientation, opportunism, disunity, and painful human unfulfillment as the major characteristics of the country.

Norman Levine wrote a novel of a young man coming to knowledge about his surroundings and severing domestic and local roots. *The Angled Road* takes Levine's narrator from Lower Town in Ottawa to Europe and back to the beginning of a McGill education. In 1958 Levine's narrator returns to Canada from residence in England, returns to confirm the rightness of expatriation. Where in *The Angled Road* the narrator leaves a condition of local and domestic failure, in *Canada Made Me* the narrator confirms a national incapacity to provide sensitive human beings with a basis of real community and growth.

In 1961 Levine published a novella called ''The Playground,'' presenting — without any significant sense that a basis for community and growth had been found — a picture of the world an expatriate had found in Cornwall, England. In 1970, Levine's narrator, this time a Canadian expatriate living and writing in England, examines a life that is not financially successful and in which the world of community and growth is as small as the family unit. In *From a Seaside Town* Levine may have written his most technically successful novel so far, but he seems to make clear that the world to which his fictional character fled many years ago is no more certain, no more rich in value, no more purposeful than the world he found so repugnant as a young man desiring a world where he might take the shape of a rich and meaningful culture.

Perhaps the lesson of the novel is that human aspirations can never really be fulfilled, that the small, intimate life is ultimately the real one. Joseph Grand is a travel writer who is trapped and cannot travel. He looks about him and measures the relations he has with family and friends. Anne Collins calls the work ''one of the best novels ever written about a writer at a dead end.''[21] Robert Fulford wrote of it that there ''appears to be nothing on the page, or next to nothing, yet the effect is powerful. *From a Seaside Town*, about a writer's marriage, is a novel that's haunted me for years.''[22] The writer in the novel is an observer, even of his own life. The friends he depicts are seen at a psychological distance; communication with them is not of a quality to suggest deeply shared understanding. Indeed, Levine says himself of *From a Seaside Town:* "The novel needs the fabric of society. I tried to show that this fabric was the family and friends. Concentrating on that and showing by all the little everyday details the larger things."[23]

He goes to Canada — another return — to visit his aging mother. The relation with her is arms length. As the narrator says in a footnote marked by an asterisk: "We don't talk much mother and me. We never have."[24] His mother lives in a well-supplied establishment for senior citizens. Together they go to see the narrator's incurably ill father in a nursing home in West Ottawa. The depiction of the characters is painful; the prose is spare. A sense is conveyed of the limitless miles that exist between people — even members of the same family. But despite that, or because of it, there is a tone of compassion and sympathy for the human lot.

When the narrator moves out to picture other Canadians, he parodies, creates the bizarre, at the same time as doubts about the basis of his own judgement rise in his mind. The narrator admits he had run away from Canada, but he admits he envies what the country has to offer:

> The steady job, the regular income, kids going to the schools one went to. One could have a stake here. Pure Spring. Esso. Player's Please. And the steeple of a church rising above the houses and the buildings. MacDonald's Export. The train increased its speed and gave that smooth hum of a whistle like the bass part of a mouth organ. Passed empty fields with trucks abandoned in the snow. The glare from the snow. Washing hanging out. The long winter underwear. Then by an open crossing with the red arm flashing in and out like a heartbeat, the cars waiting on either side. Why can't I settle for this? Why isolate myself in a cut-off seaside town in England, that I don't even like? (p. 150)

In a footnote to a comment immediately preceding that passage, the narrator admits that when he left Canada he had attacked the country in his writing: *"the violence, the mediocrity of the people, the provincialism, the dullness . . . And all the time I wanted to be there"* (p. 150).

Maybe that comment says enough about the characters Norman Levine has depicted in his novels. Maybe it says something, too, about the expatriation that so much of his work revolves around. Successive narrators fail to find a basis of value for their lives outside Canada. But Levine has edged them to a place where they recognize they cannot control reality nor dictate the terms even of their own daily existence. In so doing he seems to have freed himself to write with greater compassion, even while he claims that people are "just tourists here. I think life is meaningless, but we give it meaning through our drives."[25]

Certainly one of Norman Levine's drives has been to place himself in relation to the city and the country in which he was born and from which he launched his adult life. All ironically, then, a part of the freedom he has gained to write with greater compassion and depth has come, in both long fiction and short, from his slowly achieved willingness to give its due to the place he so rancorously left and so absolutely abandoned as a hopeless experiment. That is not to say that Levine has grown more sanguine about the future of Canada, but he seems to have come to terms with the great difficulty of finding any place that satisfies the heart's deepest longing for home.

Notes

1   Norman Levine, "In Quebec City," *I Don't Want to Know Anyone Too Well* —, London, MacMillan, 1971, reprint Ottawa, Deneau, 1982, p. 8.
2   Mordecai Richler, "Introduction," *Canadian Writing Today*, Middlesex, England, Penguin, 1970, p. 19.
    Note: Norman Levine graciously read most of this article to assure the correctness of facts reported. He asked that I report he has been a friend of Mordecai Richler for some twenty-odd years.
3   *Ibid.*
4   Norman Levine, "A Canadian Upbringing," *I Don't Want to Know Anyone Too Well* —, Ottawa, Deneau, 1982, pp. 111-112.
5   Norman Levine, letter to Robin Mathews, April 15, 1983.
6   *Ibid.*
7   Anne Collins, "Norman Levine portrays a Canada that causes a sinking feeling of recognition . . . ," *Books in Canada*, January 1983, p. 28.
8   Letter to Robin Mathews, April 15, 1983.
9   Norman Levine, "The Visible World," interview with Carol Fagan, *Descant*, Spring 1983, p. 75.
10 Norman Levine, *The Angled Road*, London, Werner Laurie, 1952, Toronto, McClelland and Stewart, 1953, p. 46.

11   Anne Collins, *op. cit.*, p. 28.
12   Norah Story, in Wm. Toye, (ed.), *Supplement to the Oxford Companion to Canadian History and Literature*, Toronto, Oxford University Press, 1973, p. 189.
13   Elizabeth Waterston, "Travel Books on Canada 1920-1960," *Literary History of Canada*, Toronto, University of Toronto Press, 1965, pp. 598-608.
14   *Ibid.*, p. 608.
15   *Ibid.*, p. 607.
16   Letter to Robin Mathews, April 15, 1983.
17   *Ibid.*
18   Letter to Robin Mathews, May 27, 1983.
19   Norman Levine, "The Visible World," p. 78.
20   Norman Levine, *Canada Made Me*, London, Putnam, 1958, p. 277.
21   Anne Collins, *op. cit.*, p. 28.
22   Robert Fulford, "Home Is the Writer Norman Levine," *Toronto Star*, Saturday, June 21, 1980, p. F/7.
23   Norman Levine, "The Visible World," p. 79.
24   Norman Levine, *From a Seaside Town*, Toronto, MacMillan, 1970, p. 140.
25   Norman Levine, "The Visible World," p. 76.

CAROL SHIELDS

MIDDLE GROUND: THE NOVELS OF CAROL SHIELDS

Donna E. Smyth

Middle-age, middle class: Carol Shields' fictional world is the middle ground of North American suburbia where her couples and their children take shelter. Here is no Peyton Place — although there are marital infidelities — nor even the stereotyped suburbia of mad, trapped housewives and their commuter husbands. Here are ordinary families coping with lives that are seldom dramatic but always changing, shifting as the family develops and changes.

Shields charts their lives in four novels published between 1976 and 1982. She has also published two volumes of poetry and a critical book on Susanna Moodie. Like the novels, the subject matter of the poems is a personal and domestic world. The Moodie book, published in 1977, seems to have been a spin-off from her first novel, *Small Ceremonies*, where the female protagonist, Judith, is writing a biography on Susanna Moodie. The novels, too, reflect each other in a familial fashion; Judith's sister, Charleen, is the protagonist of *The Box Garden*. *Happenstance* is Jack Bowman's story; *A Fairly Conventional Woman* is the story of his wife, Brenda. The dual novels complement each other and extend our knowledge of this suburban world where Shields uncovers an "ordered community" whose existence depends upon the individual's struggle for virtue.[1]

Virtue is a personal fidelity to the self, to one's work, to others. It is a modest, miraculous victory over the ego's temptations to posture and preen, to indulge the self at others' expense. It arises from the fictions and frictions of love between the characters. Marital love: only one major character, Charleen, is divorced. Parental love: by the middle-aged protagonists for their teen-aged children — despite the surliness and upset of adolescence — and for their own aging parents. Love between sisters and between friends.

Virtue exists in physically attractive and financially comfortable circumstances. Martin Gill, Judith's husband in *Small Ceremonies*, is an English professor; Jack Bowman is an historian. Charleen's ex-husband, Watson, has switched identities and jobs several times but remains a white, educated, middle-class male. Charleen is the only major female character who works because she has to and, even then, her part time job is as editor of a biology journal. She feels pressed by a lack of money but she's also having an affair with Eugene, an orthodontist, with lots of money. Charleen's "real" work is her poetry. Her sister, Judith, writes biographies. Brenda, in *A Fairly Conventional Woman*, is a quilt-maker. The women's creative work provides them with an identity apart from their roles as wives and mothers.

The parental generation prior to these couples is, with one exception, either working or lower middle class. The children jump class either through education or, in the case of the women, marriage. Judith and Charleen have difficulty in dealing with their mother's lower middle-class cramped lifestyle. Their mother has defined her narrow territory as the house which used to suffer from her constant decorating schemes. The daughters have rebelled against this narrowness of vision reflected in their mother's miserly housekeeping and her inability to express love. Jack Bowman's parents are a retired, lower middle-class couple who live for their son and his family's visits. Brenda's mother, presented in retrospect, is a vivid, eccentric character. She never married, she worked as a sales clerk for years, she retained the flavour of her Polish immigrant background.

For the female protagonists, the mother-daughter relationship has been the formative one. Judith and Charleen have consciously tried *not* to be like their mother. Judith has escaped into a happy marriage with Martin, a good relationship with her two children, and a new sense of identity in writing her biographies. Charleen escaped by running off to marry Watson. When he walked out on her and their son, Seth, her poetry helped her to maintain her sanity. In *The Box Garden*, she is still working through her ambivalence about her mother and about herself. In both Bowman novels, Brenda's mother has been dead for four years. Brenda has a very conventional marriage and displays little of her mother's exuberant behaviour. She worked as a secretary-typist for a few years and then married Jack, struggled with him through his graduate school days, and now enjoys their relatively affluent life and their two children. But her recently found vocation as a quilter is a gift from her mother who taught Brenda to sew.

In the lives of these women, the father is absent or a diminished background figure. Judith and Charleen's father was a shadowy, quiet man who died suddenly, leaving their mother to live out her days in the shabby house she had tried to turn into a Better Homes and Gardens ideal. Brenda, as she tells at least two people, ''never had a father'' and never seems to have missed one.

The male protagonists have close relationships with their parents. Martin Gill's parents are a likeable, middle-class couple. His father is a history professor and his mother an affectionate, traditional woman. Jack Bowman's parents adore him and, through their decency and caring, offer support even when they don't fully understand the academic-research world of the Institute where Jack works.

In her Moodie book, Shields writes of her subject:

> The value she placed on order and restraint represents a departure from American revolutionary spirit: it was not paradise Mrs. Moodie was looking for, but an ordered community, a facsimile of that which she left behind.[2]

These are also the values, implicit and explicit, of Shields' fictional world where the small ceremonies of family and social life are celebrated with quiet passion and, for the most part, good humour. Shields has a gift for conveying sentiment without being sentimental. Judith, for example, thinks about her twelve-year-old son, Richard:

> He is so healthy. The day he was born, watching his lean little arms struggle against the blanket. I gave up smoking forever. Nothing must hurt him.[3]

The parents alternate between a desire to protect and the knowledge that their children must enter an adult world that will inevitably hurt them as Richard is hurt when his English pen pal and first love stops writing to him. Particularly in *Small Ceremonies* and *Happenstance*, the children are fully developed characters and not simply stage props for the adult theatre. Love for these children plays as much of, or even a greater role, in the lives of the protagonists than sexual desire and/or love. Yet the tensions of living together are neither masked nor glossed over. When Jack Bowman's son, Rob, is surly with him, Jack reacts:

Jack felt the room rock. For a fraction of a second — it
couldn't have been more — he was sure he was going to
kill Rob. His right hand jerked upward and with horror
he saw he was still holding onto the paring knife. So
this was how it happened, kitchen murders, blood on
the floor, bodies falling, blind unreasoned passionate
rage.[4]

But, in Shields' world, Rob is not murdered: he is sent to his
room without supper. Like most parents, Jack controls his anger
and is then ashamed of it. Reason over passion is essential if the
"ordered community" is to survive.

Brenda Bowman, too, rejects passion in favour of the ordered
love of her marriage to Jack and for her children. Monogamy is
not a fashionable virtue. She and Jack know about the sexual
couplings and changes in the lives of their friends and colleagues
but neither of them has been touched by it. They are both
curiously innocent. Jack's previous sexual experience with the
ubiquitous Harriet Post is seen as an aberration, a happy accident that allowed him to play the experienced partner on their
wedding night. When Rob asks his father, "Have you ever — ?
I mean after you married Mom did you . . . you know . . . with
someone else?" Jack replies:

"Never." The force of declaration in his voice almost
took his breath away; so many small dishonesties in his
life, so much false posing and faithlessness but now and
then an exhilarating chance to tell the truth. "Never. I
can't tell you why. But to make a long story short, I
never wanted to. It's too complicated, but never." (H p.
196)

Brenda's refusal to actually make love with Barry, the metallurgist
she meets at the craft guild conference in Philadelphia, is more
complicated. Their relationship is tender, loving, but not con-
summated. They end up sleeping together without making
love: "The trouble is I can't disconnect," Brenda said. "I don't
mean just marriage vows. I mean my whole life."[5]

Such restraint is part of virtue without being self-consciously
virtuous. Brenda adds, with the typical Shields "wry"
touch; "Of course it makes it easier that I got my period this
morning."

Shields' protagonists are frequently self-mocking. When Judith
finally confronts Furlong about the supposed theft of her novel

plot, she calls him "an evil swine" and, although very angry, also hears how odd it sounds:

> Where had I got that word — swine? It is a word I haven't used since — since when? Since 1943 at least, since those fantastical early Forties, the war years, when the villains in our violent-hued comic books were resoundingly labelled swine by the hero, Captain Marvel, Superman, Captain Midnight, whoever it might be. *(SC,* p. 125)

Sometimes this self-mockery becomes self-doubt. Jack Bowman suffers such moments:

> He had let his hands fall to his sides, seeing clearly as he dropped them, a vision of himself, a soft-looking Saturday-morning man, husband and father, responsible, honest, a trifle bulky in a tan trenchcoat, a man defined by nothing at all except the invisible band that connected him to the woman he had just brought to the airport and waved off, the woman in the red raincoat. The husband of the woman in the red raincoat. *(H,* p. 26)
> What was missing was a vividness and direction that was the essence of style. Could it be, Jack sometimes wondered, that he and Brenda were people who had no real style of their own? *(H,* p. 43)

Brenda, going through her own mid-life crisis, suddenly becomes self-questioning. At the age of 40, she is off, for the first time, on a trip of her own. After a long period of apparent tranquility, she is changing:

> Whatever it was that had come into her life during the last year or so had brought frustration with it. A restless anger and a sense of undelivered messages. *(FCW,* p. 49)
> Part of it, she senses, was regret, for lately she had been assailed by a sense of opportunities missed. Events from the past reached out and inspired fruitless feelings of resentment. *(FCW,* p. 55)
> Or it might mean — and a new wave of anger overtook her at the thought — it might mean that all her life had been a mistake. *(FCW,* p. 56)

Through the catharsis of the conference and her pseudo-affair with Barry, Brenda discovers a new, fledgling self and reclaims her life. One of the marvellous scenes in the book is when she marches off, down the snowy city streets, to an interview with

a reporter, wearing one of her own quilts because her new coat
has disappeared:

> Ah, *gorgeous* Brenda Bowman, striding along, or rather,
> being borne forward on rails of blue oxygen, her boots
> kicking out from the brilliant folds, punching sharp
> prints in the wafery layer of snow. Ms. Brenda Bowman
> of Elm Park and Chicago, gliding along, leaving a streak
> of indelible color on the whitened street and trailing
> behind her the still more vivid colors of — what?
> Strength, purpose, certainty. And a piercing apprehen-
> sion of what she might have been or might still
> become. (*FCW*, p. 135)

In this scene we glimpse the potential of unused life. Brenda
is being drawn from the private sphere into the public world. Her
conference trip is a rite of passage between Brenda, the traditional
wife and mother, and Brenda, the artist/craftsperson who has a
separate and individual identity in the outside world. This other
Brenda will not sever, however, her ties from the earlier woman
self. She will preserve an historical continuity between these
selves by *not* jettisoning family and friends.

This evolutionary change is the opposite of Watson's many self
changes which required him to cut off his past selves, family and
friends to become his new self. Although we only see Watson
from Charleen's point of view, there is little doubt that Shields,
the writer, also disapproves of him. All of Shields' protagonists
are suspicious of the Dionysian impulse to discard continuity for
the present moment. Charleen, especially, is profoundly conservative and austere in her estimation of her friends, the Savages,
and her comments about the "pome people."

This rejection of Dionysian passion is typical of Shields'
characters but does not mean they are not capable of eccentric
behavior. Martin Gill does his weaving despite Judith's warning that people will think he's crazy. After a blizzard, Jack
Bowman walks miles home through the snowy, city
streets. These characters also have a sense of the small, absurd
miracles which make life tolerable: the stories of the unexpected
peach and the box of stationery which Judith and her friend Nancy exchange are symbolically important to both women.

Most of Shields' characters are "nice" or strive to be so; it is
another aspect of virtue. They are almost untouched by political
passions and that public dimension of life. The "ordered com-

munity'' is exclusive in that the outside world is only tangential to the lives of the characters. Apart from their own communities, there is no sense of social responsibility or commitment and little feeling of involvement in the sweeping changes that typify modern life. The families watch the news on TV in the same frame as they watch old Betty Grable movies. They are untouched, untested, and they obscurely know it. Judith begins her story: "Sunday night. And the thought strikes me that I ought to be happier than I am" (SC, p. 1). Even though Charleen reveals Watson as a fraud, she is still wistful over the possibilities he once represented. Jack Bowman wonders why he has no style.

The novels are carefully structured and each contains within the structure a reflective device about ways of writing/creating. Not only is Judith writing a biography of Susanna Moodie, she has also written an aborted novel. In this way, Shields plays ironically on the trials and tribulations of fiction writers in the very process of writing her own novel. Charleen's poetry is never directly presented to the reader but her rejection of the ''pome people'' reveals, by comparison, an aesthetic credo based on objectivity, reasoned passion:

> To pretend that dreams are generated whole out of some
> vast, informing unconsciousness is to imagine a comic-
> strip beast (alligator, dragon?) slumbering in one's
> blood. The inner life? I shrug again. The poet has to
> report on surfaces, on the flower in the crannied wall, in
> coffee spoons and peaches, a rusted key discovered in
> the grass. Dreams are like — I think a moment —
> dreams are like mashed potatoes.[6]

Jack Bowman's struggle with his historical manuscript is funny but also a means of exploring, on a more intellectual level than the other novels, the individual's relationship to the historical moment. It is Shields' and Jack's passion to explore that moment as it is embodied in the lives of ordinary people.

Brenda's quilts in her novel are an effective visual metaphor for her creativity. Perhaps because they are so concrete, they seem more vital, more absorbing than the literary preoccupations of the previous novels. They infuse A Fairly Conventional Woman with energy just as the quilting room infuses the Bowmans' house with a new sense of life.

In this latest novel, Shields' writing seems more assured. There are touching, funny, unexpected scenes, juxtapositions, slices of dialogue. She has a dramatist's ear for how people talk. Whereas in the earlier novels there is a tendency to point out the moral, in *A Fairly Conventional Woman* Shields trusts to her characters and her own sense of craft.

Shields' fictional world has been compared to Jane Austen's; the cultural differences between the two are, however, more striking than the similarities. Charleen, reflecting on herself and Judith, concludes:

> So here we are, three generations of paired sisters; had we been shaped by a tradition of kindness and had our sensibility been monitored by learning, we might even have resembled Jane Austen's loving, clinging, nuance-addicted chains of sisters with their epistles and their fainting spells and their nervous agitation and their endless, garrulous, wonderful concern for one another. As it was we were stamped out of rougher materials: dullness and drudgery, ignorance and self-preservation. Our father too had been a man without ancestors: to go back three generations was to find nothing but darkness . . . .(*BG*, pp. 123-24)

This kind of self-honesty marks all Shields' characters as they struggle for virtue on the "middle ground" of life. It marks Shields' writing, too, with an unmistakable stamp. Her fiction is unpretentious, gently probing and mocking, loving and entertaining.

Notes

1 Carol Shields, *Susanna Moodie Voice and Vision* (Ottawa: Borealis, 1977), p. 73.
2 *Ibid*.
3 Carol Shields, *Small Ceremonies* (Toronto: McGraw-Hill Ryerson, 1976), p. 9. Hereafter *SC*.
4 Carol Shields, *Happenstance* (Toronto: McGraw-Hill Ryerson, 1980), pp. 65-66. Hereafter *H*.
5 Carol Shields, *A Fairly Conventional Woman* (Toronto: MacMillan, 1982), p. 210. Hereafter *FCW*.
6 Carol Shields, *The Box Garden* (Toronto: McGraw-Hill Ryerson, 1977), p. 110. Hereafter *BG*.

DAVID HELWIG

DAVID HELWIG'S KINGSTON NOVELS: THIS RANDOM DANCE OF ATOMS

Diana Brydon

David Helwig's Kingston tetralogy fulfills the function his central character, Robert Mallon, had hoped his abortive book on the FLQ crisis might have served: to suggest "the kind of spiritual weather of the time" and of the place — Ontario in the 1970s.[1] In conveying Robert's sense of "being a helpless observer while the universe took a new turn," these novels also convey Helwig's devotion to the accidental.[2] They ask why Canada seems to be "a country where history can't happen," but less to deplore this inadequacy than to affirm a view of life in which everything remains forever unresolved.[3] And they ask questions about responsibility and justice, art and truth, in a manner that suggests that their chief focus is a moral one, even as they deny their readers the moral certainties of authorially endorsed judgement.

Helwig's characters inhabit a specifically Canadian cultural environment: they read Canadian books, attend Canadian movies, discuss Canadian sport and politics, listen to the CBC. But their lives also reveal how what Robert thinks of as "that old Canadian world out of Chekhov and Ibsen" (*S*, p. 50) has given birth to characters who seem to be permanently "spiritually unemployed" (*S*, p. 159) in a world they perceive to be nothing more than a "random dance of atoms."[4] These novels champion Freud against Jung, unresolved dualities and the accidental against monism and the significant journey. Their form therefore can seem at once both inconclusive and overly schematic, for their rejection of resolution derives from their acceptance of stereotypical dualities.

Less overtly ambitious and less complacent than Hugh Hood's *A New Age* cycle (which shares some of Helwig's concerns but not his approach,) Helwig's tetralogy acknowledges its Ontario bias, turning its regionalism into a strength. Kingston is the centre of this fictional world. Almost equidistant from Toronto, Ottawa and Montreal, Kingston is ideally placed to observe the business, political and cultural capitals, both French and English, of the country, even as its own buildings reflect their power structures. The city's landmarks — the lake and the buildings that represent the Canadian institutional establishment — are always there in the background of the text, giving definition to the apparently random personal lives in the foreground. For Helwig's Kingstonians London, England, remains a distant dream of civilization that establishes an ideal external frame of reference. In contrast, their proximity to Lake Ontario reminds them of the inescapable presence of the natural world in Canada, while the looming edifice of the Penitentiary reminds them of the unregenerate within themselves and their community.

Helwig's time focus is also more narrowly defined than Hood's, covering a ten year span in the lives of his characters. Where Hood attempts epic dimensions, Helwig is a miniaturist. And he makes this miniaturist's attention to detail within the modesty of a small canvas an integral element in his style. The flatness of his prose imitates the rhythms of the everyday lives he takes for his subject, while the violence concealed beneath the surfaces of these lives erupts in the image patterns of the elements that he borrows from Tom Marshall's long poem to Kingston, entitled *The Elements,* and in the seasonal patterns that establish the individual tone of each book in the cycle.

The epigraph to the first two books of the series, *The Glass Knight* (1976) and *Jennifer* (1979), establishes the rationale for this modesty, claiming it as an integral part of the cycle's moral concern — to find and maintain a middle way — and of its political concern — to assert the responsibility of the individual in an ideal society. "We must not pursue complexity nor great variety in the basic movements, but must observe what are the rhythms of a life that is orderly and brave . . . .": this fragment from Plato's *Republic* recalls Northrop Frye's Canadian ideal of the Peaceable Kingdom, of a country devoted to peace, order and good government, valuing decency above brilliance. The novels show how this ideal is undermined by the often unrecognized violent urges within all their characters, even as the most admirable of them hold to it as an ideal. Its disappearance from the last two books, which have no epigraphs, perhaps implies its disappearance from our society.

The epigraph also suggests the focus on character, on the rhythms of a life, that distinguishes the first two novels in particular. *The Glass Knight,* with its implications of a fragile chivalry tilting against windmills, describes Robert Mallon, a middle-aged editor in the process of adjusting to his divorce from his wife of many years, Jennifer, and it describes his young mistress Elizabeth, obsessively concerned with her own fragile sense of identity, with her chastity and with her guilt over an abortion. The second book, *Jennifer*, follows the adjustments of perception and direction made by Robert's ex-wife Jennifer after the divorce. These novels share an epigraph, similar subject matter and a season — fall, moving into winter — that seems to reflect their common preoccupation with growing old and growing up. Robert, Jennifer and Elizabeth are all defined by what they choose to read in the opening pages of these novels. Robert re-reads Freud's *Civilization and its Discontents*, while Jennifer turns for the third or fourth time to "read again her own character" (p. 24) in *Middlemarch*, and Elizabeth finds a mirror for her own anxieties in the journals and poems of Saint-Denys-Garneau. Together, the first two books present two lives, moving apart from the common base of marriage, into alternative futures — of comfortable domesticity for Jennifer (her daughter says of her and her new husband that they are preparing to settle placidly into old age) and of continued frustrated exploration for Robert (with Elizabeth as a distorting mirror image), leading to his suicide in the final book of the series, *It is Always Summer* (1982).

Clearly, for Robert at least, the last title seems ironic: summer is not his season. But for the younger generation, summer seems to hold promise of the harvesting of happiness. Cindy, Robert and Jennifer's daughter, is now grown up, ten years after the events of the first two books, and true to her name ("Lucinda, meaning light," thinks Robert at one point) in her relationship with the mysterious Paul does shine with fulfilled love. Cindy and Paul are given the last words of the cycle, significantly turning the focus outward after the inwardness of the first two books.

> They lay close together, touching.
> "You're lovely."
> "No, you."
> "You."
> "You."
> "You." (S, p. 203)

Impossible to tell who speaks which line: the two have become one yet retain their individuality. Unlike the "me" generation of their parents, they avoid "I" to master instead the far more difficult task of saying "you."

The passage recalls the very different sequences in which Robert puzzles over his identity, and those in which Elizabeth, his doomed young lover, attempts to construct her fragile sense of self. In *The Glass Knight*, Elizabeth wakes and rises:

> her eyes moving slowly around her, feeling surfaces, saying I am, I am, I am, until it almost seemed that the walls would fall toward her . . . . She turned slowly, taking in the room, feeling the surfaces. I am. I am. I am. Elizabeth. (p. 34)

Elizabeth's destructive seeking of her identity through the reflections of her physical surroundings and of the people she meets disrupts the lives of all around her and eventually leads to her brutal rape and murder. Her death by fire is paired with Robert's suicide by water, the parallelism further enforced by Helwig's insistent identification of Elizabeth with water and Robert with fire. Together, her martyrdom and his self-destruction reveal the futility of attempting to flee the physicality of life solely through either cerebral or spiritual endeavour. In Robert, the fiery intellect drowns itself, while in Elizabeth the spirit drawn to air and water is consumed by raging earth and fire. In contrast, the physical love of Jane and Burtch, linked with earth, survives to parallel that of Cindy and Paul, linked with light.

These patterns are invoked by Jane's browsing through Tom Marshall's long poem sequence to Kingston, *The Elements*, in the opening pages of *It is Always Summer*. The poem and the novel mirror one another, reflecting similar concerns in a way that adds further resonances to Helwig's cycle, but at the expense of making it appear overly schematic. *It is Always Summer* becomes the key unlocking the flat realism of the other three novels to reveal hidden mysteries in the simplest elements of ordinary lives. Elizabeth's obsession with the Gnostic heresies indicates the kind of reading beneath the surface appearance of things this text seems to invite, even as her fate suggests the dangerous inadequacies of her kind of reading.

The introduction of additional characters — Jane and Burtch, their circle of friends, and Paul and Cindy — moves the cycle away from the claustrophobic inwardness of the first two books outward gradually toward a community of sorts in the last two books. The repercussions of a single life expand like ever-widening circles in a pool. The eternal perspective that in *It is Always Summer* has been established by Marshall's invocation to the "marine city of my dreams where it is always summer" yields in *A Sound Like Laughter* to the temporal perspective of two springs on the verge of summer (in Part One and a year later in Part Two). These springs introduce a restless mood of unceasing motion that leads nowhere. Where summer promised a false calm and the island a false refuge in *It is Always Summer*, spring offers a false sense of renewal in *A Sound Like Laughter*. The Kingston novels, then, begin with a qualified nostalgia for the certainties of the past — whether they be Platonic conceptions of the relation of the real to the Ideal, medieval chivalric values, Freudian analysis, nineteenth-century realism in the manner of George Eliot or romanticism à la Garneau — and conclude in irony.

In *A Sound Like Laughter* the major figures of the other three books assume minor roles on the periphery of lives that until this novel had themselves been perceived as peripheral. The kaleidoscope turns, the perspective shifts, and we see differently — not only Robert from the outside, but also another side of Kingston, more desperate than the genteel strivings toward order and bravery of the Mallon family. The lives of four unsavoury characters intersect in ritual patterns of lust to raise questions first suggested by the title. If "a sound like laughter" is not laughter, but only like laughter, then how do we identify a sound that is laughter?

How can we know the real? How can we live it? — most of the characters in this novel are fakes, living lies — and how can we represent it in art? Helwig's *The King's Evil* (1981), written during the period he was working on the tetralogy, addresses this question more directly, casting light on issues approached tangentially in the series. Dross is researching a radio program on forgery for the CBC. He asks, "if a fake is as beautiful as an original, what is the difference between them?"[5] In *A Sound Like Laughter*, Michael Remmnant went to jail because he failed to see a difference. An art dealer, he sold forgeries and fake antiques without viewing his act as criminal. He saw himself as innocent until he was charged and convicted. Similarly, his mistress Anne helps him rob a house and sell marijuana to finance her education toward a law degree, without accepting that morally these actions may disqualify her from practising law, whether or not she is caught. She decides that she can obliterate the past through an act of will. All she need do is convince herself of her innocence and "she would come out of it smiling. One way or another, damn it, her story was going to have a happy ending" (p. 230). As Dross says of his own situation, "it was necessary to invent history in order to invent the future" (p. 83). All Helwig's books explore the consequences of such beliefs, not only for the individual but also for the society in which he or she functions.

Anne's confidence that she can re-write her own story at will contrasts with Jennifer's more mature awareness that "this random dance of atoms would not obey the laws of story-telling" (*J*, p. 178). And in contrast to Anne's easy rejection of her past lies Robert's belief that "you can't turn your back on history" (*GK*, p. 116) even though, or perhaps, because, he feels that "he and Jennifer were imprisoned in a past that left them mute" (*GK*, p. 141). In this fictional world the very possession of a questioning intellect condemns some to silence and to impotence while the lack of a conscience frees others both to speak and to act.

Dross's contention that "there are millions of world-historical individuals" (p. 92) appears to be Helwig's also. Anne's fakery parallels that of Ernest, who fights dirty to obtain a favourable tenure decision at the university despite his knowledge that his work is second-rate and therefore unworthy of support. Anne's denial of her past contradicts Marianne's obsession with possessing the past through collecting heirlooms and family stories (*SLL*, p. 20). Appropriately, it is Anne and Michael, the two outcasts who ruthlessly attempt to dispense with their pasts, who rob Marianne of the objects that represent her ownership of an inherited security. In Marianne, however, that tradition of stability has already been betrayed; it exists in external form only. It seems inevitable that these two unattractive couples should swap partners near the end of their story. Their various lusts for power appear to be interchangeable. In *It Is Always Summer*, Wayne Burtch had wondered whether

> perhaps worldly ambition was only an alternative
> language for the inevitable quest. You couldn't stop try-
> ing to outreach yourself, one way or another. You
> became rich or famous, or you let your lechery carry you

away, or you spent your life in deeper and deeper anger
at how the world had failed you (p. 152).

This theory seems to sum up the picture of life that emerges from
the novel sequence. Each character represents in his or her individual way the repercussions of a single historical situation, in
which the pragmatism appears to have replaced any notion of
an absolute and selfishness responsibility. It is a world in which
meaning is arbitrarily assigned rather than intrinsically determined, in which Anne can make sure that her story will have a happy ending, not to satisfy any reader's need for justice or aesthetic
completion but only to satisfy her greed. The irony, of course,
is that her happy ending is not everyone's and probably not
Helwig's. *It is Always Summer* exposes the emptiness of her success in a brief vignette of overheard conversation in which the
clairvoyant Elizabeth shudders away from the hell Anne unknow-
ingly inhabits: ''she looked at the shape of the two bodies, male
and female, the flames all around them, bright, dancing . . . If
they discovered her, they would drag her from her safe darkness
and throw her body on the fire . . . (p. 177).

Helwig's skill resides in his ability to juxtapose these various
alternative perspectives on a given situation without explicit
authorial commentary. Beneath the surface bantering of a summer party the Gnostic mystic sees an apocalypse of cannabilistic
destruction; but the reader sees that her interpretation is no mo.e
priviliged than anyone else's. How does one choose between
Elizabeth's hysterical millenarianism, Robert's gloomy Freu-
dianism, Wayne's resigned pragmatism, Jane's earthy hedonism,
Charlie's lechery, Anne's opportunism? The list is endless. As
a novelist, Helwig wishes to include rather than exclude, to
celebrate the infinite variety of life; but as a moralist he seems
disturbed by the tendencies in life itself to destroy the rare and
beautiful. Meaning emerges from the clash of opposing viewpoints, while Helwig appears to reserve judgement. He is particularly good at rendering conversation and argument, during
which the characters themselves debate the meanings of the
words they use and the value of the concepts those words represent. Despite the intelligence of much of this talk, however, it
always ends in futility. No one's mind is changed; no one is
moved to take positive action. Everyone feels powerless to act
beyond the personal level of private ambitions.

The FLQ crisis focusses attention on this malaise. There are various responses, from indifference, through support to outrage; it becomes the topic of idle dinner table conversation; but not even the politician in Ottawa let alone the average citizen in Kingston feels capable of participating in the decision-making process or influencing policy. Robert's plans for a book presenting the responses of representatives of various regions and interest groups to the crisis evaporate. And life goes on. It is a damning portrait of a complacent society, doomed to mediocrity by its refusal to value, or perhaps even conceive, of disinterested action in the public interest. But it is also an intelligent consideration of how the intellect can paralyze, particularly in a society that distrusts its insights. The powerlessness that the more sensitive characters like Robert, Jennifer and Elizabeth feel to effect positive change, and the arbitrary power that characters like Anne, Remmnant and Marianne presume in their blind selfishness to wield, appear to be different sides of the same coin: life in a modern world that according to Nietzsche's prediction has gone "beyond good and evil."

Kingston, best known for its penitentiary, provides the ideal setting for a consideration of what divides the criminal from the law-abiding citizen. *A Sound Like Laughter* asks what separates Anne and Remmnant from Ernest and Marianne, suggesting that it is nothing more than respectability and the degree of security that money brings. Similarly, *It is Always Summer* asks what separates the respectable lawyer Burtch, who occasionally gives way to a violent rage, from the prison guard, Carl, who graduates from petty crime to murder. Although both are violent, Burtch has learned how to direct his aggression in socially acceptable channels; Carl has not. Curiously, despite his violence, Carl is presented as passive, a victim. Of the two intellectual father figures Robert struggled with in vain, Marx's analysis seems more applicable here than Freud's, although this is an insight that Helwig's commitment to impartial recording prevents him from pursuing.

In *Jennifer*, the judge Tom justified his support of the death penalty, by arguing that "if you throw away the vocabulary of two thousand years, refuse to talk about good or evil, just insist on talking about sickness and immaturity, you reduce us all" (p. 166). Helwig's Kingston novels depict the reduction of humanity that Tom deplores but they also show the inadequacy of his language (of absolute good and evil) to cope with the reality of the violences within everyone, and of the complications that a class system and market economy introduce.

Tom stands for the self-righteousness and genuine uprightness of the old Presbyterian world that once defined Ontario, but as a sign of its declining influence Tom himself remains incapable of holding to his values, abandoning his first wife, against all his principles, for Jennifer. Tom's judgmental world is the same world that gave birth to Robert. Robert thinks: "There was no love in that dark house where he had learned to speak" (S, p. 189). Robert's childhood belongs to the familiar world of guilty repression established by Ontario writers like Robertson Davies and Margaret Atwood. Helwig's cycle relegates that world to a lost past. Like Margaret Atwood in *Life Before Man*, Helwig considers the legacy of that world to the Canadian sixties and seventies and its interaction with American liberal individualism. Helwig's Kingston novels describe a society breaking out of the framework established by his initial epigraph from Plato's *Republic*, but with no alternative consensus about values to replace it. Through his art, he creates the kind of "derangement of vision" (S, p. 106) that his artist figure Elizabeth believed characterized poetry — shifting in perspective that enables his readers to see their time and place from the outside rather than from within, as a random dance of atoms rather than the daily struggle to get by.

In addressing questions of morality and communal responsibility, Helwig places himself in opposition to the fashionable trends of much contemporary writing. His work seems more at home in the strong Canadian tradition of literature informed by moral and political concerns. Like Margaret Laurence, Rudy Wiebe and Hugh Hood, Helwig employs the novel form to reflect upon "the spiritual weather" of his time and place. But unlike them, he is not a didactic writer. Although his novels invite interpretation, they provide no resolutions — only a series of endless problems.

The apparently bland surfaces recorded in these novels break open to reveal great complexities in even the most ordinary events, but the atoms of which they are composed continue to dance before our eyes, refusing resolution. Whereas *The Glass Knight* and *Jennifer* seem obsessively open-ended, *A Sound Like*

Laughter and *It is Always Summer* seem obsessively schematic, yet on closer examination, each remains opaque, teasing the reader with hints at some meaning that is never delivered. Helwig's novels present his view of life. He says: "I see the world as fragmentary and as a mess and a hodge-podge, and those don't seem to be negative things about the world; but I don't seem to be at ease sorting them out too much."[6]

For the reader who enjoys attempting to sort such things out, Helwig's novels provide considerable exercise. But the reader who seeks certainties of any kind — political, moral or aesthetic — will find Helwig irritatingly elusive. The Kingston novels are not great fiction — they are exhaustible; but they are more interesting than they first appear, much like the city that inspired them.

Notes

1   *The Glass Knight* (Toronto: Oberon, 1976), pp. 100-101. Hereafter referred to as *GK* within my text. The other novels in the tetralogy are *Jennifer* (Toronto: Oberon, 1979), hereafter referred to as *J*; *It is Always Summer* (Toronto: Stoddart, 1982), hereafter referred to as *S*; and *A Sound Like Laughter* (Toronto: Stoddart, 1983), hereafter referred to as *SLL*.

2   "A Sense of Grace: David Helwig," in Jon Pearce, *Twelve Voices: Interviews With Canadian Poets* (Ottawa: Borealis, 1980), p. 35.

3   Ibid., p. 37.

4   This phrase of Jennifer's first appears in *Jennifer*, p. 178. It seems to be her version of Robert's favourite quotation in *The Glass Knight*: "Time is a child moving counters in a game" (p. 7). It is picked up again in *It is Always Summer* in Elizabeth's perception of marriage as a cannibalistic dance (p. 110) and later in Wayne's speculation that he, Jane and Elizabeth "were like the particles of an atom obeying the fixed laws of the universe, but soon they'd come ashore at the party into the anarchy of human feeling" (p. 155). Wayne seems given to falsely separating order and anarchy, history and eternity (see p. 203), whereas the text suggests that such easy divisions are suspect, that the anarchy of human feeling" is just another manifestation of the "random dance of atoms."

5   *The King's Evil* (Toronto: Oberon, 1981), p. 10.

6   Pearce, p. 34.

HUGH HOOD

MATT COHEN

"LAYER ON LAYER": A READING OF HUGH HOOD'S *A NEW ATHENS*

W. J. Keith

Most readers would agree, I suspect, that Hugh Hood's *A New Athens* is written in an attractively flowing style that combines freshness of outlook with spontaneity of expression. Yet most of the literary-critical comments that have hitherto appeared suggest an imposed, potentially rigid formal structure. Hood himself, in an interview with J. R. (Tim) Struthers, asserts a structural debt to Wordsworth's *Excursion:* "The largest of (Coleridge and Wordsworth's conversation poem), *The Excursion,* I've imitated explicitly, almost from point to point, in the opening chapter of *A New Athens* which is a big excursion, a modern representative of a great genre."[1]

Though fairly obvious, the general Wordsworthian hint is valuable, but it is possible that particular connections with *The Excursion* loom larger and prove more interesting to the writer than to the reader. Margaret's ruined cottage in Book I may well have provided Hood with an inspiration for his forays into "a kind of instant archaeology" (p. 6),[2] and Hood himself has shown how Mrs. Codrington's vision of the New Jerusalem in his final chapter derives from a passage at the end of Book II of Wordsworth's poem *(ECW,* p. 74). None the less, the more overtly didactic aspects of the later books of *The Excursion* seem to me — and I write as a fervent admirer of Wordsworth — more ponderous and monotonous than Hood's poised and subtly varied prose narrative.

Doubtless in response to Hood's insistence on the numerological significance of the chapter-divisions in all his fiction, other commentators have offered ingenious but somewhat heavy formal interpretations. Thus John Mills, in "Hugh Hood and the Anagogical Method," observes that the novel "is divided into four sections which are suggestive, though not strongly, of the four elements — earth, water, fire (of the Pentecostal sort), and air (into which the figures of Mrs. Codrington's last painting triumphantly recede)" *(ECW,* p. 104).

And Lawrence Mathews, developing Hood's remarks about literature as "a secular analogy of scripture" *(ECW,* p. 32), favours a more specifically allegorical account in "The Secular and the

Sacral: Notes on *A New Athens* and Three Stories by Hugh Hood'': "A New Athens" is ordered by means of a clear biblical structure. Chapter 1 corresponds to Genesis, Chapter 2 to the prophetic books, Chapter 3 to the Gospels, Chapter 4 to the Book of Revelation" *(ECW*, p. 228). There is merit in both these suggestions; I cannot help feeling, however, that they have the unfortunate effect of restricting the novel's free movement within a formal strait jacket. They imply that the structure conforms to a pre-existing model and so neglect the extent to which it arises out of its own organic coherence.

While I am happy to acknowledge a debt to both these writers (Mills, in particular, goes on to make a number of brief but cogent observations), I would prefer an approach that begins, as it were, on the novel's own terms. And I find a clue not in any discussion of *A New Athens* but in Robert Lecker's examination of the first novel in the *New Age* cycle, "A Spirit of Communion: *The Swing in the Garden.*" Lecker writes:

> Although *The Swing in the Garden* is full of documentary importance, it does not satisfy on the documentary level alone. Hood himself denies that the work is strictly documentary, and hints at a method of approaching the text when he notes that the work should be conceived of as a "documentary fantasy" which tries "to give an exact account, in the most precise and credible detail available, of something that is purely imaginary. 'Imaginary' in the sense of 'envisioned' or 'made into art.' *(ECW*, p. 189)[3]

Much the same could be said about the subsequent books in the series, and *A New Athens* seems particularly well suited to an approach that combines a consideration of different physical, literary, temporal, and psychological "levels" with an emphasis on "vision" and "art." What I propose to attempt in the following pages may at first sight seem elementary, but I hope that it will lead to a better understanding of the novel's tonal and formal unity: at the risk of appearing to proceed by means of somewhat simple-minded plot-narration, I shall try to indicate how Hood controls and vindicates the shifts in Matt Goderich's mind and memory.

A New Athens begins with Matt Goderich setting out on a walking-tour in the country north of Stoverville (Hood's imaginative transformation of Brockville), and the first major image we encounter is the familiar one, especially to southern Ontario residents, of straightened and modernized roads replacing earlier surfaces. "Sometimes," he remarks, "you can see an earlier roadbed cutting a sharp curve around a knoll a hundred feet off, while new paving lies above it on the wider, more direct course" (p. 6). This image recurs later in the chapter when, on following Mrs. McCrady to the site of the disused Forthton station, Matt notices "traces of paving under the gravel" (p. 46). This is precisely the effect that gives rise to the phrase "instant archaeology."

But the first main event in Matt's walk is his discovery of "broken old creases in the shoulder of the highway and certain strange upheavals in the tarred surface" (p. 6). The buried past here insists upon obtruding into the present. The road in question is Highway 29, once known as the Victoria Macadamized Road. Hood, as we might expect, makes artistic and symbolic capital out of this (historical) roadmaking son of Adam, and the idea of one name being replaced by another yet still existing — if only in the minds of historians — suggests levels of another sort: both circumstances point up the wider implications of what are at first literal images. After discovering "at least four different layers of resurfacing" (p. 7) on the highway, Matt then notices a "strange earthwork" (p. 8). The experience reminds him of days spent tracing thousand-year-old footpaths in England, and we follow the movements of his mind as he thinks back via the Wessex novels of Thomas Hardy to ancient legend and folklore:

> we haven't the culture-memory of the people who live
> in Angla-land (sic), layer on layer on less discernible
> layer on faint mark on mere suspected prehistoric spume
> of cross-hatched human purposes, or have we, or have
> we? Who tarred over those scratches on the road-
> way? How much past is past? (p. 11)

The unifying imagery of layer and surface is now fully established, applied not only to the humanly adapted and controlled landscape in which he finds himself but to the configurations of Matt's own mental consciousness.

What he soon comes to refer to as "the barrow" (p. 12) is eventually recognized as the disused roadbed of the Stoverville, Westport, and Lake Superior Railroad. By old-world standards this indeed represents "instant archaeology": the remains date back no further than three generations and were not abandoned until some fourteen years before the date of Matt's walking-tour. Moreover, Matt had himself observed the last ceremonial run of the railway in question; a student in the University of Toronto Art and Archaeology course, generally shortened (shades of Noah?) to "Art 'n Ark" (p. 38), he was "up the highway looking for the ruins of an old farmhouse (shades of Wordsworth's Margaret?), said to have been built before the beginning of the nineteenth century" (p. 36). What he stumbles upon at that time is not the ruins from the past but an historic moment in the present — and at the same time he gains a first glimpse of his future wife.

These two events, the walking-tours of 1952 and 1966, combine to create a Wordsworthian "spot of time"; or, in Matt's words, "this place intersected with that time" (p. 18). This invoking of Wordsworth's name is by no means arbitrary on my part. A specific reference to the poet has occurred on the previous page as if to prepare us for the dramatic moment of recollection and recreation. Wordsworth has always been a powerful force for Hood. In 1961 he wrote no less than three short stories with Wordsworthian titles: "A Season of Calm Weather" (published in *Queen's Quarterly* in 1963), "Fallings from Us, Vanishings" (the opening story in *Flying a Red Kite*) and the unpublished "From the Fields of Sleep."[4]

All these quotations are drawn, significantly, from Wordsworth's "Immortality Ode," which also provides the opening phrases in the title of an important essay, "Sober Colouring: The Ontology of Super-Realism," collected in *The Governor's Bridge is Closed*. It is also worth noting that references to Wordsworth occur in all the *New Age* novels published to date with the exception of *Black and White Keys* (where the association would not be appropriate). Hood follows the conspicuous practice of George Eliot in constantly alluding to Wordsworth as a way of indicating the particular intellectual and imaginative tradition to which his fiction belongs.

A more elaborate invoking of Wordsworth appears later in the chapter at the site of Forthton station. In another flashback, Matt remembers going with his wife to visit Tintern Abbey, mainly on account of Wordsworth's famous poem that includes the ruin in its title if not in its text. The Goderiches make their way up a trackway to obtain a distant view of the abbey-ruins in the belief that they are folowing the actual footsteps of the poet. They discover, however, when they examine the path more closely, that "the damn thing was an abandoned rail-line" (p. 49). In this English instance, which contrasts with the Canadian experience while at the same time complementing it, the disused railway is later in time than either the abbey-ruins or the Wordsworth who wrote the poem. And, predictably, Matt goes on to consider the older Wordsworth's complaints about the coming of railways and to discount the poet's fears: "*Pace* Wordsworth, the railways were never invasive, alien; they were new in their beginnings. We turned them into antiquities as fast as we reasonably could" (p. 51).

But this Wordsworthian flashback is introduced by a passage that is not only central to the whole subject of our perception of the Canadian past but extends our understanding of Hood's artistic procedure. Matt is disturbed that he had never previously recognized the Forthton station for what it was: "What bothered me about this terrible recognition was the way in which the evidence of past things lies before us, trailing clouds of meaning . . . and we miss it" (p. 46). "Trailing clouds of meaning." The allusion is, of course, to the "trailing clouds of glory" line in (yet again) Wordsworth's "Immortality Ode." The Wordsworthian statement lies, as it were, below the surface of Hood's multi-layered text in much the same way that the SWLSRR roadbed lies beneath the tarred surface of Highway 29. We begin to see how this imagery of layers and surfaces provides a key to the whole form and structure of the book. We might say that the Tintern "digression" (for want of a better word) is indicative of the layers of Matt's mood; and, by extension, the way in which the fiction is made up of an elaborate series of inter-related actions and reflections is indicative of the layers of Hood's art.

It is at this point that Matt meditates on "the almost infinite possibilities of recession" (p. 43) and considers "the strange double-treble optics of the superimposition of the present on many, many pasts" (p. 45). This has already been demonstrated in my discussion of the "spot of time" during which Matt in 1966 is carried back to the past of 1952 when he had witnessed the last run of a railway that opened in 1888. Yet, when the 1952 event was itself the present, Matt was searching for the ruins of a *pre*-nineteenth-century farmhouse. The remark about infinite possibilities of recession is made (within what is itself a flashback) when Matt is interviewing the current owner of an historic house and discovers that the owner's great-grandfather, who built the house, was born in the same year that Wordsworth and Coleridge published *Lyrical Ballads*. And here I may perhaps be forgiven for extrapolating some from Hood's text and noting that "Tintern Abbey" (which first appeared in *Lyrical Ballads*) itself depends upon a temporal recession between the present of 1798 and Wordsworth's previous visit to the banks of the Wye five years earlier.

Within the same section Matt recalls being told a local story by an old inhabitant "about the day it rained on the church picnic and the congregation just about had to swim home — which happened 75 years before I learned about it, *the tale resurfacing in my informant's imagination* as though it had happened the week before" (pp. 139-40; my italics). Matt's own imagination links the anecdote with traditional flood-narratives ("Art 'n Ark" in another manifestation). Much earlier he had remarked how the folk-mind can link legendary tales with orally-transmitted memories of historical events "on the same *level* of reality" (p. 11; my italics). I suggest that Hood subtly introduces these metaphorical phrases to show how our habitual processes of language themselves contribute to the subject he is exploring. Metaphor bears witness to layers in language that suggest resemblances to those other layers of earth and mind studied respectively by archaeologists and psychologists.

I cannot, of course, continue to discuss the later chapters with the same degree of detail that I have used in examining the novel's opening section, but this imagery of layers and surfaces looks forward conveniently to the second chapter where a ghost-ship replaces the ghost-train as a powerful symbol of the inter-relations of past and present. We learn later that the ship in question was built "in 1824-5, and scuttled as redundant thirteen or fourteen years later" (p. 195); the inconspicuous link with the fourteen-year span between Matt's walking-tours in the first chapter is almost certainly deliberate. Matt and Edie catch a glimpse of the ship under the ice in the dying moments of 1952 after a skating-scene that recalls a well-known Wordsworthian account in the first book of *The Prelude* and is heralded by another quotation from Wordsworth four pages earlier (p. 104). The ship is lying beneath the surface of the St. Lawrence River, and is only visible at certain privileged moments when suitable light-effects converge. For Matt and Edie the miracle happens; it is the occasion on which they become engaged, thus connecting by way of their personal romance with the episode of the ghost-train when Matt saw Edie "for the first time" (p. 63).

"The phantom. Really there" (p. 114). These are the words in which Matt describes what might be called the natural super-naturalism of the ghost-ship. A little earlier, an important con-versation that looks forward to some of the major preoccupations of the latter half of the book alludes to the building of the St. Lawrence Seaway, which is described as "a pressing example of the interpenetration of reality by vision" (p. 102). The phrase could be applied with equal appropriateness both to the ghost-ship and to Mrs. Codrington's paintings, which combine the vi-sionary and the local in a way that has since become popular (and perhaps been vulgarized) under the term "magic realism."

For Matt, her paintings are examples of the way "vision obliterates fact" (p. 108); realistic perspective is ignored, but an effect of "coherent unity" is none the less achieved. The con-nection is made quite specifically when one painting, The Stover-ville Annual Regatta, is described as communicating "a living at-mosphere, and at the same time a distinctly submarine, aqueous impression, as if the viewer were seeing the town through light reflected off water, maybe even from under water" (p. 109). In other words, Stoverville is seen as if from the viewpoint of the phantom but real ghost-ship.

Images of layer and surface are less prominent in the third chapter. None the less, various issues that have coalesced around this imagery, matters concerning art and history, continue to develop. Centred upon Matt and Edie's wedding, the chapter shows Matt coming to know Edie's family, and a reference to "primordial Codringtons" (p. 154) suggests the layered genera-tions evident in familial as well as local, social and national histories.

And the chapter also contains an account of Matt's frustrating relation with "the South Nation Village project" (p. 161). As chief historical consultant, he protests at the inclusion of a "kind of Upper Canadian hotel, in fact almost a motel" (p. 164) designed to accommodate tourists and their cars. He finds that he cannot prevent the absurd anachronism since the franchise-chain "in-sists on an on-site" and the chain in question is "American-owned" (p. 165). So modern political realities can distort and vulgarize an historical vision. But at least Matt learns something from the experience. "We can't actually live in our own past. All we can do is remember, love it, and try to understand it" (p. 166).

Matt is roused from his irritation by Mrs. Codrington's bringing another picture for his critical response. In the ensuing artistic discussion she complains that most modern Canadian art is "cut off from the world of vision" (p. 171). She herself is concerned with "sacred art," "the art of revelation" (p. 170). In her paintings real people (the Mayor of Stoverville, the local M.P.) are represented in fanciful guise, and one feels that this blending of the visionary and the real is close to the essence of Hood's own art. This point is, I believe, underlined in the final chapter when her paintings are gathered and arranged after her death to comprise the "permanent display at the Codrington Colony for the Encouragement of Visionary Art" (p. 216). "Twelve in all," Matt remarks, and we remember the number of projected novels in Hood's *New Age* cycle.

In the fourth and final chapter the emphasis falls squarely upon the archaeological recovery of the ghost-ship and its restoration as an emblem of the past, and on the timeless relevance of Mrs. Codrington's art, where action "occurs in space, and outside it, simultaneously," and where she succeeds in communicating a "vision of the heavenly and eternal rising from the things of this world" (p. 211). In this artistic discussion, levels and surfaces are replaced by interconnecting planes, but the basic principles of argument remain the same. On the general significance of this section, I am in substantial agreement with the findings of Mills and Mathews; the former asserts that Mrs. Codrington's paintings "seem to act as the visual equivalent of Hood's own technique and viewpoint" *(ECW*, p. 110), while the latter argues that, "in Matt's analysis of Mrs. Codrington's painting, Hood is also explaining how he wants his own work to read" *(ECW*, p. 227).

I would add only two footnotes. First, as an amplification of Mathews' point, we may detect another Wordsworthian analogue, since the discussion between narrator and Wanderer in Book I of *The Excursion* on the subject of Margaret and her cottage may be seen as Wordsworth's explanation of how his early poetry ought to be read.[5] Second, Hood has signaled the connection between Mrs. Codrington's art and his own in a detail that Mills and Mathews do not appear to have noticed. He makes

her insert a little touch of Matt Goderich into her
masterpiece: "The seventh figure is that of a man with face
obscured, not old, about my height and weight" (p.126).
One is free to speculate on the relation between this figure
and the amount of Hugh Hood that is transformed into Matt
Goderich for the purposes of the fiction.

I am further convinced that Hood intends us to make connections between Mrs. Codrington's art and his own by the fact that
the just-quoted remark about her work presenting a "vision of
the heavenly and eternal arising from the things of this world"
paraphrases his reasons for admiring Wordsworth. He praises
"We Are Seven," for example, because "there, in that poem, is
an ordinary and quotidian reference related by poetic meditation
to a great religious truth" (ECW, p. 79). A thorough reading of
A New Athens shows how "sacred art" (whether Wordsworth's,
Mrs. Codrington's, the poet Maura Boston's or Hugh Hood's)
reveals the visionary below the surface of the real, and sometimes
vice-versa. It is a quality that unites the prehistoric painters of
Lascaux (pp. 34, 60) with the best of the present day, and it also
links ancient and modern societies. Even the novel's title, in
terms of literary layers provided by Alexander Pope and Frances
Brooke, connects classical Greece with nineteenth-century Ontario. Matt Goderich is at pains to explain that the (historical)
alteration of the community's name from Farmersville to Athens
is neither presumptuous nor ridiculous:

> What they had done wasn't to insinuate that their
> village was as great, as central to culture as the city of
> Athena, but only that their schools were in the tradition
> of the Academy, that human culture is continuous, that
> a Canadian school two generations removed from the
> wilderness is the same kind of school as the Academy,
> that human nature persists, remains self-identical
> through many generations of superficial changes. (p. 59)

In conclusion, I should acknowledge that my reading of the novel
has been, to some extent, selective. Like any interpretation, mine
has emphasized one aspect and has doubtless underestimated
others. Thus my approach has laid stress on literature rather than
the fine arts, though the novel itself is concerned with painting
and references to visionary-cum-realistic painters, from Durer to
Stanley Spencer are significantly more frequent here than
elsewhere. Besides, Wordsworth is by no means the only writer

to be an important inspiration for Hood. Proust is a strong presence in his other fictions, and it is surprising that, although *A New Athens* is clearly a book about the discovery of lost time, and although Proust is named on several occasions in *The Swing in the Garden, Reservoir Ravine,* and *Black and White Keys,* he is never specifically named here. One suspects, however, that his influence can be felt "below the surface." Dante, mentioned twice in the text (pp. 168, 170), seems prominent, named or unnamed, in all Hood's later work, Joyce pares his fingernails inscrutably in the shadows, and even Stephen Leacock (complete with his own ghost-train) takes a bow here as a token Canadian (p. 25; cf. *The Swing in the Garden,* chapter 4, and *ECW,* pp. 25-7).

But I would argue that Wordsworth is absolutely central: the Wordsworth for whom common things were "apparelled in celestial light," for whom the poorest leech-gatherer can be seen as "a man from some far region sent" by "peculiar grace," for whom the meanest flower that blows — and Matt picks a large posy of them in the first chapter — can "give / Thoughts that do often lie too deep for tears." Moreover, following through the developing imagery of the "Immortality Ode," *A New Athens,* though a sun- and light-filled book, is also a deeply probing one that, as in the serene scene that presents the death of Mrs. Codrington, keeps "watch o'er man's mortality." Yet for Hood, Wordsworth provides not only an attitude and an imagery in "Space/Time and the Matter of Form" when he finds *The Prelude* a more promising clue to Hood's form than *The Excursion (ECW,* p. 140). But I would not, as Duffy does, speak of "looseness of form" *(ECW,* p. 142) — except as a necessary balance to the rigidities of elemental or scriptural reference. What this Wordsworthian form allows, rather, is a freedom of intellectual movement between times and places that allows for a remarkable variety of tone and is unified by the continuing development of an individual mind.

No less Wordsworthian is the strong sense of local place. In Hood's case, however, this manifests itself in an exhilarating emphasis on a specifically Canadian experience which is firmly present without any trace of shrill nationalism. The layers that are uncovered are those of Ontario history. Matt's thesis, we remember, was called *Stone Dwellings of Loyalist Country;* with his wife he is preparing "an illustrated guide to eastern Ontario architecture" (p. 36); and in later life they see themselves as "recapitulating . . . the constitutive, essential story of life in the colony which takes on larger dimensions. He lays claim to the title of "first prophet of the Canadian style," and remarks: "There must be something in my guts that is finally Canadian" (p. 120). We might say, indeed, that in the last analysis, both above and below the surface, A New Athens is as quintessentially Canadian as Wordsworth's poetry is quintessentially English.

Notes

1   J. R. (Tim) Struthers, "An Interview with Hugh Hood," in his edition, *Before the Flood: Hugh Hood's Work in Progress* (Downsview, Ont.: ECW Press, 1979), p. 62. This collection, originally a special issue of *Essays on Canadian Writing*, contains many of the best discussions on Hood to date. Subsequent page-references indentified in text as *ECW*.
2   All references to *A New Athens* are to the first edition (Ottawa: Oberon Press, 1977), and will be identified, as here, by a simple page-reference in text.
3   Lecker is quoting here from Hood's remarks in Robert Fulford, "An Interview with Hugh Hood," *Tamarack Review*, No. 66 (June 1975), p. 66.
4   For a reference to this last, see Struthers' Bibliography in *ECW*, p. 234. For Hood's discussions of Wordsworth, see *ECW*, pp. 28-9, 62, 74-75.
5   I have argued this point so far as Wordsworth is concerned, in *The Poetry of Nature: Rural Perspectives on Poetry from Wordsworth to the Present* (Toronto: University of Toronto Press, 1980), pp. 32-5.

TWO NOVELS BY MATT COHEN

John Mills

Over the last decade or so Matt Cohen has established his reputation as one of Canada's more interesting and important
writers; interesting because his talent is a restless one which
drives him to attempt in each work a different form and angle
of vision; important in that, a regionalist, he is taken seriously
by his country's critics as a writer who is succeeding in illuminating aspects of that most elusive hypostasis — the Canadian Consciousness.

His first two novels, *Korsoniloff* (1969) and *Johnny Crackle Sings*
(1971) are amusing, playful works which read as though the
author is engaged in an exercise, a sort of flexing of literary mus-
cle. They are rather typical of their era in striving to capture the
nascent oxygen feeling of the sixties decade — its combination
of social turbulence, liberation, and fragmentation where ex-
uberance and energy were celebrated for their own sakes in short
novel after short novel published by the small presses of those
days and where pop-singers became, perhaps for the first time,
symbols for a whole generation and thus *people to be reckoned with.*

A more solemn note creeps into Cohen's writing in the book
of short stories *Columbus and the Fat Lady* (1972), and one story
in particular, "Country Music," presages in theme, tone, and
character some of his later, regionalist narratives set in the
Kingston area of Ontario. These stories, and the two novels
preceeding them, are interesting and worthy of attention but they
do not prepare the reader for the long, ambitious, Faulkneres-
que *The Disinherited* nor for its sequel, *The Sweet Second Summer
of Kitty Malone.* These strike me as Cohen's best works. His
other writings, particularly *The Colours of War* and *The Wooden
Hunters,* are certainly not without interest — the former for pat-
ches of slightly mad, surreal charm and the latter for its painstak-
ing rendering of B.C.'s rain-forest landscape — but in neither case
do Cohen's narrative virtues compensate for what I take to be
his chief fault — a tendency to strive for emotional effects in ex-
cess of his ability to motivate them adequately. This results in
a form of sentimentality more or less under control in the first
two books mentioned.

I would like to start this essay, then, with a brief discussion
of *The Disinherited.* Formally, this novel is a variation on the sort

of fiction dealing with the fortunes of a family over several generations: one might therefore expect the book's subject matter to
include conflicts between these generations, challenges to familial
traditions, problems relating to inheritance, changes in ethics and
values as one decade merges into another, and so on. Cohen's
novel does not disappoint these expectations. The name of his
dynasty is Thomas and it has farmed a stretch of land in the
neighbourhood of Kingston, Ontario, since the middle of the
nineteenth century. The action begins with the heart attack of
the incumbent patriarch, Richard, and much of it involves his
reminiscences between the time allotted him from his apparent
recovery in a Kingston hospital to his death. These reminiscences
are interspersed most skillfully with two other narratives, also
developed with time shifts and dramatic breaks, the first concerning Richard's son, Erik, and the second his adopted son,
Brian. But the novel's fulcrum is the relationship between
Richard and Erik — the disjunction between their perceptions,
attitudes towards life, and ways of being in the world.

What Richard has inherited is a mystique of the land and an
attendant romanticism of hard work — a kind of heroic world-
view. It has reached him from his grandfather, also named
Richard, through his own father, Simon, and it is the appropriate
disposal of this land, now that he is ending his life, which
becomes a major obsession. The making of his will is pro-
blematical because Erik is incapable of running the farm nor does
he want it. Brian is capable, wants it, but it seems undesirable
and even unnatural for the farm to be left to an adopted son —
as though Richard and some of the other characters in the book
feel that there is something untribal is thus disinheriting "the fruit
of his loins."

Though inheritance and primogeniture are Richard's main concerns in the novel's present, the content of his reminiscences is
quite different; it centres on the conflict between himself and his
own father, Simon and, as seems appropriate to Richard's land-
and-tribe consciousness, the conflict is sexual in nature. Simon
is represented as a sly, physically unappealing, knife-wielding,
manipulative and domineering man known throughout the
neighbourhood as a womanizer. His most enduring relationship
is with a neighbour named Kathleen Beckwith (later Malone) who
in turn seduces the young Richard so that father and son wind
up sharing the same woman. The key episode in Richard's life

begins with Simon's visit to the Beckwith house during a snowfall, aware that the footprints ahead of him are made by his own son who is actually lying terrified in an upstairs bedroom. Kathleen sends Simon on his way and later Richard himself leaves but not before Simon has made explicit the literary and psychological basis of this rivalry with his son:

> "According to the Greeks now, a man didn't think at all. He just remembered everything he knew, because he used to know everything before he was born."
> "It's getting late," Katherine said.
> "Now just the other night, " Simon said, "I was reading a book that says there is a mind in your head that you don't even know of. It has a will of its own and remembers everything you forget. It's the same idea the Greeks had only about the lower things in life."
> "Now this man said there exists in every man's head the desire to kill his own father."
> "Now."
> "A man brings up his children to honour their parents, not to kill them. And he expects people to honour that enterprise and not to make it difficult."[1]

There follows the most powerful scene in the book. Richard returns home and Simon provokes him, over the supper table, to violence which might have ended in tragedy had not Steven, (Richard's brother, destined to die in a tractor accident) intervened, getting a knife-wound for his trouble. The episode ends with Steven wounded, Simon nursing a broken leg, his betrayed wife, Leah — Richard's mother — coughing a consumptive's blood in the doorway, and Richard through this act of rebellion, emancipated from his father. The entire situation is piquant and intrinsically comic as well as mythic but Cohen chooses to treat it not in the manner of farce but with a kind of melodramatic portentousness which is nevertheless convincing.

The battle between Richard and Erik is conducted at a different and, fittingly, more sophisticated, level. The tribal rivalry between father and son is replaced by a conflict of values. Erik is a very different person from his father, though his sexual encounter with Rose, a mysterious "single parent" living in a broken-down, bush-encroached house (who reappears later, in Kingston, as a fortune-teller) parallels to some extent Richard's seduction by Kathleen. At the age of nineteen or so and as a college boy, like his father, he is aware mostly of his need to be free of the farm and family. He thinks in terms of escape, though it is not clear to him what he wants to escape to. He is a gangling, morose individual whose alienation and lack of affect extends to college, his girlfriend Valerie, to his sex life with Rose, and to the job he has accepted at the University of Alberta. Cohen says of him:

> . . . he gave the impression of being vaguely ethereal,
> of being cautiously balanced in his movements — as if
> he didn't quite trust the reality of his body and was
> carefully shepherding it through the necessary
> obstacles. (p. 23)

His concept of the land, is, by Richard's standards, reductive. To him it is not much more than a park, a lung for the city, and not a place where survival is determined. He knows that the sort of farming his ancestors were involved in is outmoded and that the farming of the future will be done by huge conglomerates of an impersonal kind. Conversation therefore, between Richard and Erik is stilted and falters badly. They irritate one another profoundly and Richard's grandiose cliché that "a man has to know his destiny" elicits from Erik no other response than wearied contempt:

> "Oh Christ," Erik sighed, starting to get to his feet
> again then slumping back in his chair. "No one has
> destinies any more," he said. "They live in apartments
> and breed goldfish." (p. 146)

This perfectly encapsulates Erik's view of the world and the passage that immediately follows it creates physical analogues for his spiritual and emotional alienation:

> The courtyard was emptier than ever, mid-August
> doldrums, and the sun shone flat and hot on the black
> asphalt. Around the edges of the courtyard, and slowly
> encroaching on the middle, were crumpled up chocolate
> bar wrappers, old newspapers, crushed milkshake car-
> tons. There were only a few parked cars there, all of
> them seeming dusty and familiar. (p. 146)

This is perhaps typical of Cohen's technique. He seems infinitely resourceful when it comes to finding coefficients in the outer world for his characters' inner states, particularly when those states are melancholic, exhausted, and spiritually vacant. The wrappers and cartons seem to suggest the triviality of the modern civilization (in which the pinnacle of heroic action is goldfish breeding) which is fast encroaching on the land and the stalwart people who have used it as a measure of their humanity. The flatness and tawdriness of this bleak, asphalted scene in all its sterility enhanced by the melancholy, dying fall of the sentences, suggests the emptiness of the new generation who have yet to discover a metaphysic to replace that of "individual destiny."

In the long course of his dying, Richard recollects Simon's anecdotes about a mysterious cousin of his own father who arrives on the farm from England in the previous century. This cousin is a poet of sorts and an evangelist who calls himself a clergyman, though no one has (or presumably would) ordained him. He has, however, been "slain in the spirit" and, though many of his activities seem driven by a lust for instant gratification, thus perceives the world and human affairs as informed and penetrated by the Paraclete. Cohen creates diaries for this dubious character, and parts of them are included in the narrative structure. The poet thus describes his seduction of Simon's mother (there is a child of this union — a hydrocephalic son named Frederick) and communicates his sense of mission as one who heals through love. Probably the most imaginative and original sections of *The Disinherited* occur at the end, with Richard dead and buried and fought over and with Erik torn up by a broken bottle wielded by his half-brother. The poet's diaries here describe his own ordeal prior to his arrival in Canada.

> After they arrested me in London they took me to the prison. At the end of a week, they threw me out on the streets again. Then I went towards the river thinking I might find a place to sit with my wounds immersed in the water. There was a girl who saw me & the blood that was caked on my clothes & skin. She took pity on me & took me to where she lived. (p. 219)
> This is God's universe & man is meant to walk upon the land & breathe the air & join his flesh with others so he may be with God. (p. 222)

Erik too, in this final chapter, is described as a passive object arriving in Toronto after his fight with Brian "shuttled from the train to the subway and then disgorged by the subway onto Bloor Street" (p. 210). Here he is shoved around by the throng and pushed at one point against a wall which catches "on the wounds he has brought with him." He is stopped later in his aimless wanderings about the city by a young girl who takes him back home with her. In the next day or so Erik moves through the streets of Toronto casually encountering people, objects and events suggestive of madness and despair. He tries to affirm himself by pronouncing his own name aloud. He had even suggested a permanent liaison with Rose but she ignored the suggestion because "he was obviously incapable of letting anything pass in or out of his own boundaries, that he was simply saying it out of boredom" (p 218). Back at the girl's apartment he picks up the poet's diaries again and reads how their protagonist and *his* young girl embark on a ship crowded with emigrants and how he saves the life of a dying man by lying against him saying:

> This is God's universe & man is meant to walk upon
> the land & breathe the air & join his flesh with others so
> he may be with God. (p. 222)

The poet's actions are interpreted in a more profane light by the Captain who accuses him of "buggering a dying man." He is tied up, his scars and old wounds noted, and a promise made to him that if the dying man lives then he shall go free. The man lives, and the poet becomes accepted as the saviour not only of the man but, since storms have sunk other boats in the flotilla that started off from England, of his ship. The captain befriends him and bestows on him a ring claimed to have the magical property of reminding its owner of his dreams. This ring now becomes the property of Erik who seems thus to have inherited not the farm, or the land, but the Poet's function as Wounded Healer.

The very last pages in the novel are obscure partly because it is not clear what Cohen intends by this parallel between Erik and the poet, partly because the prose becomes elaborate, quasi-poetic, and muddied as to syntax and image, but mostly because Erik himself is one of those characters (almost a caricature of "the sensitive young man" of first novelists) who seem to mean much more to their creator than they do to the reader. Erik may be a youth of profound significance to Cohen; to me, at any rate, he comes across as a surly and graceless bore. What I think happens in the last scene is that, by slipping the ring on the girl's finger and feeling it scrape his wounded back as they make love, he is suddenly able to grieve for his father, for the poet, even, and to perceive himself as the recipient of their different gifts.

The relationship between Erik and Brian, one of enmity, is a given of the book and not explored. Cohen appears to be content to let the details go — probably because he sensed that to make them more explicit would be to distract the reader from his central themes. Nevertheless, he is unable to resist expending a whole chapter on Brian's boyhood adventure involving his being stolen by his real mother and kept a virtual prisoner in her house, from which, however, he is able to escape for long enough to befriend another boy whose chief claim on the reader's attention is that he has already burned down a school. Brian and he burn the former's prison house in a conflagration which kills the boy and burns Brian seriously, scarring him for life. This chapter is interesting and exciting but it is not clear to me how it fits into the novel's overall scheme. As a separate episode it appears irrelevant. Brian is said to resemble Richard in general bulk and doggedness; Erik in face and intelligence. Perhaps Cohen means to suggest that Richard's basic wholeness, strength, and endurance are somehow separated out into these fragmented and incompatible half-brothers.

The Disinherited, despite its weaknesses of over-writing and its tendency to the encyclopaedic, remains a fine and ambitious novel. Its highlights are the fight between Richard and Simon, Brian and the fire, and the poet's diaries. The physical descriptions of sickness, nature, the city, etc. are vivid and powerful and inner states, such as boredom, alienation, and joylessness are rendered so believable that the final impression left by the book is one of melancholy and pain. It is as though Cohen were aware of all the agony and human destructiveness in the world but can fit these evils into no metaphysical framework — thus he finds little room for their opposites — joy, healing, and delight.

Some, though not all, of these problems are resolved in *The Sweet Second Summer of Kitty Malone* and the attempt to affirm life is here less tentative. This novel is more sparsely written and the incidents chosen with greater discipline. The general outline of the book is thus simple and more clear, though there is no loss of creative energy. The novel's structure resembles that of its predecessor in that the central character, Kitty Malone — a woman just past forty, is sent to hospital for an operation on an ovarian cyst. While she prepares for this surgery she relives her past in her imagination just as Richard Thomas did. The "present" in the novel involves her lover of some twenty years standing, Pat Frank, a character who appears peripherally in *The Disinherited*, and the decision he and Kitty make to get married. The narrative is balanced carefully between a description of Kitty's early marriage to a Toronto cab-driver (by whom she has a son) and subsequent separation, and Pat's relationship with his father, brother, and alcohol. Though the novel is nominally centred on Kitty it's subject is Pat's regeneration.

Pat, and his twin brother, Mark are wedded mostly to alcohol and have thus neglected their patrimony, a plot of hard-to-cultivate soil with a built in propensity (as in all the land in Cohen's fictional Ontario) to revert to dense bush unless tended with care, honesty, and sobriety. Yet, as the novel opens, Pat begins to contemplate his own past and he feels a sense of unwonted openness:

> It seemed that he never slept any more. Ever since
> the winter had started to melt into Spring he had been
> waking in the middle of the night to discover himself,
> breathing the dark air, slow and careful, drawing it
> through places in his body that had slept for
> decades. The air sifted through him until it turned his
> life transparent, until he felt himself turned into the boy
> he had once been, felt his whole young body green and
> reedy, the force of the spring earth pushing though it,
> making him tingle like a seed, ready to explode.[2]

This sense of renewal brings with it a vulnerability, a set of strong yet "soft" emotions he was hardly aware of possessing: he wants to "explode with love and tenderness." He remembers that he believed, many years before, that he had pushed Kitty away from him because her life was ahead of her and that he had lost, though only a decade older, "whatever propelled lives forward." Now it seems as though Kitty's sickness coincides with his desire to affirm his own life, to claim her finally, but the logic of his new consciousness requires that he atone for the past.

Pat's rejection had forced Kitty to fly to Toronto, marry out of loneliness, have a son, then leave hastily to return to the country village (called "Salem") from which she had run. She renews, on a sporadic basis, her relationship with Pat but, until the "present" of the novel, it is mutually destructive and filled with violence. Her son, Randy, is himself at that point in life where, like Erik in the previous novel, he feels it necessary to define himself against those people who have brought him up — Pat, Kitty, and Kitty's brother Charlie, and their mother, Ellen. Like Erik he is an unattractive personality, whining and malicious with an added component of sadism. The knowledge that his mother is marrying again, and to the despised and drunken Pat, precipitates the key action of the book — the

drunken brawl in the pub which culminates in Randy's running
over Charlie with his truck in the parking lot. He also beats up
Pat and Mark — both too old and racked with alcohol and
unhealthy living to put up much of a fight. Pat's effort to avenge
this defeat, by going to Toronto to confront Randy, brings about
the atonement for which he has unconsciously been seeking, for
Randy and his father beat Pat mercilessly then throw him outside the apartment building with the garbage:

> Even as he wiped the dirt and blood off his
> pants . . . he knew he would let them get away with it,
> that what he had taken from his own father he was giv-
> ing to young Randy. And that what Randy's father had
> given him was his only reply to the theft of Kitty, the
> damage to his child . . . . (pp. 208-209).

This entire episode, which is stretched over a considerable portion of the novel, is narrated partly through Pat's own consciousness, and is then interspersed with the story of his own
assertion of himself against his father, and partly through his
brother Mark. It is a most skillful and satisfying performance. The novel, in fact, is filled with good things: Pat's
ecstatic, though hesitant, affirmations, the pastoral scenes of
Mark, fishing, swimming, walking over his parcel of land, and
the dramatic scenes themselves. What is most attractive about
this book is Cohen's sympathy with characters who tend at first
glance to strain the reader's sympathies. They seem mindlessly
self-destructive, yet they are intelligent and sensitive. It is as
though some of the pessimism and world rejection has flowed
over from the first book — men and women who are sensitive,
Cohen might be saying, have no other recourse in this life than
to seek a means of destroying themselves. Yet *Summer* flows with
vitality and communicates, with some reluctance, a zest in these
people who, in middle age and after many years of morose and
negative stances towards life, have "come to themselves" sufficiently to commit themselves to one another under the redeem-
ing power of love.

Cohen is a novelist of great and growing abilities. His real
strength lies in his powerful and accurate rendering of landscapes
and cities and in his capacity to make them believable symbols
of emotional states. I do not think his descriptive powers are exceeded by anybody writing in Canada at this time. Yet technically
speaking, though he inherits the advances others have made in

the medium of fiction, he is not himself an innovator. The play with angles of narration and syncopated prose in his early novels was a function of its time and not, it seems, a major or constant part of his growth as a writer. His attempt to break away from fairly straightforward representationalism, the unfortunate *The Colours of War* with its incoherent purpose and cluttered plot, was an attempt to blend realism and fantasy and was, in my opinion, a failure. So it is as a representationalist that Cohen commands attention. His basic themes, as set out in *The Disinherited* — generational conflict, the assertion of personal freedom, the struggle with the bogie of meaninglessness — are the great themes of the novel as an art form since it began. In *Summer* he develops these themes with increasing confidence, greater control, more convincing dramatization, and with enlarged feeling for the predicament of his characters. The pessimism which seems callow in the first novel and which charges his prose with a certain dreariness, (though the narrative technique of both books is extremely playful), is muted in the second and compensated if not by a "yes-saying" finale, then at least with a "perhaps."

Notes

1   *The Disinherited* (Toronto: McClelland and Stewart, 1976), pp. 56-57. All further references are to this edition.
2   *The Sweet Second Summer of Kitty Malone* (Toronto: McClelland and Stewart, 1979), p. 9. All further references are to this edition.

FROM BUBBLING FROG TO BURNING RING: ONTARIO IN THE FICTION OF HOOD AND COHEN

Wilfred Cude

There are books we might call history-haunted, works spun out of societies yearning for some significant touch with the past. Thus the genre we know as historical fiction has become increasingly rich and cosmopolitan, extending beyond the confines of its traditional boundaries, moving out into the realm of the conventional well-made novel. In the standard sense, the genre has concerned itself with the sweep of history on the grand scale, depicting the turmoil of major events through a perspective encouraging reflection upon the character and behaviour of central figures. The present century has witnessed a wide proliferation of novels of this sort, with the productions of Robert Graves, John Fowles, Gore Vidal and William Styron earning attention and acclaim. Here in Canada, however, only a few authors have ventured in this direction with any real force: Rudy Wiebe and Timothy Findley are the artists who spring most readily to mind. Far closer to the Canadian norm is a more understated stance towards history, the consideration of a harsh, routine and fundamentally unportentous agrarian past from the perspective of an essentially middle-class present. Representative of this development, though each characteristic in its own stylistic fashion, are the novels of Hugh Hood and Matt Cohen: specifically, in an intriguing study in contrasts, *A New Athens* and *The Disinherited*.

Potentiality rather than actuality is the theme linking these two otherwise quite disparate writings, the possibilities of the thing emerging rather than the tangibilities of the thing achieved. By looking backwards, Hood and Cohen contrive to look ahead, a trick of narrative perhaps best appreciated by examining Vidal's use of a similar device in his own latest novel. Cyrus Spitama, the voice of *Creation*, is grandson of Zoroaster and ambassador of Artaxerxes the Great King. Languishing in a ceremonial post on the periphery of the Persian empire, simultaneously cursed with blindness and blessed with unimpaired memory, he dictates to his inquiring nephew the impressions of his remarkable seventy-five years. With great relish, he discourses upon the

opulence of the East, of Persia, India and Cathay; and with marked distaste, he broods over the inadequacies of the West, of rustic
and poverty-ridden Greece and the distant frontiers of Italy. For
Cyrus considers himself virtually exiled in Athens, compelled to
endure the rant of Herodotus, the intrigues of Thucydides, the
bustle and clatter of the clumsy artisans directed by Pericles up
on the Acropolis.

> Although I never saw the old Athens — and cannot of
> course see the new Athens — I am told that private
> houses are still built of mud brick, that the streets are
> seldom straight and never wide, that the new public
> buildings are splendid if makeshift — like the Odeon.[1]

As he lingers lovingly on the Persian past, dourly dismisses the
Greek present, and continues oblivious to the Western future,
Cyrus comes to embody a sophisticated failure of the imagination: a refusal to assess potentiality. "You are a part of this narrative, young and insignificant as you are," he deigns to advise
his scribe, the student Democritus: "after all, you have stirred
my memory" (p. 10). Vidal's impish interplay of character, setting and event is underscored when Democritus draws the narrative to a close, providing a brief sketch of his own atomic theory
and the outcome of the Peloponnesian War; and, with this concluding twist, we are inspired to contemplate the present as past
to the future. So, too, we must respond to the novels of Hood
and Cohen: in both *A New Athens* and *The Disinherited*, we are
invited to take the present as a fragile bubble, bobbing precariously along down the evershifting stream of time.

As Hood is aware, the very title *A New Athens* tempts the asperi-
ty of some latter-day Cyrus Spitama, schooled in the mores of
a culture transmitted from the old Athens through recurring
waves of migration. Athens to Rome, Rome to Paris, Paris to
London, London to Boston and New York: so the flow of peoples
and cultures went, finally washing north as well as west,
depositing settlers along the fringe of the Canadian shield. And
there in Ontario, after the farms were cleared and the settlements
linked by river, road and railway, the rustic populace gave
thought to "building churches and schools — the elements of
civilization — places to worship and to learn." In their pride of
accomplishment, the burghers of Farmersville, Ontario decided
to celebrate the elevation of their municipality to a "seat of learning": they renamed their village *Athens*. And who would not

smile at such rural ostentation? "When I first heard of this," Matt Goderich confesses, "I considered it a ridiculous presumption on the part of those good Athenians — the grand name, as somebody remarks, for the mean thing."[2]

But Matt, the narrator of the novel, is an art historian who has come a long way spiritually from the time he first entertained the conceit of a new Athens. Even as an undergraduate, he had responded to "the Janus-headed impulse of the historian, the looking before and after" (pp. 58-9). For him, the looking began a long way before, with the revelation of the cave paintings at Lascaux.

> I had never been so moved and stirred in my life as by this sudden communication which I've spent most of my life since deciphering: men are at all times and places, if they are truly and fully men, the same in their art, their religion, their science. The men of 30,000 years ago, sitting at the tip of an iceberg which dropped off into unimaginably ancient prehistory, in possession of an artistic technique that must have taken ages to develop — since no refined artistic technique springs fully formed into existence from nothingness — were men just like me. (p. 35)

With his mind ranging up from the caves of Lascaux, Matt finds the disparities between the old Athens of Greece and the new Athens of Ontario less and less lugubrious as his own years slip by.

The novel takes us with Matt as he wanders across the region surrounding Athens, following a trail of cultural artifacts back and back. The mature Matt is alert to "the strange double-treble optics of the superimposition of the present on many, many pasts" (p. 45), and sees with eyes, mind and spirit the unfolding of history around him. "How, how, is time involved with value?" (p. 34) he asks, of himself and his absent father as he explores in memory the campus of Victoria College at Toronto. The answer was not to be found at the University, which became for Matt a point of departure rather than arrival. An "intense antipathy to the university establishment" (p. 32) had driven his father out of the academic life into politics with the CCF, and something of that same antipathy motivated Matt to leave in his turn, seeking time and value elsewhere than in "the long, corrupt flirtation" he had "carried on with the universities." A signal success with his Master's thesis, entitled *Stone Dwellings of Loyalist County,* nerved him to seize his destiny in his own hands: "I finally got the courage together *not* to finish my Ph.D., *not* to mix into the academic game and sink myself and my conscience in the process of institutional teaching and learning" (pp. 119-120).

Chance and choice take Matt instead to the corner he would make his home, the angle of southeastern Ontario where the waters of the Great Lakes rush into the St. Lawrence. "It was a long time before I became convinced that life in Canada would permit a Canadian to become an art historian, or at least to become one without spending most of his life away from home" (p. 69). The austere elegance of the stone dwellings of the region, patterned after the architecture of revolutionary America, crafted in the style of the masons and carpenters of loyalist America, humanized with the generations of settlers who were born, raised, married and gathered to their ancestors under the same roof, proves the most persuasive and decisive factor. Yet it is not only the artifact on site, but the artifact in time as well, that conspires to hold Matt in this remote pocket of history.

> Round about that time the whole damned body of
> modern history seemed to disconnect itself from
> everything that went before, from the time of the second
> world war and after right back to the ancient
> world. The sixties began with a roar and a rush of
> rockets; the age of space began on a tidal wave of
> change. (pp. 177-8)

From the paintings of Lascaux to the lunar footprints, man's imagination left imprints of value over time. What better place to observe this and to meditate upon it, than among those dwellings shaped of primal stone upon the lip of our glacial-scarred shield country? Matt Goderich, graduate in "Art 'n Ark," has properly found his niche.

No small part of realizing potential is the accurate assessment of current reality, a process that Hood initiates and sustains through the musings of his peripatetic narrator. "He was a remarkable person, in the same way that we are all remarkable," Matt notes of his father-in-law: "he seemed perfectly ordinary and unimpressive, maybe a bit dull, until you paid attention to him" (p. 99). This is a value judgement the reader comes to apply successively to Mr. Codrington, to Matt, to the region about Athens, and to the fabric of the entire novel. In the course of applying this judgement, we cannot avoid concentrating on the personality of Matt Goderich, who must at the outset strike most of us as a monument of pomposity. "Now I don't want to seem too stuffy about this," he intones, explaining why he did not permit his exploratory grapplings with a pretty young girlfriend to proceed to seduction: " . . . later generations of teen-agers and people in their early twenties have introduced less restrained and allegedly more honest forms of sexual play, not necessarily to their benefit" (pp. 77-8). And that is our Matt, neatly encapsulated, whatever we choose to make of him.

"You're a bit of a pompous ass, Matthew, and not the husband I'd have chosen myself for Edie," May-Beth Codrington informs him, in a flare of Pentecostal counterfire to his Catholic weightiness: "but you're innocent and good, and I suppose I'll have to settle for that." So must we all, especially in the light of May-Beth's immediate qualification. "I said you were a pompous ass," she snaps tartly, as her son-in-law blunders verbally towards the erudite: "I didn't say you were stupid" (p. 172). The distinction is necessary, since Matt's manner might blur the appraisal May-Beth so keenly offers: her son-in-law was endowed with the wisdom to choose virtue. "I'm not an artist," he sighs: "I'd like to have been one but I'm not" (p. 38). In compensation, he becomes a shrewd appraiser of societies through artistry, imparting to his impressions his own gentle human touch. From buildings to babies, he strives to get it right. "He had a charming laugh, throaty, surprisingly deep for a baby," Matt records of his infant son: " . . . think of a bubbling frog, and you'll have it" (p. 186). Hood's own pronouncement upon his narrator is conveyed in May-Beth's tumultuous last painting, the apocalyptic triptych entitled, "The Population of Stoverville, Ontario, Entering Into the New Jerusalem," a work artists and critics laud as an enduring achievement. At the feet of the risen Christ are "seven of the elect of Stoverville": and the seventh figure, Matt relates matter-of-factly, "is that of a man with face obscured, not old, about my height and weight" (p. 216). This is one judgement upon our non-artist, rendered in artistic permanence for posterity: and so, in a new Athens, time becomes involved with value.

As with stuffy Matt, so too with stodgy Ontario. "History has many cunning corridors, sometimes allowing us to see ourselves coming out of doors at the extreme other end of the dark passage"

(p. 42). Illumination in the dark passage can be obtained from flashes of value, often emanating from uncommon old artifacts that only now we are learning to prize. "People's dwellings are the best guide to their character" (p. 42), Matt reminds us, while he fondly catalogues the virtues of the fine stone homes scattered around Athens. Lovely as those structures are, they function as inducements to draw Matt's eyes beyond, to touches of the fantastic and poetic in the discarded and the disused. Ambling along the grass-covered embankment of an abandoned railroad line, he rejoices that "in Canada we haven't moved far from the wilderness, hadn't gardened up the whole damn place, blacktopped it into a huge parking lot." The grassy roadbed is a conduit to the past, to the last day of the railway which was the first day of his love, and from thence back to the time of Riel and Athens' unrealized ambition to expand Westwards. "Some of our railways had the grace to fail" (p. 61) he reasons, linking in recollection the perspective from this embankment to another prospect overlooking Tintern Abbey from the "straight, evenly-graded walkway" of the defunct "Monmouth to Chepstow Rlwy" (p. 49).

These vantage-points lead Matt naturally to another, on the frozen surface of Canada's first and mightiest commercial and cultural route, the St. Lawrence river. There, gazing in rapture through ice turned green-gold by moonlight, Edie and Matt stand transfixed in the presence of a faery spectacle.

> The phantom. Really there. The ghost ship. Holding hands, we moved apart and stood looking from bow to stern and back, the design of the starry boat delivered to us from ancient metal in the moonlight, from solid emplacement in the muddy, sandy bottom of the river, these stars poured their light upward, copper-green. The image deepened out, solidified, held . . . . (p. 114)

No less entrancing than the spectacle, ultimately, is the reality revealed years later by a team of divers and archaeologists. The ghost ship was the *Duke of Clarence*, one of a squadron of gunboats built by the Royal Navy in the Kingston shipyard, commissioned around 1824 and "scuttled as redundant thirteen or fourteen years later" (p. 195). It was a warship that never fought a war, and stodgy Ontario raised, partially restored and housed the vessel, a singularly eloquent symbol for the nuclear age. "The possession and use of our history isn't a simple matter," Matt ruminates: "rather one of the most subtle and difficult matters to comprehend in our lives" (p. 165). While he works with his materials, we see gathering about him not only the relics of the old but the artificers of the new: painters, writers, poets, actors, drawn by the romance of cultural regeneration. Around Athens, Ontario.

Once *A New Athens* is set aside, the reader might be excused for wondering — in a flight of whimsy — if Matt Goderich numbered among his artistic friends a writer with the disconcertingly steely insight of Matt Cohen. For the Ontario of *A New Athens* is the same Ontario of *The Disinherited*, only very much otherwise perceived. Potential to Hood means growth, a community evolving to cultural maturity: potential to Cohen means dissolution, a family devolving into dissipation and decline. The one perception is classic, the other is gothic; though the settings remain identical, the seeing is different, beginning with style and culminating with philosophy. Where Hood elected to use the more personal and subjective first-person narrative frame, Cohen decided to rely upon the more detached and objective third-person mode. Each stylistic choice is appropriately skilled. With Hood, the narrative frame is focused, always emanating from the warm yet studied innocence of Matt Goderich. With Cohen, the narrative mode is fragmented, drifting from consciousness to consciousness, tracing through assorted living memories the disintegration of the Thomas family over four generations. *The Disinherited* starts with the impressions of Richard Thomas, on the day of his first heart attack; then it proceeds both forward and backward from there, opening further vistas by the inclusion of other memories, recollections of other characters minor and major; then it finishes with the responses of Richard's only son Erik, inspecting and assessing the increasingly attenuated quality of his sterile academic life through the diaries of the late Reverend William C. Thomas, poet, mystic and cousin to Erik's great-grandfather. The novel is a web of memory, biological histories, broken only by the intrusion of the diaries — memory turned artifact, preserved in manuscript for the future, now the present becoming the past.

Though the theme of the disinherited is implicit on every page, the actual source of the novel's title is not revealed until the very end of the work, as Erik Thomas glances through the diaries of the Reverend William C. Thomas. The writing is somehow evocative of his own father's hand, "large and square and careful": and there, in the Reverend's account of his voyage from England, is the passage that reverberates throughout the book.

> Our ship was one of twelve & when we came across
> the ocean in this apostolic convoy we were like an army
> of the dispossessed. We had thought ourselves better
> than our nomad ancestors who had wandered to Europe
> from Mesopotamia & Africa, but now we too were
> disinherited & forced to seek out a new world; & so we
> closed the circle on our past.[3]

The circle on our past must ever be closed anew, a point *The Disinherited* reiterates unceasingly. For the diary is the sole legacy of Richard Thomas to his son; the farm that had consumed the vitality and passions of three generations of Thomases remains in the custody of Richard's wife Miranda, to be worked by their adopted son Brian as long as he chooses to do so. And Erik himself, disinherited by an act as much of his will as his father's, must wander dispossessed through an alien urban world. Cut off from the farm by his education, his resentment of his rural past, and his father's death, Toronto is "immediately a ghetto for him; there is nowhere left to go except other cities which would all be the same city" (p. 210).

The conflict between Erik and his father was just the most recent seizure in an emotional convulsion racking the Thomas men for generations. Fittingly, the last act is played out within the context of Richard's terminal illness — a disease of the heart, pitting organ against organ, leaving "the marks of this battle" (p. 135) on the victim's face. Erik, visiting his stricken father in company with his mother, Brian, and Brian's wife Nancy, sees only Richard "lying in his bed and trying to force them to accept his will about the farm" (p. 33). Years earlier, Richard had offered his son the farm: "You're my son. I made it for you." At that time, Erik refused: "You made it for yourself" (p. 28). The exchange masked a deeper antagonism, one having nothing to do with the land. Starkly, Richard counters from his hospital bed his wife's insistence that he decide about the farm, reading a marked passage from the diary of the Reverend William C. Thomas.

> God has said that the land is His and can belong to no
> man and therefore how can one man give what is not
> his to another man who cannot possess it. (p. 138)

The diary articulates what Richard had glimpsed in a drunken vision, that the farm was merely "the camping place of some nomadic tribe that had escaped the European forest for this new world and its instant hospitality and was strung out with their animals on the ancient glaciated shield of the continent, waiting for history to make them whole again" (p. 155). Not for the farm did Richard tear at his only son, even as his vitals warred among themselves.

From the days of his solitary autumnal meanderings about the county, searching for anonymity as a teenager in the family car, Erik "wanted only to get away from everything." His goal was "to have time pass quickly so that he would be away from home finally, somewhere where he was not known" (p. 13). He attains something of this goal through the academic life, appearing to his father almost as an alien being, one who has wilfully distanced himself from strife, from passion, and therefore from life itself. "Erik seemed to live only through words and his head so that his body was already vestigial, threatening to grow old before it was ever claimed by this world" (p. 104). Richard viewed this development with contempt, eyeing his son's body "thin and unbroken, cut off from anything that grew": to him, Erik has degenerated, becoming a man of "virginal bony arms that could belong to a senile old priest, rattling in their sockets, denying everything" (p. 138). Erik himself shares this concern, at least subconsciously; near the novel's end, he wakes out of a dream that "he was the perfect man, floating through space in a glass ball" (p. 169). And yet, Erik and Richard alike saw in the farm a dead end: "a purposeless self-preservation to milk the land every year, enough to fill their bellies and their bank balance, nothing more, a straight trade, body for earth, three generations of bones to feed the land" (p. 143). Erik left, that he would not repeat the same primitive drama enacted between Richard and his father, the embittered lecher Simon Thomas. And Richard, in a moment of honesty, acknowledges this was so. "Simon Thomas would've drowned him," Richard thinks of his son, the last of the Thomas line: "would have drowned everyone if he could have gotten away with it" (p. 187).

Behind the animosity between Erik and Richard, then, there lurked the Oedipal quarrel between Richard and his father. Both men had taken Katherine Beckwith, a local girl, as mistress: and both men had fought viciously over her on the night of Leah's

death, on the night Richard lost his mother and Simon his
wife. "Now this man said there exists in every man's head the
desire to kill his own father" (p. 56), Simon tells Katherine in
her home that night, certain his son is listening upstairs: and
later, in the kitchen of the dying Leah, the two men
fight. "Richard saw the flash of metal, could hear it moving by
his head, whistling like a slow train . . . . " (p. 128). This quarrel, too, had been a long time in the making — itself a dark
derivative of a still earlier sexual struggle, between Simon's father
Richard Simon Thomas and his mystical cousin, the poetic
Reverend William C. Thomas. To this struggle, over the affec-
tions of Richard Simon's wife Elizabeth, Simon had been a
vicarious, furtive, and perverse witness. The poet had recorded
the affair in the Blakean prose of his diaries, which Simon found
shortly after the death of the author: and he kept them close until
the time of his own death, when they passed into the keeping
of his son. The poet's words have therefore stalked the Thomas
men for three generations, mocking their commitment to the
physical world.

> My cousin would like to be a gentleman but he cannot
> succeed even in pretense. There is violence in his house
> & he cares for nothing but money. His body has been
> removed from God & it makes his wife suffer. (p. 81)

Along with Richard Simon's farm, the diaries move down
through the years, each testimonial in its own way to the twisted
skein of materialism and passion that constitutes the Thomas inheritance. Richard's decision to withhold the farm but bestow
the diaries is calculated to disrupt at last the circle that has spiraled
increasingly inward on his tormented line. Disinherited, Erik is
also free. His father has given him that which he truly desired,
the right to follow the poet into a distant world, to discover
himself amid terrors and marvels: voyaging alone, from Kingston
to Toronto to Edmonton, from the farm to the university — and,
possibly, beyond.

Accompanying the diaries was a ring, "a strange gold ring that
had a small green stone set in its crown" (p. 115), talisman from
the poet's cruel and marvellous era. Originally the property of
a Moroccan enchantress, it passed into the hands of a tyrannical
sea captain, who paid for it with his own blood and then gave
it to the poet.

> . . . the stone was the source of the power; & it made
> him bend closer & closer to it until the light had the
> brilliance of a sun & it shone from the stone with this
> deep & penetrating brightness which was absolutely
> round & surrounded by a halo of exquisite
> violet . . . .   (p. 237)

Love-token of the poet to Elizabeth Thomas, it is offered by Simon Thomas to Katherine, who rejects it; and Simon drops it into the coals of Katherine's stove, whence Richard later retrieves it, "blackened and lumpy" (p. 217). Elizabeth and Katherine had themselves been enchantresses, luring the poet and Simon and Richard, weaving magic out of the stuff of passion. But the logic-ridden Erik is proof against such women, eluding the palm-reading Valerie and the fortune-telling Rose: austere in his bloodless isolation, he at last removes the ring from the diaries and slips it on the finger of a nameless pregnant girl. "Put it on the second-last finger of her left hand, wedding band, wondered if this was the poet's intention, to have the ring passed through the family this way, as a sign" (p. 238). And in the girl's belly, there stirs another life, another of the disinherited. And magic and reality once again close the circle, the burning ring of passion driving the Thomas men.

"Think of this thread as the entire course of a life monad," an Indian sage tells Cyrus Spitama, hurling an unwinding ball of string up to the rafters: and, upon its collapse to the floor, he points his moral. "That . . . is the story of our existence" (p. 170). Hood and Cohen might be inclined to agree, for each has depicted history as something of a skein of time. A knitting together or an unravelling apart: *A New Athens* celebrates the one, while *The Disinherited* mourns the other. Yet either view is tenable, and both together can serve to inform the scrutiny of our past. With writings such as these, the past lives in our imaginations: and now and in the future, thus enhanced, time becomes involved with value.

Notes

1   Gore Vidal, *Creation* (New York: Ballantine Books, 1981), p. 8. All subsequent references to this work will be given in parentheses in the text.
2   Hugh Hood, *A New Athens* (Ottawa: Oberon, 1978), pp. 58-9. All subsequent references to this work will be given in parentheses in the text.
3   Matt Cohen, *The Disinherited* (Toronto: McClelland & Stewart, 1976), pp. 219-20. All subsequent references to this work will be given in parentheses in the text.

AUDREY THOMAS

MARIAN ENGEL

THE GIRL WHO WOULDN'T GROW UP: MARIAN ENGEL'S *THE GLASSY SEA*

Clara Thomas

> But for one fleeting moment I was back in the rose-
> world, inhaling all the mysteries: I felt the metaphysic
> and the crowns and thorns were around me again and I
> wanted to get into the heart of them all . . . though I
> never became, had the faith or talent or grace to become
> (and never will have, dear Philip, never will have, you
> must understand) the Keeper of the Roses, for one mo-
> ment I was at the heart of the roses and of the
> universe.[1]

In Part I, "Prologue," Sister Mary Pelagia of the Eglantines, an Anglican Order of London, Ontario, is at the threshold of a new life. Before she resumed her calling, which she has just done as the book opens, she was Rita Bowen, called Peggy, wife of Asher Bowen, Toronto lawyer and politician; later she was Rita Bowen, discarded and divorced wife; before that for ten years she was Sister Mary Pelagia of the Eglantines; and before that she was Rita Heber of West China Township near Sarnia and the St. Clair river in south-western Ontario. A very large part of *The Glassy Sea* consists of a letter Rita Bowen wrote to her friend Philip, Bishop of Huron, called by her "Philip Yurn" because of a long-standing joke between them on the vowel-slurring Ontario voice that also makes "Trawna" out of Toronto. After the ceremony dedicating the re-opening of Eglantine House with Mary Pelagia its Sister Superior, Philip and Anthony, a young priest and Philip's assistant, leave and Mary Pelagia begins by reading the letter she wrote to Philip the previous summer.

Part II, "The Letter," is her life's story. Its writing was a part of the process by which, in her forties, she finally came to see that she must wake up, live and act, that the dream world of the roses she describes in its first pages has been her chosen refuge all her life. She has never really been awake to reality, neither as a child and young girl, nor for ten years as a Teaching Sister with the Eglantines. When the Order was decimated by age, illness and catastrophic accident and Mary Rose, the Superior, decreed that she go back into the world, she fell almost immediately into marriage with Asher Bowen, a nightmare of his — and her — making. After that, banished to a lonely, decrepit farmhouse in P.E.I., she lived in a dream existence, contentedly away from the challenges, ordeals and scars of daily living:

> I think he must have been looking for a cheap, grim and
> isolated place and by a *miracle* found this . . . I keep prow-
> ling my territory; *I have to keep my eyes on it in case it disap-
> pears.* I'm like God protecting Bishop Berkeley's tree; if I
> don't watch it, the tide won't come in, the estuary won't
> fill and empty to its own thrilling rhythm, one that no man
> but me can tamper with (I play God you see). (p. 16, italics
> mine)

Rita Bowen makes a magic, protected kingdom of her rickety
farmhouse, the nearby shore and the mosquito-infested Mac-
Moan's road, "full of roses." But Philip will not let her dream
away the rest of her life. He insists on keeping in touch with her,
sending her books and then writing to her, asking her to help
him reopen Eglantine House. "The Letter" ends with her refusal
and her plea, "But leave me here, please, to dream my redemp-
tive dreams" (P. 144)

Part III, "Envoie," moves us back to the book's beginning,
Mary Pelagia in the parlour of the quiet house remembering what
happened after she finished her letter to Philip. Summer ended
and there were no more roses. With winter came the nightmare
again, when Rita Bowen, alone and cold in the house by the
shore, came to the very borderline of despair and the rejection
of life: "Life, I decided, is a sentence between
brackets . . . . With my shoulders swathed against the drafts
in every piece of cloth I could find in the house, and my feet in
the oven, I found that I wanted that end bracket to come fast"
(p. 146). Then Philip sent Anthony, his emissary, to persuade
her out of her dream turned nightmare. At first she was angry
and resentful; finally, after three weeks of discussion, she
capitulated. She agreed to return to London as Mary Pelagia,
and to rebuild the Order. Eglantine House will be reopened as
a hostel for embattled women:

> I want a core of women helping other women to put
> their lives (their souls we shall leave to Dr. Margaret
> Charters and the novice mistress) in order . . . If I can
> organize us efficiently, if we can do an eightieth of the
> work they do at Nellie's hostel in Toronto we can justify
> the faith that provided our income. (p. 163)

What used to be the rose garden of Eglantine House will become
a playground for children, but "Lord, will you allow us just a
little garden in spite of the playground? Funny. The chapel still
smells of roses" (p. 167). And so Sister Pelagia, poised to begin
again, ends her story.

As she did with *Bear*, Marian Engel has built this novel on and through a strong web of lore and literature. The rose symbolism is all pervasive and in benign contrast to the brittle, shining hardness of *The Glassy Sea*. When Rita Heber was a little girl in the United Church on the French Line in West China township she had identified herself with R. Heber, the writer of the hymn "Holy, Holy, Holy." She had been especially captivated by the verse beginning "Holy, Holy, Holy, all the saints adore Thee / Casting down their golden crowns around the glassy sea: 'I was in there with the cherubim and the seraphim. I had to be. I knew I belonged there'" (p. 19). So Engel begins the strong apocalyptic theme that runs through the novel, climaxing in "The Envoie." Chapter four of the Vision of St. John in the Book of Revelation deals with "Things which must be hereafter," with the jewel imagery of God on His throne, "like a jasper and a sardine stone: and there was a rainbow round about the throne, in sight like unto an emerald;" with the four and twenty elders wearing crowns of gold; with the "sea of glass like unto crystal" before the throne; with the "four beasts full of eyes before and behind" attendant upon the throne, who "rest not day and night, saying Holy, Holy, Holy, Lord God Almighty, which was, and is, and is to come." In verses ten and eleven the four and twenty elders cast down their crowns before the throne, saying, "Thou art worthy, O Lord, to receive glory and honour and power: for Thou hast created all things, and for thy pleasure they are and were created" (Authorized Version). The chapters that follow describe the time of death and judgment, the destruction of the destroyers of the earth.

In "The Envoie" Rita Bowen's rejection of life moves her into a horrendous apocalyptic vision of the relation between men and women as total, destructive war, its outcome the killing of all women at forty-five and of those who have not borne a child at thirty.

> Evil thoughts occurred to me, evil malicious
> thoughts. They must dispose of women, I
> thought: they want it that way. We must give them
> their heads: this is what they want, a world free of
> women who are past their nubile best, who are capable
> of thinking, who can direct them, who bring guilt and
> repression to the world. Women brought sin, they
> believe that, their hearts and their balls believe it, they
> act it out every day of their lives, treating their
> daughters like toys and their wives like encum-
> brances. Therefore let them get rid of women. (p. 148)

Rita's former husband, Asher Bowen, dust and ashes, the converse of life, or the cruel epitome of the pagan god Ashtaroth, is to play the anti-Christ in Rita's dire scenario of final destruction: "Asher, I thought, from his high righteousness, Asher alone can legislate this true casting down of gold crowns. Asher shall hold up the flaming sword. Asher shall be the one elected for the destruction" (p. 150).

But the biblical apocalypse does not end with its terrible vision of destruction. It ends with the vision of a new beginning and the invitation to partake of it, with water and the tree of life:

> Revelation Ch. 21, 22:
> Then I saw a new heaven and a new earth . . . And I saw the holy city, new Jerusalem, coming down out of heaven from God, prepared as a bride adorned for her husband; and I heard a great voice from the throne saying, "Behold, the dwelling of God is with his men. He will dwell with them, and they shall be His people, and God himself will be with them . . . Then he showed me the river of the water of life, bright as crystal, flowing from the throne of god and of the Lamb . . . There shall be no more anything accursed . . . And night shall be no more.

Accordingly, Rita's cruel vision is not the end: "I was banking, finally, on some kind of ending to the plan; on limitations; somewhere in my black, angry, jealous heart there was still room for a small eternity: a resurrection" (p. 152). Rita's capitulation to Philip's plan for her and for the Eglantines is a chance for her new heaven and earth, her participation in a new beginning.

Rita's story also conforms to the strong and powerful fairy-tale motif of *Sleeping Beauty*. Rita Bowen dreams away her summer among the roses; the prince who finally awakens her is Anthony, Philip's emissary, though she is not awakened to conformity and marriage, but to selfhood and the strength to risk going back into life. In *Reinventing Womanhood* Carolyn Heilbrun has interpreted the Sleeping Beauty story in a way that exactly fits the significance of its motif in *The Glassy Sea:*

> Analysts, of course, to a man (and woman) see the universe as revolving around male destiny: attachment to it, rather than imitation of it, constitutes female destiny. But let us translate those princes who keep awakening and discovering the girls in fairy tales. Suppose — and what else does one do with fairy tales —

that the prince in *Cinderella* stood, not for the girl's need
to love a man, transferred in proper Freudian fashion
from papa to husband, but for her other self, that
"masculine" part of herself, externalized in the story, to
which she must be awakened to achieve adulthood. So,
too, the prince in *Sleeping Beauty*. The mother is dead —
that is the early attachment to a mother must cease, as it
must for a boy. Then, the prince kisses Sleeping Beauty
awake, but not to matrimony and "living happily ever
after." No, to her selfhood, to her ability to live out her
own destiny."[2]

As we see from Rita's letter to Philip, the pattern of escape,
that most primary of all female fantasies, has dominated her life's
choices in every major way. At the wedding of her friend
Christabel and her cousin John she "fainted dead away. I got
a new start in life before they did . . . I suddenly saw, I remember
my knees saw as they crumbled, that the marriage would be a
disaster — and perhaps that most marriages are disasters — and
arranged with my consciousness to absent myself from the pain
of this vision" (p. 58). She was sick at home for the summer,
close to her mother as she never had been or would be again,
and when better, she studied for university examinations with
Mr. Laidlaw, the Anglican clergyman who introduced her to the
beauty of religion, to the Eglantines, and to her second, more major, escape.

Once acquainted with the nuns and their commitment to the
firm but gentle and civilized Rule by which they lived, she soon
longed to join them. Her reception into the Order was not
without a lengthy struggle, however. Her many discussions with
Mary Rose, the Superior, were searching and extremely hesitant
on Mary Rose's part. This good and very intelligent woman
seemed to know from the start that the vocation Rita thought she
had discovered in herself was doubtful. Mary Rose was like
Shaw's Archbishop in *St. Joan*: "Child, you are in love with
religion." Joan: "Am I? I never thought of that. Is there any
harm in it?" Archbishop: "There is no harm in it my child. But
there is danger." As Rita recognized years later in her letter to
Philip, hers was "a quest for simplifications, patterns, styliza-
tions." To her the Eglantines were "peace and bliss . . . . It
wasn't faith that got me to the nunnery, it was taste" (p. 65). Her
mother's furious, accusatory "ructions" on her announcement
that her destination after university was not the Ontario College

of Education but the Eglantine Order marked the final psychological separation from the mother that Carolyn Heilbrun describes as necessary, but with a difference that delayed her maturing until much later in life. For Rita chose Mary Rose in her wisdom and goodness of heart as another, and stronger, mother figure, though Mary Rose, recognizing both Rita's need and its perils, did what she could to keep Rita partly in the world. She insisted on her finishing university, going to O.C.E., paying back her family for what her education had cost them and then, after Rita's joining the Order, she had her teach by day in the London schools while also living the life of the other nuns in Eglantine House.

So for ten years she was a partner in both worlds, though to her the outside teaching, however conscientiously done, was tokenism only, the price she paid for her sense of protected security with the Eglantines. Because of the deeply-embedded puritanism that Mary Rose divined in her, she named her for Pelagius, the theologian who preached that we must save ourselves without the grace of Divine intervention and are damned if we commit a single sin. In time the other nuns became old and sick, except for Mary Cicely, who could not give herself any longer to the Order and died tragically in a car crash, having run away with a young gardener. More and more Mary Pelagia took on the organizational and physical burdens of running the house. Mary Rose became too ill to carry on and decided that Mary Pelagia must go back into the world: "She told me she thought there was no future for me here; I was too young to remain with a dying Order. I cried and cried, but I knew she was right. My spiritual life had died — if it ever existed — in the practical details of the house" (p. 93).

Mary Rose arranged Rita Heber's return to the world via Maggie Hibbert's house in Toronto where she worked as an *au pair* girl. It was a bewildering, frightening, but stimulating awakening for her. When, very shortly, she met, fell in love with and married Asher Bowen, who came from her part of the country and whom she had admired from afar at High School, she was acting out the female romance, she was the Sleeping Beauty, he the awakening prince. That it was a false story without foundation in reality and that Asher was a false prince, completely tied to his own male pride, expectations and anxieties, was speedily evident; and the birth of their baby, "Chummy," a hydrocephalic, provided Rita, now Peggy, Asher's name for her, with another escape route which she took. She submerged herself entirely in Chummy's life and treatments — "I was content with my new obsession." Asher went into Ontario politics and so they went on uneasily until Chummy died at five years old. Rita could not accept his death. "On the Monday Chummy's doctor phoned Asher at the Parliament buildings because I had gone to the clinic as usual. They sent me away somewhere for a rest" (p. 127). When she got back Asher had found another woman: "Peggy, I've led you a terrible life. I admit it. I want to set you free. Couldn't he see that the last thing I wanted was to be free?" (p. 127). Then followed a frantic and abortive series of darts into useless escape routes — drink, analysis, sex and flight — and, finally, divorce and exile to the shore.

On one of her desperate flights Rita ran away to the house that Asher had bought as a weekend retreat and that had belonged to her uncle Eddie, close to her own old home. Here Marian Engel overtly introduces *Rumpelstiltskin*, another fairy tale of an imprisoned princess. At the farmhouse Rita slept away her time until one day she awakened to find a strange little man watching her — "little round eyes, little round glasses, a yellow beard and a little knitted cap on his head . . . he was about the size of an elf and I often wonder if I dreamt him" (pp. 130-132). For some time, "I don't know how long it lasted," her sleep was punctuated by love-making with Oliver, this stranger, by eating the "rooty soups" he made and by the sounds of the carpentry work he was doing in the kitchen. When her meagre supply of money ran out and he realized that she couldn't get anymore, he flew into a rage; "then he did a little dance like Rumpelstiltskin, and began to scream about the world being full of decadent capitalists, vile deceivers" (p. 132). He left the hiding-place cottage, went to Asher's office demanding money and so gave away her whereabouts. Rita was partly his prisoner, as was the princess in *Rumpelstilktskin*, but he was also a benefactor: every so often he disturbed her dream and his sexual skill reminded her that she was still alive, female and responsive. His was a brief episode only, and by no means a real awakening.

Philip, Bishop of Huron, plays the *deus ex machina* in Rita's story, far from God-like, in fact guilty on their first meeting of crashing and destructive bad taste. After her marriage, pregnant with Chummy, she and Asher encountered him at a dinner party at

Maggie Hibbert's: "Then you looked at Ash over Maggie's peonies. 'And how,' you asked, 'does your husband enjoy being married to one who was once the bride of Christ?'" (p. 108). That was the moment when Rita, looking across the table at Asher, realized that he not only resented her, he hated her. To me, Philip's speech denotes a mind-boggling crudity on his part that is scarcely credible, but Marian Engel writes it in as the context of Rita's continuing friendship with Philip, and as motivation for his stubborn refusal to let Rita Bowen dream her life away: "You became my friend, my consolation" (p. 108). As Philip leaves her in the Eglantine parlour, about to start her new life, he admits his guilt from the time of that first meeting: "'I feel better now.' 'Why?' 'Because if I robbed you of a certain amount of your past, I have given you a future'" (p. 11). Insensitive enough to have said it, he is also sensitive enough to be aware of the damage he did. So Philip was the agent of Rita's long-delayed awakening, but in a final and satisfyingly feminist turn, we find that he in his turn has been Mary Rose's agent: "So I am Mary Pelagia again. Sister Superior. As Sister Mary Rose indicated I ought to be in a last, flattering, and moving letter to Philip" (p. 165). *The Glassy Sea* was published in 1978 and Heilbrun's *Reinventing Womanhood* in 1979. Without any connection whatever, it is certain that each writer would be gratified to find such a congruence in the other's thesis, thoughts and patterns.

Marian Engel's own mind and imagination play easily with literature and philosophy, in fact a good deal like the mind and imagination of Rita Bowen. But *The Glassy Sea* is by no means overloaded with its themes and motifs at the expense of its credibility. Engel has evoked the background of Rita Heber with an authority of detail and frequent infusions of humour that are convincing and, to me at least, who also grew up in southwestern Ontario, totally authentic. All the elements are familiar, sometimes funnily, sometimes painfully so: Mother and Father, poor, proud, decent and hard-working; Kenny, the brother who was killed in the war and Stu, the wild one; Shirley, the sister, worldly-wise within the confined limits of the world she knew; their awe of education and yet their fear of its making their child "different"; the narrowness of their society and their religion; and above all, their confused mixture of pride in, resentment of and bewilderment at "Rita the Dreamer." The Baptist university she enters on a scholarship — after a great family crisis — is not named McMaster, but must be; in any case its strange combination of seductive intellectual freedom and repressive social *mores* was certainly built into Western as I knew it and, undoubtedly, to all of the other Ontario universities in those still inhibited post-war years. And totally credible is Rita's overpowering need to escape — idealistic, romantic and beauty-hungry, there was nothing in past or present and nothing she could see in the future to answer her dream.

The structure Engel devised for *The Glassy Sea* sets up, sustains and fulfills the pleasurable suspense of a mystery story. At the end of the Prologue, as Mary Pelagia begins to read over her letter to Philip, the two questions ''Who?'' and ''Why?'' dominate the reader's response. Who is Mary Pelagia? Why did she join the Order, then leave it; above all, why has she come back again? The answer to ''Who?'' is largely contained in The Letter. ''Why?'' can only be satisfied by reading ''The Envoie'' as well. At the end, I think, most readers will turn again to reread the Prologue, as I did. ''Who?'' is satisfied by the story of Rita Heber's life as she wrote it down for Philip. It is not a confession, nor does it end with a change of heart, a new decision. Rather it is an explanation and a confirmation of the decision to refuse Philip that Rita made before she began to write to him. But ''I am having to see things as they are,'' she says as she writes and the writing is part of the process of her maturing. Her capitulation and the answer to ''Why?'' comes only in The Envoie, as Mary Pelagia remembers the end of the summer world of dreaming by the shore, the coming of the winter world with its stark and terrifying visions of destruction, the saving arrival of Anthony, their three weeks of discussion and, finally: ''It struck me again as it had at the table that reaching out physically was irrelevant; that my hunger was not wholly physical any more than it was wholly spiritual, that what I wanted was not Anthony and not God, but something else. A world . . . I must use the rest of my life'' (pp. 157, 162). Much good mystery writing shares another strong element of *The Glassy Sea*, the author's knowledgeability about unfamiliar and intriguing life-patterns, in this case the precision of detail Engel provides about the history of Eglantine House, its Sisters and the life of the Order. The suspenseful forward thrust

At the end she is setting up a half-way house for women, but Mary Pelagia will be fully alive within it. Her effort will be to help these women heal themselves and so to go back into the world, not to escape permanently from it: "I will do this work for the good of my own immortal soul; but I will do it also knowing that I came here out of a need, not to serve, but to belong" (p. 164). She is wary of pride and, especially, of power, which is so strongly a part of the male world: "Now I have power, only a little power, but with power comes risk. I am afraid" (p. 13). She is going to exercise the power, however, and take the risk. Moreover she knows, and recognizes the irony of knowing, that the organizational, practical and working skills which she has and will exercise are her legacy from the background and family she repudiated so often and for so long:

> I am standing in front of the Heberville church belting out "Fling out the Life-Line." I am the bloody-minded Martha that my mother was, Grammacrae was. God give me grace to taint my bloody-mindedness with love. (p. 165)

Notes

1   Marian Engel, *The Glassy Sea* (Toronto: McClelland and Stewart, 1978).
2   Carolyn Heilbrun, *Reinventing Womanhood* (New York: W. W. Norton, 1979), p. 145.)

A PEOPLED LABYRINTH OF WALLS: AUDREY THOMAS' *BLOWN FIGURES*

Louis K. MacKendrick

Several techniques employed by Audrey Thomas in her monumentally complex novel, *Blown Figures* (1974), are suggested in her earlier and later fiction, and these exploratory or dislocatory mannerisms have a significant application. The keynote is that of a structural division of the narrative line, or voice, into discrete psychological stances, or into episodic or anecdotal segments, which cohere in the larger story.

In her first novel, *Mrs. Blood* (1970), the narrator, identifying herself as both "Mrs. Blood" and "Mrs. Thing," alternates between what Thomas has called the visceral woman and the objective distanced woman;[1] in the later stages of her confinement and miscarriage the narrative becomes a virtual collage of voice, with a fracturing of the temporal and linear into what are essentially fragments of consciousness. Though this novel sounds true to the psychology of the character, it nevertheless reads as a literary construct, and its form most immediately anticipates that of *Blown Figures.*

In *Songs My Mother Taught Me* (1973) both the "Songs of Innocence" and the "Songs of Experience" are divided into episodes, self-contained incidents closely centered on a topic or theme, though the narrative segments have linking motifs which can take the obvious form of repeated words or phrases, a manner greatly amplified in *Blown Figures.* Thomas' recent novel, *Latakia* (1979), follows a similar form, its distinct divisions of narrative tied by its narrator's emphatic reversion to particular topical concerns. Two of Thomas' stories also reflect her interest in expanding the psychological and technical ramifications of conventional story. "Ten Green Bottles" (from *Ten Green Bottles*, 1967) is written in a literally elliptical style, as well as being considerably literary in its allusions and metaphorical structure; in her stories Thomas is often willing to make figurative analogies evident. Again, "The More Little Mummy in the World" (from *Ladies and Escorts*, 1977) mixes the present, memories, and ironic intercalations from a tourist lexicon almost surrealistically in a sequence of implications while still remaining true to the fundamental expectations of the short story.

Such selective examples may hint at Audrey Thomas' concern with the separations of a narrative voice — what Joan Caldwell has called her "splitting" techniques [2] — and in its breakdown as a representation of the mind at hazard, a practice taken to an extreme degree in *Blown Figures*. As Robert Diotte has observed in his study of *Mrs. Blood, Songs My Mother Taught Me,* and *Blown Figures,* "the dominant structural techniques throughout the trilogy are juxtaposition and discontinuous narrative. The flashback, the dream, the substance of memory predominate in the trilogy, and Thomas' style, allusive and adaptable, tends towards the anecdotal."[3] In effect, *Blown Figures* is the epitome of narrative mannerisms Thomas had used and would use; rather than being self-consciously avant-garde the novel means to convey the quality of a supercharged, troubled mind and its ways of saying. Her techniques express the reality of her often fretting tellers.

Blown Figures is both psychologically and poetically structured. Though it may at first appear as an intermittent stream of association or dissociation, close attention shows the frequency and relative consistency of the iterated elements of this structure, which operate both as a realistic psychological self-portrait of the protagonist, Isobel Carpenter, and as the connections of a literary fabrication. Thomas' story alternates irregularly between a nearly linear narrative and a series of fragmentary impressions which conclude most chapters; these include cartoons, newspaper stories, advertisements, recipes, nursery rhymes, metaphorical observations, African chants, literary citations, and quotations from particular African rituals. The technique of disarrangement complements Isobel's perception of Africa as "the broken, the divided land."[4] A variation of this manner may be seen in the many parenthetic comments that are inserted in the more traditional narrative, though its complete independence from both an intrusive narrator and the protagonist's mind is questionable. Though the novel's sheer physical impression may be one of a gigantic rebus, reverberations accumulate between its fragmentary portions while connections of theme and image become apparent. A purely literary analysis of *Blown Figures'* incidents, characters, and associative fragments shows the novel's exacting internal logic; however, its extraordinary density only permits the presentation of representative motifs or themes as indices to its substantial world of words.

In considering her title Thomas has said, "it just goes BOOM. That's why it's called *Blown Figures*. It just goes out."[5] As a closer correspondence to Thomas' practice Isobel may be suggested as a figure blown by every wind of memory and psychosis. However, there is also the literary figure, the figurative, which in the novel is blown out of all proportion — perhaps in contrast to Isobel's surname, which ironically signifies a joiner or maker. In whatever case applies, *Blown Figures* is an explicator's paradise, or nightmare.

Audrey Thomas has identified the narrator of the novel as mad,[6] which to a large extent justifies its perplexing organization "more around images than along lines of narrative," according to George Bowering.[7] A definition included in *Blown Figures* seems appropriate: "'A roaring of tense colours and interlacing of opposites and of all contradictories, grotesques, inconsistencies: LIFE'" (p. 388). Thomas, however, has said that her fiction is "very controlled, extremely structured although it might not seem to be when you pick it up and it falls all over the place."[8] In simple terms, the structure is evident in Isobel's recurrent compulsions and images, and in the narrator's repeated verbal gestures, allusions, and use of forms of analogy — if in fact these can be separated for the novel's two personalities. Even the very disposition of the narrator epitomizes the apparently miscellaneous technique underlying the fiction's subscription to meaningful fragments, whose existence in any chapter demonstrates no strictly cause-and-effect order.

The narrator — who will hereafter be identified as female — achieves an independent and often reflexive character. Though she may well create Isobel and an imaginary journey to control her own chaos, as Thomas has suggested,[9] her subjective concerns are often with writing itself. (Thomas has said that *"Blown Figures* is a novel about writing a novel."[10]) At the outset the reader is invited to "Consider Isobel" (p. 11), a postulate or a fabrication, and the truly controlling, even arbitrary, voice is apparent even in what Isobel sees: "Once a child's wagon full of potted geraniums pulled by an unseen hand. (My hand, Isobel, my hand.)" (p. 14). This form of the narrator's random self-assurance recurs frequently. Her control of the protagonist's every move is declared emphatically: "Ah, Isobel, I who mould your head like a waterpot, how carefully I arranged you that hot September noon on the verandah deck of the H.M.S. *Pylades*" (p. 118). Her remarks, however, need not be literally parenthetic, but direct and participatory:

> I can do anything I want with Isobel. I can make her fat or thin, like a funhouse mirror. Give her an elegant back — she always wanted an elegant back — a lisp, a limp, a missing finger, a wart on the end of her nose, a lover, a husband, a dead child. Imagine her now . . . . (p. 140)

When Isobel feels that she is dissolving piecemeal on a bus, losing her identity, the narrator gratuitously comments, "How silly you are Isobel, I could rub you out like a chalkboard. Do you not understand that none of this is real? Solving. Dissolving, it is all so pointless . . . . I spit on you" (p. 227).

> Frozen like this, as in a snapshot, we pause for a minute to examine the scene. A white woman in a long striped dress, very pale. (Or shall we place two little hectic spots of colour, high up, one on either cheek? It's possible; anger is sometimes good for the complexion.) . . . Given this snapshot, what sort of story would you put to it? . . . (Frozen, for an instant, in a snapshot, how would you construe this scene? . . .) (pp. 141, 142, 144)

A number of rhetorical questions suggest alternative interpretations from the perspective of the scene's purely physical arrangement.

The narrator can tease Isobel cruelly, especially by reference to her miscarried child. There are sometimes protective justifications of such sadism: Isobel is not treated as blameless nor is she accorded much sympathy: "How arrogant you are with your demands for continuity and your fear of change" (p. 159). It is in fact the narrator's own problems, which Isobel is perhaps focusing or working out as a fictional surrogate, that are never completely distanced; one of many allusions to Beatrix Potter's *The Tailor of Gloucester* reveals the possibility of her dependence on Isobel: "If I become ill and cannot finish, what will become of my cherry-coloured coat?" (p. 269).

The burden that the character bears for the narrator is evident in "Ah, Isobel, how do you like belonging to another person's dream?'' (p. 301). Isobel only seems to be allowed a fiction's traditional independence from blatant narrative management; she never has her freedom from a superior critical personality: "I watch you in the courtyard of the Hotel de Bull and truly I blush for your stony-heartedness" (p. 413). But the dominant attitude, or tone, seems one of cruelty as an offshoot of frustration, as in an aside on Isobel's expiatory journey and the husband left behind:

> Oh Isobel, you fool! . . . I marvel at this idea of yours
> that you have really undertaken this journey to exorcise
> your demons. Don't you know that the journey, as well
> as the exorcism, is of no use whatsoever; and if you
> think you are going to prove to Jason how brave and
> well and strong you are, then you are very much
> mistaken because at this moment he does not care one
> way or another what is happening to you . . . . (pp.
> 218-219)

An ironic citation from *King Lear* enforces the essence of this approach: "Isobel, at any second I can pluck you like a paw-paw from a tree. However, I will let you dance a little longer. 'Ripeness is all'" (p. 477).

At times the narrator's seemingly incidental reflections are directed to a Miss Miller. Of this intangible character Thomas has said, "She's simply a reference point — a kind of old-fashioned confidante, someone the narrator talks to . . . ."[11] Barbara Godard may overestimate this external referee as "a symbol of that analyzing and organizing force taking over Isobel's experience and turning it into narrative":[12] Miller has no "effect" on the narrator, however randomly she may be called up to be co-conspirator, sympathizer, or object of resentment. She makes no response, and may function peripherally as merely a psychological projection. Some of the narrator's summonings of Miss Miller seem direct reflections of her own madness.

The novel's first sentence introduces the character to its significant symbols and technique of repetition: "Cripples, one-eyed people, pregnant women: we are all the children of eggs, Miss Miller, we are all the children of eggs" (p. 11). The narrator may occasionally confess, plaintively, an insecurity to Miss Miller, or be cautionary: "The traveler who has returned from a journey may tell all he has seen, Miss Miller, but he cannot explain all"

(p. 94). Characteristic feelings of superiority may be exercised against the unresponsive Miller, who may be called on to witness the chaos of consciousness — "So many memories, Miss Miller, things flow about so here!" (p. 145) — and hear the central notion of the tug of fate: "Once a man has stepped in the stream, Miss Miller, there is no more time to think of measuring its depth" (p. 157).

The narrator may also rhetorically seek advice, and in the next breath recognize her mind at odds with itself: "Don't speak to me, Miss Miller. I am sure I shall split!" (p. 190). Like Isobel she is concerned about her own ceremonial end, and at times even sounds like her self-torturing subject: "Oh Miss Miller no one went against me; I went against myself" (p. 342). At times she manifests complete, uncryptic sense, identifying the confidante as "only a sort of something in my dream" (p. 297) and confessing, "Ah Miss Miller, how can I tell? I am not of that country and was never there to see" (p. 322). The final address to this figure is another allusion to *The Tailor of Gloucester* — "NO MORE TWIST / MISS MILLER / NO MORE TWIST" (p. 545) — with its all but completed coat: this parallels the novel's open-endedness with the apparent disappearance of Isobel into the African landscape, possibly as a witch.

Isobel's journey is both forward and backward, from Vancouver to Kumasi, "the City of Death, the city of broken dreams" (p. 110), and into selective memories ranging from childhood, through prior experiences in England, and to her earlier time in Africa with Jason. Though the past is now out of her reach, her trip persistently activates it as, perhaps, a security. The incidents of Isobel's journey are related relatively straightforwardly, even at times with complete objectivity; there are, however, occasional parenthetic or impressionistic intercalations in the form of dreams or compulsive image-clusters. These last may be free associations but are nonetheless always thematically related obsessions from her subconscious. Correspondences appear everywhere to Isobel. Her African memories constantly intrude upon her immediate consciousness. Thomas' definition of African novels, "the only kinds there are," is important here: "What I meant there was the sense of the other, the dark side of ourselves, the nightmare side of ourselves, where everything is too big, or too bright, or too beautiful, or too overwhelming."[13]

Much of *Blown Figures'* "straight" narrative, then, is strongly underscored by symbolic and thematic values that appear more dramatically in the dissociative fragments which conclude most chapters, predominantly the province of the narrator. As with all of the purely literary functions in the novel — which may be equally considered from a psychological perspective — there is a wealth of such figurative performance. An unexhaustive look at Chapter 1 alone gives some indication of Thomas' method in her fiction; its manner of association and connection begins at the beginning.

Aboard the *Pylades* at Southhampton, recorded older tunes are heard (by Isobel) or described as "musical ghosts" (p. 12), a lead-in to her exaggerated concern with her miscarried ghost-child and the propitiatory rites she did not follow five years ago to allay it. A woman's screaming baby is the first in a series of fetuses, infants, and children that will invariably impress upon her consciousness — later epitomized in the ceremony of disposing of a dead offspring carried as a "headload" (p. 202), literally and psychologically. One line from the song "Oklahoma," "WHERE THE SUN SHINES BRIGHT-LY ON THE HAY!" (p. 12), signifies her ongoing neurosis about the harsh and revealing quality of unclouded light, while another song, "Getting To Know You," ironically points up her essential isolation. The bass drum booms "GET OFF GET OFF" (p .13) to Isobel's unnaturally heightened sensitivities, the first of what may be considered omens on her prospective trip, while the boat's supposed "breakdown" (p. 12) and delayed departure are understandable as prefigurements of her own psychological dislocations throughout the novel.

Again, Isobel remembers books left her by her grandfather, which include a *Photographic History of the Civil War, Don Quixote,* and *Paradise Lost,* and these suggest her own social and spiritual trials and ambitions very leadingly. To her psychiatrist she had earlier confessed her apparently contrary fears of "Nearly everything. Transportation especially. And things that shut you in" (p. 20), so that in a real sense her quest acts as therapy for her paranoia. (Many of the transports she will encounter are named in accord with her estimate of her situation: the circuitous claustrophobic taxi *Pitié de Moi,* the lorries "Two Shadows," "People Weep to See Me," and "Life Changes.") Further, Isobel's present memory of letters from her mother which "always said

TO BE DESTROYED in the upper lefthand corner'' (p. 21) indicates her major concern with the dissolution of her personality, a persistent motif reinforced by Jason's gratuitously accurate observation, '''Isobel doesn't live . . . she exits.' He meant to say 'exists''' (p. 22). Even a stamp machine card in her purse urging "STICK TO YOUR JOB" (p. 22) is the first of many messages or life directives she receives from popular sources, and which are seen as serendipitously specific. (Ironically, in her final dream-ritual of purification Isobel learns that in any event her destiny cannot be changed, that '''The witches have eaten up your *kra*''' (p. 524).)

Isobel's having considered her family as illusionary from ''behind the invisible glass wall of her disguised madness'' (p. 22) anticipates her references to the safety of glass enclosures and bottles (especially those containing preserved fetuses), and looks back to her immediate memory of Hitchcock's film *Vertigo*, with its themes of mental breakdown and illusion. She is by nature primed for family disasters, and as she conflates various times past in the boat's pre-departure she characteristically remembers terrifying dreams, sequences that erode her determination: '' . . . the dreams she should have had hovered just outside her window, restless as shadows— holding out their arms to her 'Isobel, let us in''' (p. 28). Even her memory of a mouse in her London hotel room — to appear in later citations from *The Tailor of Gloucester* — bothered her with ''the question of his reality'' (p. 30): she is open and subject to hallucinatory experience, so that her worlds of reality and dark imaginings often merge their boundaries. Earlier distortions in her perceptions of her African environment are regarded as psychic punishments for an uncompleted ritual. Another memory of a former English lover prepares for several major themes; he had observed that ''Nothing is ever accidental or irrelevant. Nothing is ever lost'' (p. 36), which suggests the technique of *Blown Figures* and argues against the initial impression of the haphazard. Like Isobel herself, the lover gave ''the general impression of madness'' yet was ''a seeker-after-truth'' (p. 36), and the lines she recalls he recited from Dylan Thomas' ''The force that through the green fuse drives the flower'' — which stresses the mutually creative and destructive aspects of natural and human vitality — metaphorically figure her immediate condition with great aptness.

Few chapters are as long as the first. While not every portion of the novel's chronological narrative carries such a freight of ongoing or retrospective themes and structural figurations — and the foregoing is merely selective — no such part is entirely unembellished story. This is guaranteed by a considerable consistency in Isobel's sensibility, however erratic or deranged her reactions may appear at any time. There is not so much progression or development in her understanding as there is recapitulation and repetition of motifs. An indication of some of these may simplify an enormously complex fiction, and may indicate the very real order beneath a surface which seems to be highly diffracted.

In the relatively traditional narrative parts of *Blown Figures*, patterns of actual objects, as well as Isobel's ceaseless interior associations, emerge. Such ordered motifs are echoed and offset in the fragmentary, even bizarre, melange which more properly functions as the narrator's oblique commentary. Any such motif is capable of extensive illustration. The sheer weight of evidence, however, which includes cross-references and interrelations, must be taken as a given, and only the prominent patterns will be generally outlined.

On her journey Isobel is exposed, in fact and in memory, to many grotesques of body and mind, the deformed and the compulsive, the eccentric and the uncaring, who represent a failed or imperfect humanity. Such individuals may be understood as aspects of herself, as she seeks an uncertain release from "her crime against her dead child" (pp. 484-485). She considers herself a failure as a mother, overlooking her two living children, but in *Blown Figures* mothers are not seen favourably. Isobel's mother-in-law is a forbidding woman, perceived as a threat to unrestrained lovemaking and effectively characterized by an interest in crewel work and dried flowers, *nature morte*. (Ironically, the narrator invokes Miss Miller in the language of the Book of Ruth, 16, as its subject confesses her absorbing self-denying loyalty to her mother-in-law.) Isobel's travelling companion, Delilah Rosenberg, has been frequently aborted and is uncaringly pregnant anew. Even Isobel's eccentric mother wanted her daughters to walk on glass splinters (hence the recurring images of bleeding feet), and the legacy of her own impulse to leave, and preoccupation about her disappearance, is clear:

> Isobel's mother always put her hat on when she went
> out, calling over her shoulder that she was never coming
> back. Isobel would lie on her bed and listen to her
> mother's determined footsteps fade and sink into the
> cold grey pavement of the street. (p. 450)

Situations of inertia or imagined entrapment press on Isobel's consciousness, and she incessantly personifies her troubles as demons, witches, and ghosts, which represent both avenging Furies and Imps of the Perverse. She is, and has been, subject to threatening and devastating dreams, as well as to rarer, more ceremonious and positive, dream-rituals of recovery and control. Animal and insect life intrudes often upon her awareness; she reacts naturally with feminine repulsion, but such lower orders of life demonstrate her often chaotic perceptions and inability to accept life at an uncomplicated level instead of at an overcharged level. A prime example is her reaction to Delilah while waiting for a taxi.

> A tiny lizard ran across Delilah's sandalled foot; for a
> terrible moment Isobel thought the child had somehow
> slipped out from Delilah's pants-leg and was scurrying
> away. (pp. 162-163)

Blood is often present in Isobel's mind, logically associated with her earlier African miscarriage, but also hinted at through the many appearances in the novel of the colour red and related hues. Blood is both a threat and an index to a more formal and primal existence suggested by the African ceremonies excerpted, perhaps for Isobel's benefit, by the narrator. Glass barriers and containers, associated with refuge from oppressive reality, also figure in Isobel's mental makeup, and are epitomized in her swimming at Dakar: "she submerged herself every few minutes, jellyfish floating, suspended, safe as a baby in a bottle" (p. 110). Glass signifies Isobel's wish to escape the demands of her mind and body, but it is also associated with her wish for, and fear of, intangibility: "By the time they reached the border she would be all gone. There would be nobody. No body. Personne" (p. 168).

The idea of glass may be pursued briefly as an indication of how the literal and the metaphorical become connected in *Blown Figures*. On board the *Pylades*, at dinner, Isobel sees through the self-absorbed and uncharitable Mrs. Hankinson "as though she were made of glass" (p. 66). Visualizing the eating and digestive processes she is "made fully aware for the first time of the foulness we all carry within us" (p. 67) and of the farcical pretense of civilization. This projection, perhaps, of her own unclean condition is linked to her memory of an earlier treatment for pinworms — "her knowledge of the omnipresent worms" (p. 210) — and the remedy, a red viscous liquid. The symptoms of this parasitic infestation are leadingly given in a French description contributed by the narrator; these include "*des ecoulements de sang*," "*la nervosité, l'irritabilité et l'insomnie*" (p. 224), and eggs in the intestine. Such instances contribute to a later cautionary observation, "Garbage is one thing Isobel, compost is another" (p. 345), and their interrelations propose the novel's poetic structure.

To continue the patterns of Isobel's awareness, she records a veritable gallery of heads separated from their bodies; these clearly stand for the almost continual sense of menace she feels, as well as for the reason and balance she has forsaken. George Bowering has noted, "Headlessness suggests craziness, one guesses, and bears an acute relationship with the image of the abandoned womb."[14] The reintegration of mind and body rarely occurs. Parts of bodies are also imagined, directly related to how Isobel believes her child was removed from her, in pieces. Her intense recognition at many points of "her enemy the sun" (p. 210) symbolizes the unsparing light of a clear and unclouded perspective; against this are set the ambivalent references to water, more escape than cleansing: "But water, a boat, the idea of being carried somewhere, of once having embarked the impossibility of further choices" (p. 111).

Blind or one-eyed people appear often in *Blown Figures*, perhaps demonstrable as Isobel's own imperfect vision and lack of insight, as her obsession makes her at times vividly paranoid. What she sees, and remembers, has a cast to it, a myopia of interpretation. She is the victim of feelings of vastation and distorting hallucinations, which generally dislocate temporal reality into threatening configurations. This is part of her strongly mythic awareness as well as of her fear, of her inability to view her world straightly without casting her subjective and self-accusing problems on it.

The effect of dislocation becomes total in the last few chapters, in which she seems to live a dream that, almost predictably, denies her absolution. Isobel tends to read significations in all things, as everything in the real world appears to accuse her of her guilt: "Why did things take on such awesome significance?" (p. 218). Eggs, the seeds of life, are also never far from her mind, both in terms of their importance to the propitiatory ceremonies she imagines, the eggs held by each "supplicant" (p. 487), and in their role in the interrupted cycle of life. As an extension of this image pattern, "the great conflagration of a man and a woman" (p. 393), as well as the obsessional restrictions on whole-hearted physical loving, are balanced in Isobel's present and memories. This dichotomy of fundamental life is epitomized in Chapter 10, a childhood memory of two different toilets in her grandfather's house: the recollection acts as a tangible metaphoric identity of the light and dark sides of her personality.

Another aspect of *Blown Figures* is Isobel's attraction to the etymology of words and to what are clearly their thematically apt definitions. Conversely, the narrator is drawn to puns and word-play, with an even more pointed relevance. Words which spring into Isobel's consciousness include widowhood, breakdown ("collapse, stoppage, failure of health or power, negro dance" (p. 108)), scrap ("Small detached piece of something, fragment, remnant (pl.), odds and ends, useless remains, allied to *scrape*" (p. 132)), and zero ("m. zero, naught. cipher; freezing point; starting point; love (tennis); nonentity, nobody (fam.)" (p. 114)). She is also responsive to remembered African words and phrases, which act as a simplification of her reactions and a base chorus to her perplexities.

The narrator — if it is indeed she — often puns cruelly and pointedly about Isobel's situation; one instance is "'MUM-MY.' *MUM. MOM.* Persian, wax used in embalming" (p. 75), which follows a vivid reminder of the miscarriage. The narrator is more obviously behind the play of "Nous allons / Noose alone / Nurse along / Isobel, Beware the Eyes of Mars" (p. 173) — a cryptic reference to this mother's perhaps suicidal journey, in conflict with herself, omen-ridden, and unaware of her unchangable fate. Again, each term of "Diseased / Dis-eased / De-ceased" (p. 197) has an acute relevance to the uneasy Isobel. The bitter wordplay of "TUMMY / TUMULUS / TOMB" (p. 397) only reinforces her masochistic association of life and earth, while "Marriage / Mirage" (p. 446) summarizes her only technical interest in the family left behind, her casual adultery on the *Pylades*, and the fading of all "normal" connections before the strength of her obsession. In fact, many of the fragments and juxtapositions in the novel's non-narrative sequences are ghastly jokes against Isobel.

The dividing line between what can legitimately be said to proceed from Isobel's awareness and the narrator's sometimes ironic, self-serving, and interpolative interjections is very thin. The very nature of many of *Blown Figures'* fragments makes any assignment of "source" questionable, for the narrator *knows* what Isobel knows. Some of the fragments are extremely oblique and private.

However, apart from parenthetic asides in the narrative proper, the narrator consistently (except for Chapter IV) concludes each chapter with an artful melange, a sequence of individual items each of which is allowed a full page of the novel. As John Moss has remarked, "The whiteness becomes overwhelming. The reader reads the emptiness . . . . Not since *Tristram Shandy* has the physical page been so effectively incorporated into narrative reality."[15]

What can be ascribed to the narrator constitutes a metatext. Her fragmentary associations, allusions, metaphors, and suggestive parallels act as part of generally hallucinatory intrusions into Isobel's consciousness. (It is interesting that clippings from African newspapers included by the narrator are duplicated as originally printed in the American edition of *Blown Figures* (Knopf, 1975), but not so in the Canadian edition: there the majority were simply typed out, and the visual homogeneity was not an asset to the novel's impressionistic texture.) The narrator's fragments fall into some distinct patterns — only her technique may seem to be self-indulgent — as a collage which constitutes often ironic indirect echoes of Isobel's world.

Apart from the narrator's incidental literary allusions, the majority of these are to Lewis Carroll's Alice books and to Beatrix Potter's *The Tailor of Gloucester*. Alice's encounters with surrealistic, mythically self-contained, grotesque, and threatening fantasy situations are close to the nature of Isobel's experience; George Bowering has written that *Blown Figures* is "a fiction that puts the reader in Alice's position."[16] An advertisement urging "BE TALLER" (p. 87) is succeeded by "I MUST BE GROWING SMALL AGAIN" (p. 88), signifying Isobel's fluctuations between self-control and its opposite, while Alice's directional dilemma in the hall of locked doors is implicitly linked to Isobel's claustrophobically self-defeating enterprise.

The Mock Turtle's emotionally appropriate sentence, "'He taught Laughing and Grief'" (p. 141), and the grim Duchess recommending beheading are only too pointed. From Looking-Glass land there are allusions drawn through to the arbitrary and imperative roles of Queens, exaggerated models of control, while references to the black and white kittens emphasize the schizophrenia of Isobel's condition. "Looking Glass Milk Isn't Good to Drink" (p. 442) picks up a pun on Mali Lait, and Isobel reflects on her relationship with Delilah as "being a parody or looking-glass reversal of her own distress five years before" (p. 479).

The narrator also alludes relatively frequently to Potter's classic tale, including part of its preface (addressed not to "Freda" but to "Isobel") as a dedication to *Blown Figures*. The fragments of Chapter XIII are rich here; as the narrator ambiguously confesses, "Ah, Miss Miller, I was never so good at stitching buttonholes" (p. 245) Isobel herself becomes the cherry-coloured coat. The Potter citations remind us of the narrator's function as maker, like a Carpenter, and the anxious threat of incompletion.

Furthermore, a quotation from Charles Kingsley's *The Water Babies*, about the very existence of these creatures, is apt: babies and water are re-emphasized, and the possibility of one such exotic being cut up for scientific definition reactivates the motif of fragmentary children. There are additional associations in the novel of Tom the Chimney Sweep's transformation and eventual redemption, and his obsession, "'I must be clean, I must be clean'" (p. 335), operates strongly in Isobel's context. The motif is continued: a sequence of nursery rhyme selections in Chapter XIII manages to stress a forbidding world of childhood, with threats and disasters only rarely relieved by any comfort.

The newspaper items scattered throughout the narrator's domain are ironic reminders to Isobel of the African world's imitation of her personal grief. These include a missing girl, a boy trapped by a wall, burial without a coffin, a child-theft and one refused medical treatment, a piece on deception in male-female relationships, and a columnist's reflection on a "a very thin dividing line between the inmates of our mental hospitals and those of us outside them" (p. 416). The narrator's selection of such tragedies or incongruities is not miscellaneous, and the specific application to Isobel's condition is metaphorically sound.

The advertisements chosen from African newspapers also

epitomize ironic, sometimes positive, directions to Isobel, but in a more direct manner. One for family planning is sardonic, considering the search for her lost child, as is that for Astral Cream Soap, "for the girl who has everything."[17] Isobel is urged to "Feel Young Again Fast" (p. 135), she whose more generally coherent past is alive for her on this journey, while a picture of two African boys who "can always change clothes . . . but they wear their skin for a lifetime!" (p. 186) suggests the deep-rootedness of Isobel's problem. Lorexane Head Lotion points to the psychological source of her distress, less directly addressed by De Witt's Kidney and Bladder Pills: "WHEN LIFE SLOWS DOWN / . . . Clean out your system, revitalize the blood . . . get back your health and strength . . . then enjoy life again" (p. 419). These are similar to the promises of No. 9 Bladder and Kidney Tea, and Power Tea is yet another nostrum for women's ailments, a prospect of relief and healing. (In a related pattern, the narrator makes many citations from African rituals of expiation, purification, and cleansing — including a list of the causes of miscarriage — often connected with dead children.)

Isobel is also exposed, through the narrator's discretion, to a number of advisory and admonitory voices from newspapers. These include El Mohr, who, significantly, interprets dreams, and Dolly, who counsels on romantic and sexual matters: the cry to her, "I HAVE SEX WITH A BOY OF TEN!" (p. 123), is a rude echo of Isobel's affair with a Dutch boy on the *Pylades*. "YOUR STAR TODAY" proffers direction for Libra ("Domestic and family problems will preoccupy most of you today making it impossible for you to attend to personal affairs") and Scorpio ("You may have to go on a short trip for your health's sake" (p. 422)); both signs are intimately of Isobel's condition. The various weather reports included by the narrator are another, but mild, version of the prophetic assurance Isobel so earnestly seeks, susceptible to all analogies. Elsewhere, a stern voice advises "YOU CANNOT HAVE YOUR EGG AND EAT IT" (p. 72), brutally applicable to her sensitivity to eggs. Another warns, "LOOK OUT!" (p. 101); a further announces "THE HOUR OF DECISION" (p. 395); one ironically inquires, "BLOOD-BATH WARDED OFF?" (p. 391). All have the superior overlooking quality of the several government sponsored signs in public places, the proper conduct of life.

The recipes which appear among the narrator's fragments identify victims, heads, or young creatures sacrificed to appetite, perhaps connected with a French-Canadian priest's observation to Isobel, "We have a saying here. 'You eat in Africa or Africa eats you.'" (p. 183). These seeming domestic pleasantries or formulae are, however, as indirectly meaningful as any of the narrator's selections. In a final hallucinatory chapter Isobel supposedly confesses, "'I ate the child in my womb . . . . Since then I have never been happy'" (p. 518). This comes full circle from her grimly humorous dialogue with the African doctor who attended her miscarriage: "'Rinse cycle, Dr. Biswas, that's what it is. I'll come out as good as new. Egg is the most difficult. Ask your wife'" (p. 34).

All this, and so much more. As Thomas has said, "In *Blown Figures* readers are going to have to work really hard."[18] The reader's relationship with the fiction is a working one, for it is an accumulative novel; Barbara Godard has written of "the true subject of the book, the creative act taking place in our minds."[19] All the novel's apparently random associations and patterns fit literally or metaphorically into its larger complicated figure. In one passage of complete objective sense, uninterrupted by an intense imagistic or rhetorical concentration by either Isobel or the narrator, the narrative makes its rational point:

> For five years she buried her head beneath the
> pillows: not any more. She knew what was wrong, and
> why, and what to do about it. She understood and ac
> cepted the terrible pull of the dead, knew she was as
> haunted as any old derelict house of her childhood, that
> there was within her a small ghost which had to be pro
> pitiated and set free. (pp. 193-194)

Isobel does not seem to be "squashed by the words, strangled by the sentences" (p. 193). This is total realization, a temporary release from the nightmare distortions, the key to the labyrinthine ways of her own mind.

Notes

1   Elizabeth Komisar, "Audrey Thomas: a review/interview," *Open Letter*, series 3, no. 3 (Late Fall 1975), p. 59.
2   Joan Caldwell, "Memory Organized: The Novels of Audrey Thomas," *Canadian Literature*, 92 (Spring 1982), p. 47.

3   Robert Diotte, "The Romance of Penelope: Audrey Thomas' Isobel Carpenter Trilogy," *Canadian Literature*, 86 (Autumn 1980), p. 61.
4   Audrey Thomas, *Blown Figures* (Vancouver: Talonbooks, 1974), p. 68. Further references to this edition will be given parenthetically in my text.
5   George Bowering, "Songs & Wisdom: an interview with Audrey Thomas," *Open Letter*, Fourth Series, no. 3 (Spring 1979), p. 9.
6   Komisar, 60 *passim*.
7   George Bowering, "The Site of Blood," *Canadian Literature*, 65 (Summer 1975), p. 88.
8   Komisar, p. 64.
9   Komisar, p. 60.
10   Bowering, "Songs & Wisdom," p. 9.
11   Komisar, p. 60.
12   Barbara Godard, "Dispossession," *Open Letter*, series 3, no. 5 (Summer 1976), p. 82.
13   Pierre Coupey, Gladys Hindmarsh, Wendy Pickell, Bill Schermbrucker, "Interview / Audrey Thomas," *Capilano Review*, 7 (Spring 1975), p. 91.
14   Bowering, "The Site of Blood", p. 88.
15   John Moss, *A Reader's Guide to the Canadian Novel* (Toronto: McClelland and Stewart, 1981), p. 273.
16   George Bowering, "Snow Red: The Short Stories of Audrey Thomas," *Open Letter*, Third Series, no. 5 (Summer 1976), p. 29.
17   Audrey Thomas, *Blown Figures* (New York: Alfred A. Knopf, 1975) p. 68. The Canadian edition omits the amplifying matter quoted.
18   Bowering, "Songs & Wisdom," p. 29.
19   Godard, p. 82.

REAL MOTHERS DON'T WRITE BOOKS: A STUDY OF THE PENELOPE-CALYPSO MOTIF IN THE FICTION OF AUDREY THOMAS AND MARIAN ENGEL

Wendy Keitner

During the current wave of the women's movement, Canadian authors have described a rich and complex panorama of contemporary fictional women: murderous housewife, Amazonian pig farmer, "a fairly conventional woman," nun turned feminist activist, wilderness recluse, expatriate writer — these are a small sampling of the gamut of roles women in recent Canadian fiction have spanned.

In the barely twenty years separating Betty Friedan's landmark attack on the "feminine mystique" in the early sixties and her controversial scrutiny of its apparent replacement, the "feminist mystique," in the eighties, the cleavage between woman's traditional domestic situation and her more emancipated social position has opened an important new vein in Canadian and Quebec literature. While manifested at times in the writing done by men, the impact of feminism on the literature of the past two decades in both English and French — on character, theme, structure, and style — is registered more fully and explored in more depth in the work of women writers, perhaps because their own lives demonstrate many of the same complexities that their almost unswervingly realistic fictions present.

That elusive synthesis of love and work, family and career, intimacy and power, which is the main subject of recent Canadian and American inquiries in the social sciences, is also, at present, a dominant theme in fiction written by women.[1] This marks an important juncture, for Canadian women's writing up until the sixties had been characterized by its nearly exclusive focus on domesticity — on "house and family" — alone.[2] Nowhere in the literature written in English are women's current conflicts and competing loyalties more frequently and forthrightly analyzed, perhaps, than in the novels and short stories produced by feminist writers Audrey Thomas and Marian Engel. The main women characters who populate the seventeen novels or volumes of short stories written by these two authors to date (and published between 1967 and 1981) are all involved, in various ways, in the quest for self-definition or redefinition in the turbulent socio-political context of women's and men's rapidly changing roles and expectations.

While Thomas' and Engel's central female characters range in age from girlhood to old age, cover the spectrum of single, married, separated, widowed, and divorced, and embrace a multiplicity of lifestyles — including that of single parent, pregnant mother, childless career woman, and founder of a women's commune — several of their most complex and interesting heroines (and the only ones to be discussed in this paper) are creative women caught, like their authors, between the frequently incompatible functions of lover, mother, and writer. Their collective search for freedom, connection, wholeness, and self-expression, and for a new balance between intimacy and individuation, charts the heights and plumbs the depths of the fecund — but perilous — middle ground that lies between those classical, male-defined extremes of womanhood: Penelope, on the one hand, symbol of feminine virtue and chastity, of married love and maternal self-sacrifice, a "real mother"[3] beleaguered by the ceaseless demands of others, enmeshed in a mercilessly repetitive daily routine, and required by Telemachus, as "master," to attend to her own work, "the loom and the spindle," and to leave "talking" — history and literature — to men,[4] and, on the other hand, Calypso, the "hider," symbol of sexual love and desire, holding out the offer of immortality and perpetual youth — single, free, but finally abandoned by Ulysses, and unconsolable in her island loneliness.

The fierce polarities between familial and sexual ties, and the freedom necessary to create works of art, are explored by Thomas and Engel from the time of *Songs My Mother Taught Me* and *No Clouds of Glory!* Both are *Kunstlerromans*, sprinkled with autobiographical details which trace the painful evolution of a young woman from a constricted, conformist girlhood towards greater maturity and freedom. The female North American counterparts to Joyce's Stephen Daedalus, each harbors the fervent if repressed desire to break away from the entrapments of home and country, and forge a new identity as a writer. Their quests for sexual freedom and self-expression through art are impeded by social factors which weigh heavily against women. For one thing, sharp dichotomies between women and men, and among types of women, characterize the postwar North American society — and that microcosm, the family — which the two novels, set in upstate New York and Ontario, depict. For another, romantic, maternal, and professional images of women in the pre-liberationist years in which events take place are not merged; rather, these three significant aspects of womanhood are split amongst separate and typically antagonistic characters, which foists on the creative young protagonist an unwelcome — but seemingly unavoidable — choice between limited, mutually exclusive, adult female roles.

Coming to maturity in the 1950s at the height of the "feminine mystique," both Isobel Cleary and Sarah Porlock — two intellectual and solitary young women with outstanding academic accomplishments, but no great physical beauty — see themselves through the myopic lens of their mother's constant criticism as misfits and failures; both feel miserably unhappy, to the point that they have seriously contemplated suicide. Emotional tension is generated by the antagonism and guilt which mount in the relations between the heroine and her mother, close female relatives, or mentors, as the highly sexed younger woman observes the partialness of the role, not only of dependent housewife and mother, but also of spinster career woman. During the novels' present time, the emerging writer-heroines yearn for some radical means of escape from the quagmire into which gender has thrust them.

Thomas' *Songs My Mother Taught Me*, the first-written novel of her fictionalized, autobiographical trilogy centered on Isobel Cleary,[5] traces the heroine's psychological and emotional development during the formative years from age five through seventeen. A shy, self-conscious girl, who is ashamed of her thin body with its "rat-bite" breasts, and whose favorite childhood story is *The Ugly Duckling*, Isobel gropes, now fearfully, now desperately, during her teenage years, for her valid identity as an intelligent and sexual adult female and potential poet. She instinctively rejects the model provided by her mother Clara, a domineering and embittered housewife, whose imposition of guilt, self-abnegation, sexual repression, and material sacrifice on her daughters creates a major source of tension in Isobel's maturation. The ghastly fate of reproducing her mother's wasted life is symbolized for Isobel in her two, eroded, corpse-like rag dolls, Me and Mimi, a mother and daughter symbiotically intertwined, as their names suggest, bleached featureless and rendered almost indistinguishable from each other, which she initially interprets as her totems.

Isobel is also dissatisfied, however, with the images of single womanhood presented by her sexless spinster aunts — not only the powerless, housebound Hetty, but also the self-sufficient Olive. Aunt Olive, an antithetical "public" figure, better educated than Clara and economically independent, is a university professor with a Ph.D. in English, whose income is sufficient to supply Isobel's family with a house to live in and regular loans; but she arouses instant fury and resentment in Isobel's mother, creating a gap between them that is unbridgeable. Painfully conscious of the psychological self-effacement and economic powerlessness inherent in the domestic role of housewife and mother, Isobel discovers in the example of her professorial spinster aunt an equal, if, in some respects, opposite, limitation. She feels disgust and revulsion for Clara's slack corpulence — her heavy body disfigured by stretch marks and oozing menstrual blood; but she is equally repelled by Olive's disembodied probity — her shapeless figure concealed in drab brown skirts, opaque stockings, and heavy shoes. Isobel asks herself "did I really want to end up sack-shaped, on a Greyhound bus, honorary house mother to a group of sorority girls?"[6] And the answer is a resounding no.

These older, female family members contrast bleakly with the dazzling heroines of popular romances and the slim-waisted, well-groomed models of the women's magazines of the day, so that, for much of her young life, Isobel is reduced to a state of paralysis and despair, wanting neither to be shackled by a bad marriage nor to live the half-life of an "old maid." She lolls morosely around her home, sullen, passive, and resentful, resisting the role of either mute and powerless Penelope or an isolated, if independent, Calypso. Her subjective, expressive, diary-like narrative confesses; "What I really wanted to do was to remain forever fixed . . . like the little girl in the glass paperweight at home" (p. 138).

Mrs. Blood and *Blown Figures*, the concluding novels of Thomas' Isobel trilogy, set in Africa or "MAFROKA the broken, the divided land,"[7] demonstrate the legitimacy of this fear of womanhood's fragmentation and loss. The subsequent novels, which pick up Isobel's story some fifteen and twenty years after the time of *Songs My Mother Taught Me*, present the adult protagonist as a shattered, depressed, and embittered married woman and mother, who has been lured further and further into introspection, torpor, and withdrawal. Recently uprooted from Canada to Africa, horizontal and immobile in a hospital bed, the Isobel of *Mrs. Blood* produces a complex, confusing, fragmented record of her third pregnancy which is threatened by unstanchable bleeding. Repeating the life of her own housewife-mother, whose image she had struggled desperately to resist as an adolescent, the middle-aged Isobel is defined and engulfed by unsatisfactory, traditional, domestic ties. Beneath the maternal identity, but entirely dissociated from it, another identity is only hinted at, for the intensely passionate, sensual, and poetic part of Isobel has been swamped and buried in her, trapped like "men in peat," and effectively silenced.

The split between domestic and independent woman, previously portrayed as an external conflict between antagonistic characters, is studied now as a rupture within the heroine herself. Thomas' experimental narrative presents the novel in two alternating categories of entries, according to a division in the character of the central woman, as one sees from the opening monologue. "Some days my name is Mrs. Blood: some days it's Mrs. Thing."[8] This technique both illustrates the woman's "partialness" and also emphasizes the disparate nature of those parts of which she is composed. The split suggests the fragmented nature of woman, divided, not only from other women, but also from herself, by language, tradition, religion, and law, in order to *be* for someone else.

Mrs. Thing might be woman as she is acted upon: passive, performing perfunctory roles that have blurred her identity and transformed her into object or function. Mrs. Blood, by contrast, might be woman in touch with a universal source of female strength, yet wholly overwhelmed by her reproductive capacity. Joined together, however, Mrs. Thing and Mrs. Blood still do not make a whole, since in either state the central woman is reduced to a condition in which what she is missing and lacking is always the most prominent feature of her life.

Through the deliberate biographical holes left in the formation of this central character, as well as through the incompleteness of the categories of Mrs. Blood and Mrs. Thing, Thomas directs us mainly by means of what is missing in the woman's life. Gaps and missing parts, loss and impending loss, are recurring motifs in Isobel's life and mind, and are a central clue to her dilemma. Concluding in stillbirth, the brutal memory of abortion, and silence, the novel's final gaps and negations suggest the loss of both the woman's language-making power and her potential for life.

In *Blown Figures,* set five years after her traumatic miscarriage, Isobel is haunted by the memory of the dead foetus, fearful of her crumbling sanity, terrorized by grotesque dreams, and overwhelmed by self-loathing. Although she only gradually becomes aware of precisely where she is going and what she must do, Isobel's return journey to Africa — unaccompanied by her husband and children, whom she leaves behind in Vancouver — is intuitively prompted by a visceral desire to regain the spark of life which has been ground out of her and by the need to assuage a spiritual agony that has left her overwhelmed by guilt. That this female quest figure is a version of Penelope who has "given up her archetypal role" and who now "incorporates aspects of Odysseus" has been fruitfully suggested, though not explored in detail, in earlier criticism.[9]

At first, clearly self-conscious of the "paradox" she feels herself to be — as a wife and mother she should be at home — Isobel gradually, during the stages of her pilgrimage, loses this maternal sense of guilt and fear and enters wholly into her quest for self. What Thomas celebrates is not the familiar, male, American epiphane of individuation, however. Rather, Isobel is able to reject the life-defeating impulses within her and to move beyond them only when she discovers a connection to others — specifically to other women — a life-enhancing bond which has always before been missing.

Although Isobel has a brief, superficial affair aboard the ship that takes her from England to Africa, her most important and revealing friendship is with the rather ruthlessly liberated Delilah Rosenberg, who becomes her travelling companion for a major part of her journey. Having had four abortions and now faced with yet another unwanted pregnancy, the life-loving Delilah provides both a reversal and a grotesque distortion of Isobel's predicament five years earlier in *Mrs. Blood.* The mirror of herself in Delilah is something Isobel does not wish to acknowledge, and so her response to the younger woman reflects her ambivalence: she joyously acknowledges the shared closeness of a sister, while also pitilessly condemning the irresponsible and promiscuous woman. Delilah begins to miscarry, Isobel makes her commitment to remain beside the younger woman rather than give in to the desperate need to flee;   she confirms that she shares with Delilah and all other women "a link of blood." Delilah, then, validates Isobel's need to explore her "self" through other women, rather than to separate herself from their experience, as she had done since childhood.[10]

At the end, Isobel symbolically removes her "slave" clothes and dons the traditional white calico of the African penitent, garb in which she can begin to "glow, tingle, to become electric," as she intuitively responds to the language of the drums and the horn, and as she feels the power of the god pass into the body of the priest. Isobel is revitalized by the ritual of expiation she undergoes. Our last sight of her is as she plunges into the forest on the far side of the village, healed in heart and mind. Although the narrator does not reveal what Isobel will do with her liberated self, the entry into the text by her creator at this point seems to provide a clue to the new dimension which has been opened up in the life of her thinly fictionalized central character, whose background is shared by the writer-mother heroines of Thomas' two other novels — characters whose lives begin to combine the previously divided roles of Calypso and Penelope.

The precariously shifting balance between sexual, maternal, and creative elements within the character of the writer-heroine, and the replacement of external antagonisms between women by a sense of connection, which are central themes in Thomas' writing, are explored also by Marian Engel from the time of her complex, richly humourous, and insufficiently studied first novel, *No Clouds of Glory!* This pioneering, feminist novel is the powerful first-person narration of the tough and intelligent Dr. Sarah Porlock, who jettisons her academic career at the University of Toronto in the weeks following her father's death and the abrupt conclusion of two love affairs with married men (one of them, her sister's husband), in order to "get on with (her) own writing."[11]

Set in the mid sixties, the diary-like narrative presents the highly-educated and unmarried heroine as being, in her own estimation, a freak, a fool, and a bastard. Engel's Sarah Porlock has observed the same limited and mutually exclusive images of women in her formative years as has Thomas' Isobel Cleary, but she has made the alternative choice — like Isobel's Aunt Olive — of becoming a university professor of English and has rejected the model of her mother, the stern and self-sacrificing (yet, at moments, magical) Mrs. Porlock. "I am a lady Ph.D. One of an increasing multitude, but in my own point in time and space, a rare enough bird . . . the only one at my college under fifty" (p. 8), she explains.

Initially, the novel's theme and plot seem to hinge on the almost total contrast between the protagonist —intellectual, "gutsy," and unfeminine — and her beautiful, married, near-twin sister, Leah, just ten months her elder. Linking together the two dichotomous images of womanhood implied by the "earnest and fat" Sarah, and the "feckless and lovely" Leah (who eloped young with a Venetian Entrepreneur and is now a glamorous part of international society, as well as, almost incidentally, the mother of two sons), Engel's discontinuous narration sketches episodes from the sisters' Canadian childhood — set amidst the idyllic beauty of the northern landscape, but made miserable by stifling social conditions which "forced the dialectic on us: beauty/truth, light/dark, introvert/extrovert, down to the blue pajamas and the pink" (p. 12).

The intellectual Sarah is attracted to the male-dominated realms of ideas, power, conflict, and literature rather than to Penelope's secluded, domestic, material sphere. Preferring to "bring the bone home myself, not raise babies"(p. 48), Sarah is taunted by accusations, she is a Lesbian or a monstrous female man; in jest, a friend paints her as "just a big girl with a lot of books under her belt (who), if she stays another week will grow a mustache and a beard" (p. 172). The physical unattractiveness — even the encroaching "masculinity" — of the smart and ambitious career woman is underscored by Sarah's repeated references to herself as "the homely sister," a "tatty fool," "No Rodgers and Hart girl this . . . but a vigorous, untidy — bull dike" (p. 22), and by exaggerated statements drawing attention to her preference for "manish clothes, straight hair, flat shoes" or her irrepressible "nicotine stains, warts and self-importance." These traits are summarized in her Rabelaisian self-portrait: "I ooze, booze, stink, feel human rather than feminine" (p. 88).

Like Isobel, Sarah briefly ponders her fate as a "desperate old maid," for to have a career, especially the career of writer, woman runs the risk, like Calypso, of being abandoned by both women and men. That intellectual pursuits, particularly writing, are unsuitable endeavors for women is an issue raised by the model of

Sappho in Ancient Greece, and it is given indignant articulation by Anne Finch in seventeenth-century England ("They tell us, we mistake our sex and way . . . . To write, or read, or think.")[12] The theme is pursued in Virginia Woolfe's tragic story about the fictitious Judith Shakespeare in *A Room of One's Own*, and it is explored in detail by contemporary feminist critics and scholars.[13] Working in a traditionally masculine profession, living the life of a sexual adventurer, and harried by psychological, literary, and social factors, then, Engel's central woman is wracked by doubts both about her identity and her vocation.

If Engel casts Sarah as the frog-prince of fairy tale, she leaves to Leah the quintessentially "feminine" part of story-book princess. Leah is repeatedly linked to mythological beauties, including Leda, Venus, and Minerva. Nicknamed "Lotus Blossom," she is associated with the season of summer, the element of water, and an island retreat. The beautiful, sensual, drifting Leah is everything the diligent Sarah, for much of her life, thinks she wants to be. In addition to this central fissure between "brains" and "beauty," the novel also explores another division between "domestic" and "public" woman: between the conservative, maternal, Penelope-like Mrs. Porlock, who has been married forty-one years and has raised four daughters; and Sarah's alternative, intellectual "mother," her mentor, Dr. Gertrude Lyle, who is single, economically independent, and the successful principal of St. Ardath's College but who is also described as emaciated and sexless. Sarah depicts Lyle as having "no age, shape, definition: all brains and standards" (p. 27). As in *Songs My Mother Taught Me*, but more boldly this time, the protagonist resists making a choice between highly contrasted, but almost equally unsatisfactory, role models.

Interestingly, Engel's heroine, more mature and better educated than Thomas' Isobel, has spent a half-dozen years researching the literature of her native land; she discovers that her predicament is not just individual, but that it has massive, national proportions. Not paralyzed by fear, but spurred into action by this insight, Sarah takes courage from the knowledge that certain parallels exist between her existential predicament and her country's lack of a first-rate literary tradition, so that the diary which is her narrative resonates with both feminist and nationalist undertones. Referring to the American and European "masters" of modernism — among whom she lists only one woman, Gertrude Stein — Sarah appreciates that they have provided "footsteps worth studying." But, she adds: "those of us who operate from bastard territory, disinherited countries and traditions, long always for our nonexistent mothers." Her Canadian literary research has uncovered "a few geniuses," but mostly "a host of Sarahs looking for themselves; too late finding their modes and models" (p. 8). An emerging Canadian woman playwright, Sarah is triply "motherless," then, lacking appropriate models of liberated adult womanhood, and of both Canadian and female authorship.

As Sarah gradually comes to terms with her unconventional lack of "nestyness" and her guilt over at least one abortion, she begins to understand that Leah's glamorous but hollow life as a married woman is not an ideal existence — any more than Lyle's orderly but abstract career or her mother's domesticity have been. Sarah is set free from the simple dichotomy that had seemed to divide her from normalcy and happiness. Her "notebook" points out that it is false to think "that if opposites and equals are joined, a solution will be evident, easy, and practical" (p. 12). What Engel's daring first novel illustates, finally, is not that women have become "halved," but rather that we are "atomized."

Several of Thomas' and Engel's short stories, from *Inside the Easter Egg* and *Real Mothers*, for example, illustrate how "one's self was split into too many parts: home, school, family, and the private life of the imagination."[14] This complaint, which is repeated in their remaining novels, is a new variation on the familiar theme of woman's "partialness" or fragmentation, and it sounds the keynote of feminist fiction of recent years. The desire to "have it all," which earlier writing presented as altogether impossible, is much closer to being realized in current women's fiction than previously; but stitching together the mismatched roles of Penelope and Calypso into a new, seamless whole is shown by Canada's leading women writers to be highly problematic.

In the recent novels of Audrey Thomas and Marian Engel, as well as of other authors such as Margaret Laurence, Alice Munro, Sylvia Fraser, Margaret Atwood, Aretha van Herk, and Janette Turner Hospital, fictional presentations of contemporary women who try to combine what were formerly proscribed as mutually-exclusive roles offer a striking and important contrast to the current commercial image of that "young dynamo" who is instinctively able to "tackle the old love-career conundrum with breezy self-confidence,"[15] the fresh and energetic New Woman who brings home the bacon and, smiling and sexy, cooks it too. The lives of Thomas' and Engel's writer-mother heroines expose some of the cracks in the mould of the new Superwoman.

Thomas' *Munchmeyer and Prospero on the Island*, which is composed of twin novellas centering on a male and female writer, examines the relationship between the mind of the creator and the product of her creativity, and also suggests some of the similarities and differences in the circumstances under which the male and the female writer pursue their vocation. Will Munchmeyer, the central character of the first of the two novellas, is a dissatisfied, morose graduate student in English, sometime university lecturer, and would-be writer. In his late twenties, Will is on a futile quest for a Miracle Girl to soothe his spirit and fire his imagination; he becomes increasingly alienated from his loveless marriage and from passionless sex with his competent English wife, Martha, whose awesome physical size and domestic competencies are suggested by the Brobdingnadian allusions surrounding her characterization.

Lovingly but erratically attentive to his four small children, Munchmeyer removes himself from family responsibilities, first by retreating to his basement study on the pretext of writing a novel, and later by sending his wife and children back to England. In his eyes, his success as a writer justifies this rejection of commitment to family. Finding his own situation repeated again in that of his male artist friend Tom Lodestone, Munchmeyer recognizes that "work was obviously his mistress."[16] The first novella goes on to trace Munchmeyer's ascent from the purgatory of his basement room, through a bizarre, drug-inspired trip, to a period of resurrection on the top floor of a Vancouver house.

The central character of the second novella, Miranda Archer, is a Vancouver writer in her thirties, who is in the process of composing *Munchmeyer* during a sabbatical year, paid for by the state, which allows her to retreat from technology and the press of modern society on the island of Magdalena. Told in the first person, through diary entries which are formally introduced by Miranda, the story of the second novella links the woman writer — the creator of the character Munchmeyer — to her creation, but mainly by means of contrast rather than complement.

Miranda, who bears some biographical and psychic relationship to the tortured heroine of Thomas' trilogy, is the mother of three young children; unlike Isobel in the other novels, and also unlike Frankie Sweeney in this one (a woman who has allowed the poet in her to be silenced by her responsibilities as the mother of six children), Miranda attempts to bridge the gap between Penelope and Calypso, and she largely succeeds.   In sharp contrast to her fictive male writer who abandons his family for his work, Miranda, though separate except for weekends from her sculptor husband, continues to fulfill those "elemental maternal" tasks, for she takes her daughters to Magdalena with her.

Casting herself briefly in Munchmeyer's part, Miranda thinks: "I'd be working on two novels, at least, if not more. I would have borrowed this place from my friends Tom and Maria ("Christ, man, I've just got to get away")(p. 114.) Instead of severing family ties, Thomas' writer-mother protagonist sits down to do her creative work at that crossroads of domestic interaction, the kitchen table, "a repository for books, kids' caps and toys, phone books, general clutter" (p. 122).

At times, Miranda is able to work with a rapidity and concentration that astonish her;   at other times, she is restless and bored, in need of a long walk on the beach "alone, without Toad" or else a long talk with "someone other than a dog or a kitten or a child, however charming"   — a pull away from her two year-old toddler that fills her with "terrible surplus guilt" (p. 114) which even her success as a writer does not obviate. While alienation has been identified as one of the most significant themes of twentieth-century masculinist literary tradition — exemplified here in Munchmeyer's marriage and work — its polar opposite, connection, is a major concern of contemporary women writers, as personified by Miranda.   Despite the domestic hurdles which the writer-mother must surmount in order to finish her book, and although she does encounter some resistance to her work as a woman writer who uses too many four-letter words, most of the novel's diary entries record the happiness and harmony Miranda feels in the varied realms of her life as mother, writer, wife, and friend of the older married artist and permanent island resident whom she names "Prospero." The final, joyous impression left by the second novella is, in large measure, a response to the vitality, good humour, and success of its central woman.   Her wonder year on the island has, in its deliberate echoing of the experience of Shakespeare's character in *The Tempest,* opened her eyes to a "brave new world" in which are planted "seeds of hope."

The affirmations and connections which are celebrated at the end of *Munchmeyer and Prospero on the Island* are examined from a more critical perspective, however, in Thomas' most recent novel *Latakia,* named for a Syrian port to which the writer-mother heroine, Rachel, travels briefly with her lover, the younger writer, Michael. This politically volatile and incomprehensible stopping place which frightened, bewildered, and disoriented them on their sea journey becomes a private metaphor for muddle and failure. The novel, which is written in the form of a letter from the forty-year-old Rachel to Michael, after he returns to his wife Hester, gives the woman writer's interpretation of their intense but unhappy two-year relationship.

Composing her "love letter" on the Greek island of Crete, Rachel finds it impossible to stop looking for the "eternal aspect" of their triangle; she is a self-conscious Calypso, abandoned, but not unconsolable, when her lover goes back to his traditional and nurturant wife, a woman who contrasts in almost every way with Rachel. The self-effacing Hester is an artist, apparently of no great talent or ambition, who willingly subordinates her creative work to her role as Michael's wife during the seven years of their marriage; Rachel, on the other hand, is the mother of three teenage children, divorced, feminist, independent, and a successful writer.

Michael has fallen in love with a falsely "free" image of Rachel, however, having met her at a graduate seminar conducted on the only afternoon of the week that she spent away from her children. In order to please him, Rachel temporarily denies the maternal part of herself, a distortion similar to "trying to fit into a dress that was both too small and not my style"; conversely, Rachel dressed her lover — ten years her junior, unpublished, and not at all "fatherly" — in "clothes that were too big for you, that you weren't ready for."[17] The attraction between Rachel and Michael is less their shared interest in literature than their sexual compatibility. "Just sex can be a pretty big thing," (p. 20) Rachel muses; but ultimately their relationship, which alleviates the loneliness of divorce and restores Rachel's sexual confidence, angers her children and blocks her writing.

The man plays the part of sibling rival rather than supportive father to Rachel's daughters, and he burdens her like an added child. The initial "intense electric glare" of their attraction is replaced by "long dark shadows," both of which serve only to "eclipse" Rachel's sensibility and "blot" out everything else, so that she can "see" nothing but Michael. Rachel realizes she has become the battleground for an exhausting struggle between her children, her lover, and her writing.

The egotistical, immature, and competitive Michael has never experienced the "divided attention" that goes with being a parent; therefore he expects her to be "always free to sit down and have a long talk about literature or life . . . to retreat to the bedroom and make love" (p. 21). The mature and realistic Rachel sums up the multiple and contradictory roles he needs her to perform; "You want me to be your *soror mystica,* your mystical sister, who would talk art all day and make love all night and miraculously still find time to do the housework and cook your dinners" (p. 39). When occasionally, she would give vent to her fatigue and frustration, and ask for help — for "even geniuses sometimes clean bathrooms" — he would storm out of the house, acting as if her demands are totally unreasonable and calling her a "fucking bitch."

While Michael appreciates the financial benefits of a partner who brings in a paycheck, he still needs the security of the old domestic arrangement: Man of the House and Little Woman. Michael's definition of a wife is "someone who is always there when you need her." Rachel disagrees: "No, that's the mother of a child under five" (p. 39). What she longs for is mutuality, not the old style of merging and submission for woman. Moreover, Rachel's success as a writer (her fifth book is about to be published) threatens Michael on both professional and personal levels; his work is unknown, while Rachel crisscrosses Canada on speaking engagements, and he resents that she does not take her identity from him nor sacrifice her art for love of him. Rachel realizes: "I want both (love and art), but I can't give up the second for the first" (p. 73).

Hester, an artist who has made the opposite choice from Rachel, perhaps because her talents as a painter are less than Rachel's gift, on the contrary seems happy enough to bask in reflected glory as "wife of the rising young novelist." She fulfills the mother servant function of the domestic woman, earning the demeaning epithet of "dog wife" from Rachel, who is enraged at the spectacle of Hester responding, like a mindless and obedient pet, to every whim of her "master." What Michael must choose between is not merely two women, but two ways of life and two ways of relating to a woman — a choice he briefly avoids in their short-lived *ménage à trois*. One night on shipboard Rachel reminds Michael of the classical myth: "'Odysseus rejected immortality with Calypso in order to return home. Was he not saying what you have said? 'I have to be the centre of attention.' I've often wondered, considering I was trying to hang onto you, why I chose to tell you that particular tale. I guess I was all along telling you to go back to Ithaca and chaste Penelope" (p. 148).

Thomas' formulation is more complex than Rachel's articulation of the conflict between "feminine" and "feminist" lifestyles at first suggests, for *Latakia* not only supplies a critique of the "feminine mystique," but also, in its sensitive depiction of the multiple burdens — as well as the joys and triumphs — of the central woman, it suggests some of the limitations imposed by the feminist revision. Rachel is not blind to the pitfalls scarring her track, and she announces to Michael: "I have a terrible time balancing all the demands made on me" (p. 35) in her roles as mother, writer, teacher, and lover.

She sees fundamental contradictions in the roles of nurturer of others and creator of works of art: an artist must "develop the selfishness necessary to pursue one's art, whatever happens" (p. 47), whereas "real mothers weren't supposed to have obsessions like writing or separate identities" (p. 51). Earlier divorced from her husband and now abandoned by her lover, Rachel momentarily thinks of herself as an "Invalidi," like those for whom seats are reserved in the trains and buses of Europe, those "crippled (or wounded) by war and by work" (p. 99). But, joyfully waiting for the imminent arrival of her friend Robert and her three daughters, Rachel, at the novel's end, rededicates herself to writing, responding to life's call with the lusty affirmation that "the best revenge is writing well" (p. 172).

Engel's most detailed studies of that complex and endangered creature, the writer-mother, are located in her racy, cumulative portraits of Marshallene Heber Osborne Peacock, the main character in the stories "Marshallene on Rape," and "Marshallene at Work," and "Bicycle Story" from *Inside the Easter Egg*, who reappears as a supporting character in her latest novel, and again in her sympathetic and sensitive presentation of the journalist Harriet Ross, the main protagonist of *Lunatic Villas*. The big, dark, strong, fearless Marshallene, who grows up to write the stories of the Hebers, Frasers and Macraes of the "French line," is another of Engel's large-scale, non-conforming writer-heroines, a kindred spirit of Sarah Porlock, but with an unsavoury rural background.

Marshallene has grown up "the hard way" in a family characterized by violence and tension, so that her mother Millie, brutalized by her drunken husband Walter, flees home, leaving her children — including the twelve-year-old Marshallene — to be reared by Mrs. Macrae. As Marshallene later recalls, "we were country nobodies with an ambition to scale all heights and absolutely no right to romanticism."[18] Coming from the country, Marshallene "knew about things" that other girls were ignorant of; the precocious and rebellious Marshallene, to the dismay of Ruth Ann Macrae, "walked out of the VD film they showed at CGIT, and refused to go to Normal School. She broke all the rules and God never struck her down with lightning after all."[19]

Always "a worker," Marshallene is educated out of her limited beliefs about women's role by her second "mother," Mrs. Macrae, who, widowed in the war, teaches Latin at the collegiate. Without her tutelage, Marshallene reflects, "I'd have thought six kids and the prize at talent night was the apex of existence,"[20] Instead, Marshallene, who "knew all the stories" about her family past and "therefore . . . knew who she was," as Engel notes in "Marshallene at Work," takes up the difficult career of writer, wrestling with the thought that "there ought to be a way of telling it" — the love and the deprivation and the violence.

Disowned long ago by her father for marrying a Jew and separated from her second husband, as well as from her grown son Toby, who lives on an ashram, Marshallene, an intrepid "survivor," is, at age forty-eight in *Lunatic Villas*, a successful feminist writer and acclaimed critic of Canadian society. Marshallene reiterates the split between the "self-centredness" of the writer versus the self-sacrifice of motherhood that Thomas' Rachel also articulates. She, too, plays the part of an unfulfilled Calypso, longing for an end to "this big white moonsize loneliness inside" (p. 199).

Her two marriages should have taught her better than to want another one; nevertheless, the tough and enormous Marshallene sees herself as a "blue lady" yearning for roses and romance still, even while recognizing that her career as a writer has rendered her "sublimely unsuited" for marriage. "I still want it all" (p. 198), she says, adding: "Don't make me laugh, it's unjust; don't make me cry, it isn't fair. I want to love, I want to cry, I want to eat. But I don't want to vacuum or cook. And those who want everything both ways get it no way. Two plusses make a minus. I'm therefore an island in spite of myself" (p. 199).

Harriet Ross, the complex, feminist, writer-mother protagonist of *Lunatic Villas*, also in her late forties, worries that "women are falling on their faces all over the place" (p. 154), and feels lately as if she, too, is on thin ice, "walking across the crusted snow of depression" (p. 52). A journalist who does not see herself as a "real writer" like her neighbour and tenant, Marshallene, Harriet earns her living by her pen and heads a family of half a dozen only partly related children after the sudden and unexplained death of her pacifist househusband, Tom, and her divorce from the ne'er-do-well, Michael Littlemore.

Harriet is a perplexing, diverse, and over-extended contemporary woman. She is both a reluctant Penelope and an ambiguous Calypso: Harriet nurtures six children and takes in the elderly Mrs. Saxe as well, but she claims "domesticity isn't my thing" (p. 38) and is twice challenged in court by the Children's Aid who try to wrest her children from what they deem a disorderly and unsuitable home environment; she has affairs, but feels guilty about adultery; she writes articles on a range of controversial women's issues including abortion, and also a column for a conservative women's magazine which she signs "Depressed Housewife."

Harriet is caught on the horns of the dilemma; she struggles to play the traditional parts of both father and mother, provider and nurturer, for her miscellaneous brood. Resenting her double burden, Harriet protests that she is incapable of living up to domestic standards set in the past by full-time homemakers, while she works as a professional woman to earn a living, too. She is angry at the women's magazine she works for — and guilty over her own association with it — because it promulgates the "foul gospel" that houses that belong to women who work outside the home and raise children also, should look like "personalized showrooms."

Suffering the symptoms of what Betty Friedan in *The Second Stage* labelled "feminist fatigue," Harriet blames society and also castigates herself, wondering guiltily if she has lost all her "self-control," for she longs for the simple right to stay in bed — a wish ironically granted at the novel's end when a broken ankle temporarily removes her domestic burden and confines her to a hospital bed. Moreover Harriet's domestic role clashes, not only with her professional work, but also with her romantic interests. In the half-dozen years since her second marriage fell apart, Harriet has had occasional lovers, including a fifty-year-old businessman who dreams about their uniting in a perfect marriage. His utopianism is punctured by Harriet's realistic and wry comment: "It's easy over a dinner table, Ewie," she says. "Especially in a restaurant and nobody's spilling their milk" (p. 75).

The novel focusses briefly on a teenage boy and girl of the next generation — on Harriet's oldest son, Sim, and his old-fashioned girlfriend, Mary Lou, who already wants to have a baby. Sim rejects this images of his future partner, symbolized by his breaking up with Mary Lou on the eve of his departure for university; but he also admits to feeling "kind of bad" about those young women who militantly refuse to have babies at all. He seems caught between two types of women whose lives replicate either the "feminine mystique" or its current feminist substitute. Although no solution is articulated for either mother or son, the surrealistic and triumphant ending — in which the immortal Mrs. Saxe, together with Harriet's troubled middle son, Mick, ride off into the sunset, winners of a cross-Canada bicycle race — perhaps indicates that the chaotic, eccentric, but loving home of this single writer-mother is, miraculously, on course after all.

While the popular fiction of the current era centers on poised and unconflicted career women — mostly actresses, interior decorators, and other glamorous types — the female characters who prevail in the serious fiction of Canada's leading women novelists, who include Audrey Thomas and Marian Engel amongst the front ranks, form a heroic line of imperfect and ambivalent women who struggle with both the annihilating self-sacrifices required of mothers in earlier periods and still required, and also the self-destructive syntheses or crippling abrogations demanded of career women today. What this substantial and distinguished body of feminist fiction points towards, finally, is neither a return to a romanticized past nor a simple fusion of the roles and responsibilities of Penelope and Calypso; rather, it implicitly and explicitly calls for the invention of a "new way of living" that will reshape the balance of power between women, men, and children, and blaze a trail capable of reconnecting home and workplace. The next innovations in Canadian fiction may well lie in the reconceptualization, not of women at all, but of men, in their interconnected roles as workers, husbands, fathers, brothers, sons, and lovers. Penelope must give birth to, and Calypso instruct, a new Telemachus and transformed Odysseus.

Notes

1 These range from the popular to the scholarly and include Betty Friedan's *The Second Stage*, Michele Landsberg's *Women and Children First*, Susannah J. Wilson's *Women, the Family, and the Economy*, Penny Kome's *Somebody has to do it*, Carol Gilligan's *In a Different Voice*, and Grace Baruch, Rosalind Barnett, and Caryl Rivers' *Lifeprints*.

2 W. H. New, "Fiction," in *The Literary History of Canada*, ed. Carl F. Klinck (Toronto: University of Toronto Press, 2nd ed., 1976), vol. 3, p. 269.

3 Audrey Thomas implies what measure of devotion to children rather than to self is required by traditional motherhood in the critical portrait painted in the title story of *Real Mothers* (Vancouver: Talonbooks, 1981), pp. 9-22.

4 Homer, *The Odyssey*, Book 1 (Harmondsworth, Middlesex, England: Penguin Books, 1946), p. 34.

5 Audrey Thomas is on record as saying that she wrote *Songs My Mother Taught Me* (published in 1973) prior to writing *Mrs. Blood* (published in 1970).

6 *Songs My Mother Taught Me* (Vancouver: Talonbooks, 1973), p. 83. Further references will be included in the text. For fuller discussion of Thomas' trilogy see the essay co-authored by Lois C. Gottlieb and Wendy Keitner, "Narrative Techniques and the Central Female Character in the Novels of Audrey Thomas," *WLWE*, 21 (Summer, 1982), pp. 364-73.

7 *Blown Figures* (Vancouver: Talonbooks, 1974), p. 68.

8 *Mrs. Blood* (1970; rpt. Vancouver: Talonbooks, 1974), p.11.

9 See Robert Diotte, "The Romance of Penelope. Audrey Thomas' Isobel Carpenter Trilogy," in *Canadian Literature*, No. 86 (Autumn, 1980), p. 66. Diotte seems to miss the mark, however, when he asserts that Isobel's "fatal flaw" is her "inability to control her dreams" and that her rage is inspired by "trivial incidents."

10 Thomas' novel thus explores a mode of self-definition through relationship and care, a "dynamic of interdependence," which feminist psychologists have just recently begun to study. See, for example, Carol Gilligan's discussion of the different ideologies of "justice" and "care" in *In a Different Voice. Psychological Theory and Women's Development* (Cambridge, Mass.: Harvard University Press, 1982).

11 *No Clouds of Glory!* (New York: Harcourt, Brace and World, 1968), p.

29. Further references will be incorporated in the text. The paperback edition is retitled *Sarah Bastard's Notebook*.

12   *The Poems of Anne Countess of Winchilsea*, ed. Myra Reynolds (Chicago: University of Chicago Press, 1903), pp. 4-5.

13   Sandra M. Gilbert and Susan Gubar, for example, argue that the "metaphor of literary paternity" — the patriarchal notion that the writer "Fathers" his text as God fathered the world — has been all pervasive in Western literary civilization, and they trace its deleterious effect on the tradition of English women writers in their book, *The Madwoman in the Attic. The Woman Writer and the Nineteenth-Century Literary Imagination* (New Haven: Yale University Press, 1979), see ch. 1, pp. 3-44.

14   "Only God, My Dear," *Inside the Easter Egg* (Toronto: Anansi, 1975), p. 124. Further references to this collection of stories will be included in the text.

15   Katherine Govier, "Does Success Spoil Love?" *Chatelaine*, (March, 1978), p. 58.

16   (Indianapolis: Bobbs-Merrill, 1971), p. 72.

17   *Latakia* (Vancouver: Talonbooks, 1979), p. 21. Further references will be included in the text.

18   *Lunatic Villas* (Toronto: McClelland and Stewart, 1981), p. 198. Further references will be included in the text.

19   "Bicycle Story," *Inside the Easter Egg*, p. 169.

20   "Bicycle Story," p. 171.

GEORGE BOWERING

ROBERT KROETSCH

A WINDOW ONTO GEORGE BOWERING'S FICTION OF UNREST

Smaro Kamboureli

> It beats talking back to the electrowave oven. Voice, speech, is a means of bonding or asking; it is what connects people with one another & with the world, or reaching from the post-modern world, with the universe. Adam spoke the names of the animals to make a place for himself in the new world. He was reaching with words. The post-modernist novel reaches too. The modernist novel charted this world we found ourselves in: now the new fiction tries to make contact with creatures living here. In other words, the novel is now saying. "Hey, I'm human too!"
>
> George Bowering
> "The Painted Window," in *The Mask in Place*

I

George Bowering's fiction and criticism of fiction derive their energy from the antagonism he sets up between his own art and modernism. So, I propose to use as my point of departure those essays which delineate his critical and theoretical concerns regarding the state of fiction in the present and in the recent past.

In "The Three-Sided Room: Notes on the Limitations of Modernist Realism," Bowering discusses the extent to which modernism has been contaminated by the very thing that it has tried to achieve: verisimilitude.

> There we have two cases in which what I was taught to call realism depended on one's closing one's eyes to the facts. In one case the viewer is supposed to pretend he's not watching a movie. In the other he's asked to pretend he cannot see the stage or the people in the row in front of him.
> The creatures of the modern realist novel & short story ask for a similar self-deception. One writes a book & then tries to make the reader agree that he is not reading a book.[1]

The contradiction inherent in the aesthetics of modernist realism, according to Bowering, is one that centres on visual dictation. Although modernism privileges sight as the sense that guarantees the success of representation, it also operates on the principle of blindness. The reader has to make himself invisible in order to see the reality reflected in the literary work. Or, as Bowering says of the modernist realistic novel, "Certainly it is not unrealistic to ask: if I am close enough to hear what they (the characters) are saying, how come they can't see me?" (TSR, p. 21).

It will never occur to a reader accustomed to modernist fiction to betray its conventions by asking this question. A question such as this deconstructs the verisimilitude that the modernist writer builds up at the expense even of his own presence. Bowering points out that

> the modernist novelist, whether writing in the first person or the third, does not usually bother to tell you how he knows. He will offer a first person novel that doesn't explain how it got into the reader's hands, or a third person novel that doesn't identify the person who is telling us all this. (TSR, p. 21)

> For the realists of the twentieth century it was a step into invisibility. They played the disappearing writer, & even, as I suggested earlier, the disappearing book. (TSR, p. 25)

The conventions of verisimilitude which stress referentiality dictate that the writer erase himself from the reality he represents. The novelist's invisibility betrays the pretensions of objectivity in modernism, and its claim that what is being written is not fiction but a representation of reality. In fact, the represented reality in the modern novel is not substantial but formal.

Bowering's critique of modernist realism is mainly concerned with the versions of reality that modernism chooses to imitate; his fiction, on the other hand, is concerned with those realities which modernism pretends do not exist. As he says, "it would seem to me that just about any prose fiction wants to treat something real. And it would seem that Realism is no more like the real than any previous method of making fiction" (TSR, p. 21). What Bowering objects to is the representation of reality as an absolute and immutable given condition that determines the direction of fiction. Modernist realism insists on taking place inside a "three-sided room" where the novelist can hide behind the door of the room's fourth wall. More than that, it also insists on concealing the fact that this structure is its form of expression. As a mimetic art, modernist realism repeats the received forms of a reality that is perceived in an act of blindness, an act that renders other forms of reality invisible.

Bowering as a writer refuses to play hide-and-seek with his readers and comes to the fore both in his fiction and in his criticism. Two of the points of departure from the "shell game" that he refuses to join in are James' psychological realism and Zola's naturalism (TSR, pp. 22-4). Writers such as Morley Callaghan, Hugh MacLennen, W. O. Mitchell and Margaret Laurence work, according to Bowering, with extensions of these aesthetics, whereas writers such as Jack Hodgins, Sheila Watson, bp Nichol, Michael Ondaatje and Nicole Brossard, and of course Bowering himself, stand for the alternative that he offers, that of "post-modernism."

> A realist fiction was intended to produce a window on the world. Hence the value of invisibility, or more properly of transparency. One did not so much read the novel as read through it to the world. Post-modern novels, on the other hand, are in a way decorative. If they are windows they are stained-glass windows or cut-glass windows that divert light waves & restructure the world outside. (TSR, p. 25)

The imperative proclaimed here has a great deal to do with understanding Bowering's fiction within a larger framework that encompasses "post-modernism" and the world view that informs it.

"Post-modernism" announces the need for radical thinking, that is thinking that goes to the root of the treatment of reality and language in literature.[2] In his essay "The Painted Window: Notes on Post-Realist Fiction," Bowering says that

> The reader's first experience of any story is an experience of form. He opens the book, sees the black marks, & away he goes. Formally, in that situation, there is no criterion that will distinguish fiction from "non-fiction." It is all fiction — the reality here is the book. Fictilis: (capable of being) fashioned.
> Hence the only way a story can be told is fictively. To put it more boldly: life is revealed as a fiction.[3]

Whereas modernism advocates realism as a representation of a referential nature, "post-modernism" cancels out the illusion that fiction is representational. The modernist writer creates a simulacrum of external reality while forgetting, in the process, the reality of the writing act. In contrast, the "post-modern" writer does not hide in the dark corners of the house of fiction holding up the pen as a magic wand that conjures up images of reality and erases him miraculously from the pages of the book. He does not write *about* a world that can still maintain its reality when laid flat on pages. Instead, he is aware of creating art *and* of producing an artifact.

Bowering's statement that ''life is revealed as a fiction'' draws attention to the fact that ''post-modernist'' fiction works according to a self-reflexive mode.[4] It tells stories that do not absent writing. They allow the process of writing to permeate their telling; they echo their own making, the making not of literary works which are close homogeneous entities, but the making of texts in the full sense of this word.[5] Every knot visible in the surface of a text contributes to the plurality of its meaning, its significance.

''Post-modernist'' fiction is a fiction of presence. And it takes its shape at the crossroads of two phenomenologies: the phenomenology of reality as it is being rendered by the writer's consciousness and the phenomenology of writing which gives reality its presence.[6] Both levels of reality centre on the power of language. ''The only thing that is real about language,'' Bowering says, ''is the speaking of it, the act of the one voice'' *(PW*, p. 125). Language is the locus of ''post-modern'' fiction and as such it challenges the tendency of modernist realism to silence the questioning of consciousness. The modernist writing that achieves this silence of consciousness, the ''disappearance of the author'' or the inconspicuousness of the reader, is writing degree zero. The ''post-modern'' writer tries to raise language out of its reduction to a mere referential function. He wants to re-establish the relation of language to reality. The semiotic system that he acknowledges does not pay any dues to the modernist notions which favour the anteriority of reality to language. The Sauserian linguistic signifier, while it arbitrarily points to a signified outside its own order, displays in ''post-modern'' fiction its own artificiality as well. As Bowering says, ''We see doing,'' we see the production of ''linguistic activity'' *(PW*, p. 118).

''Post-modernist'' fiction moves on lines that intersperse both territories of language and reality. This geography, however, does not determine any boundaries that cannot be crossed over. ''Post-modernist'' fiction breathes through the skin of language, a language which, as Bowering remarks, ''is interesting prior to reference'' *(PW*, p. 114), that makes the word and the world come together not in any natural, preordained work of "God's creation," but in the text fashioned by the writer's consciousness.

The play of the writer's consciousness with experience defines the reality presented in the "post-modern" novel. This play occurs on the surface of fiction. Bowering points out that "If the writer . . . becomes attentive to the surface upon which he must work, two conditions are likely to come into effect: the literal prose will be more interesting, & the reader will be called upon to actualize the work" (PW, p. 120). The surface of "post-modern" fiction affirms its phenomenological nature while it presents the dynamics of the writer's vision and the kinetics of its form. The writer, Bowering observes, works according to the "principle of creating" (PW, p. 115). Since the reality of the fiction created is the product of the writer's intentional act, that is consciousness, the principle of creating demands that the writer be constantly on the alert. The writer writes what presents itself to his consciousness. This does not mean that he does not apply any selection or discrimination to what his consciousness grasps. It is his intentionality that prevents his vision from blurring the external reality with the reality he invents. As Bowering says, "Places & characters . . . are what they are, beings fashioned of words" (PW, p. 116). The writer's experience remains unmediated and it continues its life in the pages of the text.

II

I have put "post-modernism" inside quotation marks, first because it is a term that Bowering uses and secondly because it is a term that inspires a lot of controversy. The problematics of the term, however, lie not so much in its radical aspects as they do in the fact that it contains, as Ihab Hassan says,

> its enemy within, as the terms romanticism and
> classicism, baroque and rococo, do not. Moreover, it
> denotes temporal linearity and connotes belatedness,
> even decadence, to which no postmodernist would
> admit.[7]

"Post-modernism" seems to announce the beginning of a new literary period whose origins, nevertheless, cannot be pointed to with precision.[8] Bowering is aware of this:

> The attitudes, techniques, politics, styles, artifices &
> philosophies that critics are calling post-modern have not
> sprung upon us holusbolus. The "post-" in post-
> modern does not make reference to a sharply demar-
> cated time. (TSR, p. 30)

Bowering would agree with Hassan who sees "post-modernism" as being both a diachronic and synchronic construct which finds its antecedents during and even before modernism.

Its iconoclastic ideology and inconclusive aesthetics have made "post-modernism" a "dirty" word among conservative critics. "Post-modernism" becomes less controversial[9] when we cease seeing it as a term that delimits a literary movement and start seeing it as a term that demystifies[10] many of the moder-nist assumptions that we have been taught to take for granted. Bowering, although conscious of these problems, in-sists on using the term, encouraging thus his critics to label him as a "post-modern" writer. I have some reservations in doing this not because I think he does not share the "post-modernist" concerns but because he cannot quite divorce himself from moder-nism as his frequent reminders to his readers of its failures in-dicate. The antagonistic relation that Bowering has developed with modernism prompt me to call his prose writing a fiction of unrest.

III

As a critic, Bowering sees "post-modern" fiction as the deconstruction of the innocence of realism. As a fiction writer, he is dedicated to a "practice of writing"[11] that posits itself as being more real than modernist realism exactly because it is an act of consciousness, an art of surfaces. But it would be reduc-tive to assume that Bowering, whose main objective as an artist is that he "wouldn't want to shame the language,"[12] rejects modernism altogether. Modernism is far from being as homogeneous as it appears to be when juxtaposed with "post-modernism." The modernists that Bowering disagrees with are those who turned to art as a last refuge of order and meaning in a chaotic world of fragmented experience. Yeats, Eliot, Hem-ingway, Farrell, Joyce, Woolf, are a few of these modernists who displayed confidence in high cultural tradition as a means of res-cuing humankind from the disillusions of modern society. But there are those other modernists as well, such as Jarry, Artaud,

Kafka, Beckett, Robbe-Grillet, Nabokov, Williams, who responded to the chaos of the modern world in a totally different fashion
that opened the way to "post-modernism."[13] Modernists of
this kind asserted the fact that art is merely another subjective
creation of the human mind that cannot pretend to reveal truth
and meaning in a world whose values are constantly refurnish-
ed. Bowering allies himself with this group of modern writers
to whom art offers no security or assurance. Their art insists on
being seen as an invented, made-up entity. Its processual form
is full of echoes of the state of emergency that our lives are in.

Mirror on the Floor, Bowering's first novel, is a work located,
I would say, almost with a planned deliberateness, in the intersection of modernism and "post-modernism." It is a novel that in-
vites a Freudian approach while at the same time repudiating
psychological interpretation.[14] When Andrea, who has been
seeing a psychoanalyst about her emotional problems, refuses to
discuss her past with Bob Small, her lover, he comes up with a
suggestion that shifts the reality of the novel from being merely
representational to being consciously realistic.

> "Why don't you take that tape recorder of yours, and
> unloose into it and leave it for me, and I'll come up
> when you're at work and listen to it. That way you
> could have all the time you want and pretend you're
> just talking to yourself, anyway. Also you could string
> it together for a novel if you want to go commercial on
> me. That's my idea. I really mean it, I want to know
> the things that hurt you and bother you, because I feel
> as if there's a part between us that's not you and me
> alone, but the two of us joined.[15]

Although Bob's suggestion discloses his desire for presence and
meaning, it also reveals how conscious he is of the symbolic constructs that inform their lives. His irony in this passage is a self-
reflexive irony that mocks the usual claims of psychological meaning and the verisimilitude of the modern novel.

Andrea accepts Bob's suggestion. The narrative of the novel
then shifts twice from Bob's first-person accounts and the limited
third-person point of view to Andrea's tapes: "ON: . . . :
OFF"; "ON: . . . :OFF." She reveals, too, like Bob, her
awareness of the artificiality of meaning:

> Where, then . . . with my father it must have started a
> long time before I was born, all this Freud stuff, was I a
> happy child, were my father and mother competing for

> my affection . . . Daddy-O, with the accent on the O,
> being a cipher and a rectum image, so you can see why
> I am saying this on tape, I can't say it straight at you,
> not because I'm shy or I think you are too innocent and
> bumpkinish, it is that I am just too tired of it to organize
> the way you are expected to do in conversation. (pp.
> 95-6)

Andrea decides to use the tape recorder because she can keep her narrative under control. When she reminds Bob that he can turn the switch off if he wants to stop listening, she also reminds herself of the reflexive contrivances she uses which suspend the inauthenticity of the situation and the devices of realism employed. Her narrative, although confessional, challenges the assumption that psychoanalysis can provide remedies for emotional alienation. She does not empty out the contents of her subconscious but re-works what she is conscious of. She remains on the surface and consciously uses symbols and images traditionally meant to be thought of as being submerged in a character's subconscious.[16]

Andrea's tapes, which she refuses to discuss with Bob, are a dialogue without a second voice. They are a record of her personal archaeology that covers both her past and her present. "I am doing it for me, not for you primarily . . . . " (p. 99). She becomes her own archaeologist, consciously, and skeptically, unearthing the shards of her shattered emotions. The tapes are a text within the text of *Mirror on the Floor*, and Andrea and Bob, in their conscious manipulation of the realism of their novelistic situations, are "post-modern" characters in a modern novel.

Both main characters of *Mirror on the Floor* are aware of the intertextuality of their world. The concept of intertextuality, according to Julia Kristeva, does not designate the literary influences upon, and/or the sources of, a literary work. Rather, intertextuality "désigne cette transposition d'un (ou de plusieurs) système(s) de signes en un autre . . . qui a l'avantage de préciser que le passage d'un système significant à un autre exige une nouvelle articulation du thétique — de la positionnalité énonciative et dénotative."[17] The intertextual aspects of *Mirror on the Floor* are produced by the tension that exists between the modernist and "post-modernist" devices and attitudes that Bowering employs. *Mirror on the Floor* is a novel with a well-rounded plot unravelled in a fashion that fulfills the modernist expectations of closure. It is also, however, a text that supplements the representation of the plot as discourse whose intertextual function is to make the novel negate its own direction toward resolution.

The intertextuality of *Mirror on the Floor* affects the novel in more ways than one. In one of her tapes we hear Andrea saying:

> I can't answer questions, this way you can imagine I am
> an arty show like on CBC Sunday night, and consider
> that the arty-farty stuff you miss in the rush is the in-
> tellectual surmise you are supposed to make and pre-
> tend you get it all, like college girls do in Cocteau
> movies . . . . (p. 96)

The reference to Cocteau, like the other references in the novel to Miro, Leger, Matisse, Bracque, Rivera, etc., is, on the one hand, incidental to the fact that Bob and Andrea are, as are many of the characters in Bowering's short fiction, young people who, among other things, practice name-dropping. On the other hand, however, these references play the role of modernist allusions, giving thus a perspective of depth to *Mirror on the Floor* consistent with the modernist insistence on meaning. What is interesting, though, is that all these references are to modernist artists who prepared the ground for "post-modernism." Thus Bowering declares his allegiance to both modes of writing and shows that "post-modernism" does not see

> itself as a corrective to Jamesian realism . . . . It is a
> successor. It tries to offer ways of seeing the real, while
> the older ways, because of the very success of their own
> efforts in earlier days, have grown tired through over-
> use, or even suspect because of low-energy imita-
> tion. (*TSR*, p. 24)

Mirror on the Floor can be seen as a mirror which reflects the mimetic aspects of modernism while it deflects the modernist tropes that stifle the form of the novel.

We see the same polarity between modernism and "post-modernism" when Andrea makes an effort toward consistency in the midst of her "unloosing":

> But there was one time I have to put in here to keep on
> the theme, so to speak, that is about my father if that's
> what you want to call him, because I swear he was an
> accidental sire . . . (p. 99)

Andrea mocks here the modernist search for order, but at the same time she submits herself to a psychological regression which indicates her need to find an answer to the emotions that alienate her both from herself and from the people around her. Her search for order seems to be answered for a moment when she watches from the window of her apartment the street below where

> there was absolute human order and human
> trust . . . Order. She watched for a long time and none
> of the cars crashed, none even faltered in their paths,
> waiting and accommodating one another, the cars came
> together from six directions, interstitched and moved
> away again, continuous flow inward and outward . . . A
> small bomb dropped in the middle would blow
> everything outward, evenly. A body dropped in the
> middle would jam the whole moving machine. (p. 104)

The order of the street is perceived here as a scene from a realistic novel rather than a moment of real order. Andrea forgets she is a character in a realistic novel. Her vision of reality as a machine destroyed by a bomb reveals order as an event of randomness and brings *Mirror on the Floor* a step closer to "postmodernist" fiction. Moreover, the fact that her fantasy does not include a war setting but merely a bomb dropped out of nowhere also destroys the cause and effect pattern that characterize both the world view and the aesthetic of modernism.

Before Andrea kills her mother, she leaves a note on Bob's bed:

> Don't come and visit me. I will write if they let me, and
> if I want to. Just go to my place and take whatever you
> want and give the rest to my brother. (p. 155)

The note appears in the novel in script, another texture added to the intertextuality of *Mirror on the Floor*. The handwriting is a sign that speaks not only Andrea's inner turmoil, but also the novel's restlessness. The tapes, and to a large extent the note, are texts that resist assimilation into the novel. They remain as utterances that enunciate the difference between literature and writing, between the finitude of a literary work and the process of a text.

When Bob, after reading the note, goes to her apartment, he turns the tape recorder on hoping to find the answer to Andrea's erratic actions. "If this was her way of telling me the things she found hard to say, it would be here now" (p. 159). Bob's hope reflects the optimism of the mimetic mode of writing, an optimism generated by the patterns of closure that prevent surprise and randomness from destroying the desired order. But Bob sits down calmly only to listen to an empty tape. The silence that speaks to him adds to the multiplicity of meaning in the novel.

The synthesis of the same silence with Andrea's speech in her tapes neutralizes the impact the tapes might have on the reader. The reader is given ample information to (psycho-) analyze the motives behind Andrea's murder. Andrea kills her mother fulfilling thus Freud's theories about the Oedipal complex and the pleasure principle, while betraying at the same time her consciousness that such psychological and symbolic constructs are imbued, in realist fiction, with artificiality. But it is this tension between reality and realism, presented through Andrea's consciousness, that renders the validity of a psychological reading doubtful.

The extent to which Andrea both adopts and reverses the psychological truth of the realistic novel is most evident in the scene that gives *Mirror on the Floor* its title.

> She pulled the screws out and put the full-length mirror on the floor. The room seemed to tip without a lurch and the ceiling came into the mirror a little crooked . . . .
> Poised over the mirror, she looked down ten feet above. The figure in the glass was wavering, ready to fall, to sail, to come out and away, swaying on the edge of adhesion, out of the world in a second, it was herself seen from within the glass and out to the yellow walls. (p. 62)

The mirror, with its tilted images of the room, captures Andrea's fragility and emphasizes her fall into a world where meaning wavers. As she undresses, she frees herself from the reality she disavows. She seeks the fulfillment of her desire in her ''I,'' the imaginary construct of her self that rises to join with her lowering body.

> The glass was cold under her skin. She flattened herself more, pushing away the cold, and the front of her shoulders pressed against the glass. She lowered her open mouth to the open mouth. (p. 63)

But this is not a narcissistic embrace in the strict sense of the word. Her image in the mirror is a signifier subject to the double condition of similarity and difference. During her embrace with her other, a moment of *mimesis*, Andrea has to perceive herself as being homologous to another, the image she beholds, in order to become herself. Yet Andrea designs this encounter to occur at the same time with the "intelligent masculine blues" that pour out of her tape recorder (p. 63). The music accompanies her discovery of her other, of what she lacks,[18] but it also creates a presence out of the absence of a positive "masculine" principle in her life. "Sonny Rollins licked his way through a solo, saxophone rising in melodic jabs into the air, saxophone sounds" (p. 63). It is this conjunction of similarity and difference, or presence and absence, that holds Andrea "on the edge of adhesion," on the edge of a reality that lacks cohesiveness. The mirror on the floor, that contains both her desire and its missing object, is the locus of her discontinuous reality and the inefficacy of the realism she tries to evoke.

Mirror on the Floor, although fairly conventional by Bowering standards, foreshadows his development as a prose writer. It locates him within the literary tradition at a position from which he can afford to gaze in two directions at the same time. As he says,

> This compulsive commentator (meaning himself) does not proclaim that any writing described as post-modern is free of the taint of modernism, nor *vice-versa*. For one thing, post-modernism grew out of the fiction caused by the modernists in their carving of patterns in the wood sawn for them by the Romantics & realists.[19]

Bowering's association with modernism is continuous in the sense that he redeploys its devices and parodies its claims. In this novel, he can go beyond the mimesis of modernism only by exorcising its tropes through his own use of them.

The form of *Mirror on the Floor* is shaped by the dialogic interaction among the realism of the events, the reality of the characters' discourse and the third-person narrator's voice. Bowering's interrelating of all these levels of discourse and their systems of meaning can be illuminated by Mikhail Bakhtin's concept of dialogism:

> The novel orchestrates all its themes, the totality of the world of objects and idea depicted and expressed in it, by means of the social diversity of speech types (raznorecie) and by the differing individual voices that flourish under such conditions. Authorial speech, the speeches of narrators, inserted genres, the speech of characters are merely those fundamental compositional unities with whose help heteroglossia (raznorecie) can

enter the novel; each of them permits a multiplicity of
social voices and a wide variety of their links and interrelationships (always more or less dialogized). These
distinctive links and interrelationships between utterances and languages, this movement of the theme
through different languages and speech types, its disper-
sion into the rivulets and droplets of social heteroglossia,
its dialogization — this is the basic distinguishing feature
of the stylistics of the novel.[20]

Dialogism is manifest in *Mirror on the Floor* in the plurality of
meaning that emanates from the different points of view, the
characters' consciousness as characters and as individuals, and
the tape recorder as a device capable to maintain the primacy of
speech. Bowering has Andrea and Bob revolt against the limitations imposed upon them by the monologism of the third-person
point of view chapters, a monologism which dictates that the
characters act in a one dimensional way. This monologic view
reflects, of course, the modernist mode of writing which Bowering employs in order to show how realism levels out the differences of discourses and the possibilities of meaning. Both Andrea and Bob, however, supersede these restrictions by asserting
their consciousness as characters in the mimetic world of the
novel. As Bakhtin observes,

> The speaker strives to get a reading of his own word,
> and on his own conceptual system that determines this
> word, within the alien conceptual system of the
> understanding receiver; he enters into dialogical rela-
> tionships certain aspects of this system. The speaker
> breaks through the alien conceptual horizon of the
> listener, constructs his own utterance on alien territory,
> against his, the listener's apperceptive background.[21]

Andrea and Bob act inside, and react against, the "alien territory"
in *Mirror on the Floor*, that is the realism of the novel. The
dialogue generated by their consciousness deconstructs the
realism of the novel from within by means of foregrounding its
creativity, its language and its potential for multiple meaning. This dialogue initiates another dialogue, this time inside the
characters' consciousness. In "internal dialogism," according to
Bakhtin,

> it is not the object that serves as the arena for the en-
> counter, but rather the subjective belief system of the
> listener. Thus this dialogism bears a more subjective,
> psychological and (frequently) random character,

sometimes crassly accommodating, sometimes pro-
vocatively polemical.[22]

The tape recorder is what encompasses in *Mirror on the Floor* both
external and internal dialogism. As an object of a technological
society that can both arrest and communicate speech, the tape
recorder becomes the subject that connects the monologic and
dialogic aspects of the novel. The recording of Andrea's voice is
a form of *mimesis* which, however, challenges the stasis of realism.

Bowering's dialogism affects his writing style and enables him
to reveal his dialogue with the literary tradition. His latest novel,
Burning Water,[23] which won him the Governor General's Award
in 1980, provides his readers with a supreme example of the
aesthetic dialogue that Bowering carries with the tradition.

IV

Concentric Circles[24] presents yet another aspect of Bowering's
dialogue with the tradition. This novella links Bowering with
modernism through the *nouveau roman* which first displayed the
iconoclastic elements that we now relate to "post-modern" fiction. The *nouveau roman* is often said to have marked the "death
of the novel," but Bowering's *Concentric Circles* seems to announce, quite forcefully in places, not the death of the modernist novel but of the ideology that has informed its aesthetic form.

Mel, one of the two main characters, holds a black box tightly
onto himself, a box that holds in turn the fate of his small city
(read city as the status quo that Mel wants to see radically changed). Brown, the other main character, is a painter who is too gentle to complain to the people of the store where he buys his paints
that the tubes, no matter what their labels say, contain brown
paint. As a result, his paintings are entirely brown. And, of
course, Brown is dressed in brown as well. The setting, a room
covered with newspapers, is presented in a matter-of-fact tone
that resembles the stage directions of a play. In fact, Mel and
Brown, the minister, who pays them a visit hoping to come to
an understanding with Mel's subversive desires, and Janice, the
neighbour who falls in love with Mel, evoke in their dialogue and
in their minimal action the formal qualities which undo the
naturalness of the modernist novel and echo, to some extent,
Beckett's *Waiting for Godot*.

In spite of the news that has invaded the room of action in *Concentric Circles*, the characters' attempts toward communication

fail. Yet the characters do not fail to inspire, when intended by Bowering, laughter and irony. The novella has a theatricality about it that functions on more than one level. The objects that the setting consists of, the gestures and the attires of the characters, their discourse that is meant at places to be stilted and sentimental, all these elements intend to foreground the phenomenal reality of the characters, a reality which is normally more evident on stage rather than in the pages of a book. The theatricalism of *Concentric Circles* is also a device that points to the failure of the modernist novel by avoiding its habitual forms. The theatricalism of all these elements becomes even more emphasized when the reader realizes that the characters are cast in such a way as to be emblematic of a cultural and an aesthetic ideology that Bowering is interested in portraying and undoing. In one of his rages, Mel departs on a monologue that reveals much of this ideology:

> "Oh, you artists! Oh, you leeches that suck onto the
> real objects and real emotions and real *life* of life, and
> use them to perpetrate a golding aura of art! For its
> own arty sake! Don't you know what Plato said about
> the artist? The artist should be tied in a big plastic bag
> and dropped in a deep chasm and entirely forgotten
> about. I have murderous tendencies when I think about
> the artist who doesn't care what happens to the world
> as long as he can tell about it or paint about it or dance
> about it. The Hollow Men, hah! The poet is the hollow
> man, and don't forget that. He's a creature that bears
> the outward appearance of a man, except that he doesn't
> contain meat and bones . . . . He's full of essence and
> beauty. Dung! That's what the normal man leaves in a
> thousand pots all over the country he roams. Artists
> leave nothing but symbols. Artists! Dung!" (pp. 55-6)

Mel's reaction against the solipsism of artists reveals that his own obsession with his mechanical device inside the box and the concentric circles, which capture man in their tight embrace and stifle and delay the production of meaning and knowledge, is not the kind of solipsism that could blind him with regard to the world around him out of mere selfishness. In fact, what Mel reacts against is the world view that permeates the modern artist's vision and aesthetics.

Mel, I think, is the first character in Bowering's fiction from whom we can elicit the ideological reasons behind Bowering's deconstruction of modernism.[25] When Bowering argues against modernist realism he does so because he traces its sources to humanism which was formulated in the Renaissance. Humanism postulates reason as the instrument that shapes order and abnegates irrationality, and views nature as being alien to the human cosmos. Being a humanist implies believing in an anthropocentric world, in a universe according to the principle of exclusion or elimination. A humanist displays an unshaken faith in man and in the arts, but while doing so he ignores the rest of the world. The phenomenology of the world remains for the humanist a reality of objects representing man's reason and established meanings. Bowering, as he said in his interview with Caroline Bayard and Jack David, "is not . . . a humanist."[26]

Humanism is a practice of thinking which presupposes that the world out there is the mirror image of the world that exists in the human mind. Modernist realism is an aesthetic expression of this attitude toward the cosmos. "Post-modern" fiction, although it does not always reject humanism as such, questions the validity of an approach to the world and the arts that eliminates process and the presence of things.[27] Bowering has Brown in *Concentric Circles* propose an alternative to this elimination:

> "You have to paint them (people) a picture . . . . that is
> not an imitation of life, but the life itself. You have to
> paint *them!*" finished Brown flourishing toward the
> brown minister. (p. 59)

The brown minister had initially posed as the subject of one of Brown's portraits, but he ended up in the process of painting becoming the object itself. Characteristically, it is the minister who in the very end of the novella subjects both Mel and Brown to the objectification of is interpretation:

> "These two were not the cause of their own deaths. It
> is the Tragedy of Man that he alone can not see the way
> to his salvation . . . . " (p. 66)

These words accompany Mel and Brown's elimination from the setting of *Concentric Circles*. Their subjective utterances, their attempts to open a dialogue with the totalitarian reality that surrounds them, leads to their arrest by the police of their small city. Mel and Brown's attempts to escape from the monolithic certainties of the so-called humanistic society that the minister represents are coerced. Their subjective dialogism is overthrown by the logos of the minister, logos in the sense of pronouncement and God's word.

Mel and Brown's exit from the novella is also an exit staged to announce Bowering's departure from the logocentricism of modernism. As an anti-humanist, Bowering does not exercise the authority of modern writers fostered by their humanism. He is a writer who becomes present in his fiction by virtue of the restlessness of his vision.

V

A Short Sad Book is Bowering's work that best illustrates the unrest of his aesthetics. It is a work that resists summation and challenges generic classification. "This is no novel," the narrator says in the beginning of the book. Yet, later on, he calls it a "novel" a "serial novel," a "post-modern novel," and a great number of other things.[28] Robin Blaser has included *A Short Sad Book* in his edition of Bowering's *Particular Accidents: Selected Poems* and calls it in his introduction a "poem in prose."[29] But no matter what its genre is, *A Short Sad Book* is consciously conceived as a book, complete with an index. The index, which we normally find in non-fictional works, indicates the discursive character of the book which enters, with amazingly swift and delicate movements, both history and fiction. Bowering himself says of this book:

> In *A Short Sad Book* I was trying to clear the boards and make clear a lot of my opinions that had been working up over the years on various things and say them out . . . . I just wanted everybody to know how I feel about everything. So there is a lot of measuring of relationships . . . . I was trying to get the sense of spreading the whole thing out on one big flat surface and then you might see something in the top right-hand corner that connects with something down at the bottom left-hand corner ironically or simply in order to rhyme with it or whatever . . . . That book just ends because one ran out of space or ran out of pages to do or whatever.[30]

The randomness of *A Short Sad Book* is obviously deliberate. The narrator, a young boy called George Bowering who knows more than his age implies — "I am eight years old" (p. 16) — orchestrates a multi-dimensional dialogue that explores the grammar of Canadian history and literary tradition. But the logic of this dialogue exceeds that of history and of straight fiction.

Bowering's excursions take him from his personal landscape and history, including his criticism and fiction, to the Canada Council offices and to the top of the mountain where Sir John A. MacDonald and Evangeline make love, the reality of his act of writing and the Canadian publishers' world to Margaret Atwood and Louis Riel.   His writing style echoes the meanderings of his content.   It emulates Gertrude Stein whose *A Long Gay Book* has influenced the composition of Bowering's own *Book*.[31]   *A Short Sad Book* is a cultural narrative which is determined by the interplay of opposing and contradictory semantic and ideological positions.   This interplay constitutes the intertextuality of the book, the dialogic relationship between its seemingly unrelated fragments.

Although *A Short Sad Book* works against the principle of a unified structure that solidifies the form of the modernist novel, it does create its own rhythm, a rhythm which interrelates the various surfaces of the book into a composition that demonstrates the transcience of perception and meaning.   The rhythmic qualities range from melody to cacophony.

> All this dialogue was too much for the novel. I noticed that it was beginning to speak in short sentences with periods.
> Literature fell from the skies.
> The novel withdrew itself painfully from its skin & assumed position five.
> The skies opened. (p. 72)

> I Love this country, I didn't the thirty years ago but am I I. A poet is not a dealer in a card game. Not even a poet writing a novel.
> They all do in this country.
> I held her & kissed her right on James Bay. For a moment she wriggled in my grasp. (p. 52)

The rhythmic variations are part of Bowerings's self-conscious play.   Indeed, ludism is what integrates the disparate elements of *A Short Sad Book* into a surface where they are let be only by means of competing with other elements.   I use the term ludism according to Vicki Mistacco's definition:

> as the open play of signification, as the free and productive interaction of forms, of signifiers and signified, without regard for an original or an ultimate meaning. In literature, ludism signifies textual play; the text is viewed as a game affording both author and reader the possibility of producing endless meanings and relationships.[32]

Bowering's ludism exhibits the discontinuities of his style and renders the jarring elements of his discursive narrative as comic and parodic. The syllogisms that he plays with in *A Short Sad Book* reveal that his intention is to announce the death of the sovereignty of meaning and to call for attention to the significance of particular moments.

> Now it is all beneath me when I bend over to look at it this way.
> It is extremely clear.
> I am lucid tonight.
> I am writing with the clarity of regret.
> The Red Sox lost the fifth game today. (pp. 30-1)

The clarity of particular moments in *A Short Sad Book* is constantly underplayed by the contradictory logic of other moments. The textual play, present throughout its six parts, points out Bowering's reflexive awareness.

VI

Bowering's textual play engages in its activities not only his characters but his reader and himself as well. His collections of short stories, *Flycatcher & Other Stories*, *Protective Footwear* and *A Place to Die*,[33] more than any other of his prose works, involve the reader in their textuality at a very immediate level.

The reader often plays the role of a spectator who is bewildered by the action that goes on around him, for Bowering likes to test his reader's expectations for consistency. The reader reads, for instance, in "Owning Up," about George Delsing who was a student at UBC and was found "stabbed to death with an old-fashioned quill sharpener" (*PF*, p. lll). But when he moves to the story "The Elevator," he sees George Delsing "put(ting) on his magic necktie . . . and becom(ing) a Professor-Man" at the University of Calgary (*F*, p. 12). In other stories, the reader is an alert observer seduced by the characters' outrageous dialogues. When he is perplexed, Bowering is quick to address a few words of consolation: "Gentle reader," he says in the story "Student, Petty Thief, TV Star," "recline there in the sand where there are no prints" (*PD*, p. 72).

When the story "Ebbe's Roman Holiday" promises some wild action and the reader is keen to become part of it, George Delsing (again) kindly encourages him: "Tell you what: select a favourite tie from your own 1961 and put it on me. I'm sure I won't care. I won't ever know. I want your faith friend" *(PF,* p. 140). The fact that the reader is not a sharer of the character's reality does not create problems in his active participation. And Delsing, the narrator, knows that: ''That was an aside,'' he comments, ''so you won't get carried away thinking this is real life'' *(PF,* p. 140). Participating in Bowering's fiction of unrest is sometimes easier than the reader expects.

Most of the time, however, the reader performs a role that can be frustrating, not to say impossible to act out, because of Bowering's ludism. The reader encounters himself in Bowering's fiction as a detective trying to solve ''puzzles.'' But he always falls a few steps behind the writer who detects his impulse to pin him down. ''Arbre de décision,'' for example, is full of ''authentic'' and ''fake Greek accents'' that speak softly and seductively, crudely and threatingly. They speak from within the inner ear of the principal character, Arthur Cuff. The reader, naturally, attempts to unknot Arthur's sexual fantasies and the maze of his discourse. But any effort to arrest the meaning of the story in an act of good will, an act considered to be by the modernist tradition not only worthwhile but necessary as well, is stymied. Arthur's meaning as a character is as elusive as his wet body is slippery inside his bathrobe. The puzzle of this story is not solved by the reader, but it is settled by an ''accentless Greek's voice.'' The ''cultured foreigner'' comes to an agreement with Arthur about the ''old rules of grammar'' and the ''employment of vernacular'':

> You agree with me that if we do not preserve the rules of discourse, our literature, bequeathed to us & ordered for us by the Greeks, will be murdered by us. Arthur was all at once aware of his unaccompanied nakedness. He thought of the word. Murdered? *(PD,* pp. 103-4)

The question mark that punctuates the end of the story presents Arthur as a character with a double direction: although he is a character of his own making in his fantasies, he dies not as an Agamemnon, the subliminal figure of his fantastical adventures, but as the character that Bowering has created. The same question mark that expresses Arthur's surprise at the reality of his discourse makes the reader of the story also aware that the positioning of himself in Bowering's fiction as a thematic interpreter is untenable.

Bowering often acts as a writer by assuming a reader's role. He likes telling his reader what the reader is accustomed to searching for by himself. In "Looking for Ebbe" the questers do not know why they look for him. Besides this lack of motivation, the story is further complicated by the fact that although Ebbe's mother says that he can be found "anywhere," he is nowhere to be seen in the story. The reader's interpretive problem then is to understand how Ebbe can be both ubiquitous and elusive. This understanding is shared by the narrator of the story as he admits to the reader that he faces the same problem: "I'm trying to understand him for you. It's not easy" (F, p. 26). It's not easy indeed, for later on in the story the narrator repeats that he is still "trying to get at Ebbe Coutts" (F, p. 27). In fact, this quest for Ebbe is continued in many of Bowering's stories and is one of the recurring motifs that contributes to the stories' intertextuality and seriality.

The quest in "Looking for Ebbe" for a character who is both present and absent illustrates the reader's situation in most of Bowering's fiction. The narrator as quester is identified with the reader who searches for answers. But the moment the reader becomes aware of the identification of the two roles, he feels that his detective explorations are thwarted. There is already somebody else in the story doing for him what he has been instructed by the modernist tradition to do on his own. The reader, in other words, is present in the story but given limited access to the field of action, a limitation that is part of Bowering's textual play.

The reader's relationship to Bowering is exemplified in the story "Time and Again." When George Delsing visits Mrs. Ackerman, the widow of a dead orchardist, she tells him during the course of their conversation that her husband, "from about two months after he went blind till the day he died . . . kept a diary" (F, p. 63). Delsing, as the young man who left Lawrence planning to become a sports writer and who is writing now a "great long novel on the blatant secret lives of three thousand people in Lawrence" (F, p.56), displays a keen curiosity.

> "How?"
> "On his little typewriter. He used to sit in his dark room with the typewriter on his lap and type out his diary every night. I could hear it right through the wall, very slow typing. I wanted to jump up and offer to help, it got on my nerves so much, but of course I

couldn't do that, having caused him to go blind, and get
into the peach business and never see Europe and all
that. So I used to read it the next day when he thought
I was watering the front garden."
"Can I look at . . . ?"
"No." (F, p. 63)

The husband's secret life is shared with his wife. But Mrs. Ackerman, who has already expressed her guilt regarding her husband's misfortune, does not plead guilty for violating the privacy
of his diary. She does not plead guilty, for she has to become
the reader he cannot be. Mrs. Ackerman's reading act throws
light on the darkness that accompanies her husband's blind
writing. But as a reader, Mrs. Ackerman remains silent. She
discusses her husband's method of writing enhanced by her
reading, but she does not reveal the content of the diary. The
withdrawal of this vital piece of information disappoints young
Delsing only momentarily. After all, he is writing about the "blatant secret lives" of the people in Lawrence. Like Mr. Ackerman
who did not need any light in order to write, Delsing does not
need to pry into the diary in order to write about the dead man's
secret life. The concealment of the diary endows Delsing with,
and deprives him of, the knowledge he needs as a writer. But,
paradoxically, it is the combination of revelation and concealment
that makes Delsing think of Mrs. Ackerman as "wise" and sends
him to the "gladland" of his future writing. To appreciate "Time
and Again," the reader, like Delsing, must accept the fact that
he cannot always reach what he knows to be there.

But there is a compensation for the limited access to the existing
material. The writer/quester foregrounds his presence in such
a way that although he can identify himself with the reader's problem, the reader cannot rest on the illusion that he can identify
himself with him. The compensation offered is the reader's
awareness that the writer knows he exists.

The reader's existence is not simply actualized on the edge of
fiction and the reader's reality. Bowering's frequent apostrophes
put the imprint of fiction on the reader's act and draw the reader
into his writing. The reader, traditionally being exterior to the
text, becomes interior to it. Like the Ackermans, Bowering in-
vites his reader to become a character in his fiction to the extent
that he himself becomes his own reader. The reading act prac-
tised upon Bowering's fiction is a graphic event that does not
necessarily take place outside his texts. Bowering's reading of

his own writing *in* his writing introduces the reading act as a reinscription of the text.

The reader, Bowering tells us, ''will not have time to puzzle the modernist's un/sub/pre/conscious because he has to watch where he is stepping in the conscious, in the composition. In the side-by-side'' *(PW,* p. 121). The reading act in Bowering's fiction is an extension of his ''principle of creating.'' The reader is called upon to take part in the drama of consciousness and experience that unfolds itself in the text. He becomes a character who contributes to the realization of the writing act.

Bowering often extends his role as a reader of his own fiction and gets involved in a critic's enterprise by analysing his own writing. In ''A Short Story,'' for instance, he breaks down his story into eleven components: ''setting,'' ''characters,'' ''point of view'' (the rest of the sections are easy to guess), assuming, that is, the role of an Aristotelian critic who, by definition, would not approve of this kind of fragmented writing *(PD,* pp. 23-35). Bowering does *in* his fiction what is traditionally done *to* fiction. He himself, decodes the signals and signs of his writing. Interpretation, for Bowering is ''synonymous with imagination.''[34] It is both a creative and a critical activity.

In ''Looking for Ebbe,'' the narrator, conscious of being a writer in action, expresses his doubts about the success of his activity.

> I don't think I'm telling this very well; I have the sense
> that I'm dealing with a room I see in my mind, its
> darkness in a side of my head; I don't think I'm making
> a visual presentation. Maybe that's proper.
>   Maybe the room doesn't — but that's wrong, it is real,
> though I merely make it real with these words, make it
> new, make it different, the reality may be then imping-
> ing on the mind that turns this out, this recollec-
> tion. Because I'm away from it now, hundreds of miles
> away, and the first thing I forget is the smell. It was
> bacon . . . . *(F,* pp. 14-5)

The importance of this passage is twofold. On the one hand, it draws attention to the fact that those characters of Bowering's who are writers are conscious of their act of writing and maintain this consciousness throughout their narratives at the risk of losing aesthetic distance and abandoning literary propriety. On the other hand, it accentuates Bowering's mode of writing not as a realistic rendering of experience or memory, but as a fictive act. Bowering's dialogue with his reader here is fairly indirect, but the message is clear. His fiction is not to be measured through the norms of external reality. More than that, it is not to be interpreted in the same way critics interpret mimetic fiction. His fiction is not realistic because it is mimetic; it *is* real in the sense of knowing that it is being written.

Notes

1   George Bowering, "The Three-Sided Room: Notes on the Limitations of Modernist Realism," in *The Mask in Place: Essays on Fiction in North America* (Winnipeg: Turnstone Press, 1982), p. 20. Hereafter cited as *TSR*.
2   For an exposition of the radical aspects of contemporary fiction see Raymond Federman, ed., *Surfiction: Fiction Now and Tomorrow* (Chicago: The Swallow Press Inc., 1975), Jerome Klikowitz, *Literary Disruptions: The Making of a Post-Contemporary American Fiction* (Urbana: The University of Illinois Press, 1975), Ihab Hassan, *The Dismemberment of Orpheus: Toward a Postmodern Literature* (New York: Oxford University Press, 1971), Hassan, *Paracriticisms: Seven Speculations of the Times* (Urbana: The University of Illinois Press), 1975.
3   Bowering, "The Painted Window: Notes on Post-Realist Fiction," in *The Mask in Place*, p. 116. Hereafter cited as *PW*.
4   I use the term "self-reflexive" in the sense in which Roget Shattuck uses it in his book *The Banquet Years: The Origins of Avant Garde in France: 1885 to World War I: Alfred Jarry, Henri Rousseau, Erik Satie and Guillaume Apollinaire* (New York: Vintage Books, 1968). Shattuck describes with this term the phenomenon that "Twentieth Century art has tended to *search itself* rather than exterior reality for beauty or meaning or truth, a condition that entails a new relationship between the work of art, the world, the spectator, and the artist" (p. 326).
5   For the differences between literature and writing or text see Roland Barthes, *The Pleasure of the Text*, trans. Richard Miller (New York: Hill and Wang, 1975) and *Elements of Semiology*, trans. Annette Lavers and Colin Smith (New York: Hill and Wang, 1968); Julia Kristeva, *Desire in Language: A Semiotic Approach to Literature and Art*, trans. Thomas Gora, Alice Jardine and Leon S. Roudiez, ed. Leon S. Roudiez (New York: Columbia University Press, 1980) and *Le texte du roman; approache semiologique d'une structure discursive transformationnelle* (The Hague: Mouton, 1970).
6   Bowering cites Maurice Merleau-Ponty in "The Painted Window" (pp. 117-8) to show the phenomenological aspects of "post-modernism."
7   Hassan, "The Question of Postmodernism," in *Romanticism, Modernism, Postmodernism*, ed. Harry R. Garvin (Lewisburg: Bucknell University Press; London and Toronto: Associated University Presses, 1980), p. 119.
8   With regard to the origins of the term "post-modernism" see Hassan, "The Question of Postmodernism," pp. 117-18.
9   The controversy about "post-modernism" is also due to the fact that there are a great number of terms employed by various critics to discuss identical aspects of diverse or similar authors. For example Federman's "surfiction," Stephen Heath's "practice of writing," in *The Nouveau Roman: A Study in the Practice of Writing* (Philadelphia: Temple University Press, 1972), Matei Calinescu's "age of dialogue," in *Romanticism, Modernism, Postmodernism*,

define, to great extent, the same mode of fiction.

10   For a study of the "postmodern impulse to demystify" see Alan Wilde, "Irony in the Postmodern Age: Toward a Map of Suspensiveness," *boundary 2*, Vol. IX, No. 1 (Fall, 1980), pp. 5-46.

11   I borrow the term from Stephen Heath, *The Nouveau Roman*, pp. 23-4.

12   "14 Plums: An Interview" with George Bowering and Bill Schermbrucker, Sharon Thessen, David McFadden, and Paul de Barros, in *The Capilano Review*, Vol. 1, No. 15 (1979), p. 100.

13   On the aesthetic reaction of modernism against Aristotelianism and the European middle-class ethos see William V. Spanos, "The Detective and the Boundary: Some Notes on the Postmodern Literary Imagination," *boundary 2*, Vol. 1, No. 1 (Fall, 1972), p. 147-68.

14   Freud's theories, which have shaped modernism, in spite of the attacks on them, have recovered their status in the "post-modern" and poststructuralist scenes of criticism refurbished by Jacques Lacan.

15   Bowering, *Mirror on the Floor* (Toronto: McClelland & Stewart, 1966), p. 85. Further references will appear in the text.

16   Bowering has stated many times that he does not believe in the subconscious. See his interview with Caroline Bayard and Jack David, "George Bowering," in *Outposts: Interviews, Poetry, Bibliographies & a Critical Introduction to 8 Major Poets*, Vol. IV in the series *Three Solitudes: Contemporary Literary Criticism in Canada* (Erin: Press Porcépic Ltd., 1978), p. 90, and "14 Plums: An Interview," pp. 88, 107.

17   Kristeva, *La révolution du language poétique: l'avant-garde à la fin du XIXe siècle, Lautreamont et Mallarmé* (Paris: Éditions du Seuil, 1974), pp. 59-60.

18   On the subject of the self and its other and desire and lack see Jacques Lacan, *Speech and Language in Psychoanalysis*, trans., with notes and commentary, Anthony Wilden (Baltimore and London: The Johns Hopkins University Press, 1968), and *The Four Fundamental Concepts of Psycho-Analysis*, trans. Alan Sheridan, ed. Jacques-Alain Miller (Middlesex, England: Penguin Books, 1979).

19   Bowering, "Modernism Could Not Last Forever," in *The Mask in Place*, p. 82.

20   Mikhail Bakhtin, "Discourse in the Novel," in *The Dialogic Imagination: Four Essays*, trans. Caryl Emerson and Michael Holquist, ed. Michael Holquist (Austin: University of Texas Press, 1981), pp. 263.

21   Bakhtin, p. 282.

22   Bakhtin, p. 282.

23   Bowering, *Burning Water* (Don Mills: Musson Book Company, a division of General Publishing 1980). See my review "*Burning Water:* Two Stories / One Novel: Narrative as Exploration," *Island*, 10 (Fall 1981), pp. 89-94.

24   Bowering, *Concentric Circles* (Coatsworth, Ontario: Black Moss Press, 1977). All references will appear in the text.

25   It is important to notice that although the novella was published in 1977, it was written in the 1960s.

26   *Outposts*, p. 98.

27   On the relationship of "post-modernism" and aesthetic and social ideologies, including humanism, see Richard Palmer, "Postmodernity and Hermeneutics," *boundary 2*, Vol. V, No. 2 (Winter, 1977), pp. 363-93.

28   Bowering, *A Short Sad Book* (Vancouver: Talonbooks, 1977), pp. 26,37,107,139. All further references will appear in the text.

29   Bowering, *Particular Accidents: Selected Poems*, ed. with an introduction by Robin Blaser (Vancouver: Talonbooks, 1980), p. 15. Blaser's introduction, "George Bowering's Plain Song," is brilliant in its exposition of Bowering's imagination, and although it focuses on his poetry, it offers helpful insights about his fiction as well.

30   "14 Plums: An Interview," p. 88.

31 See Blaser, pp. 16-7 and "14 Plums: An Interview," pp. 88, 101.

32 Vicki Mistacco, "The Theory and Practice of Reading Nouveaux Romans: Robbe-Grillet's *Topologie d'une cité fantôme*," in *The Reader in the Text: Essays on Audience and Interpretation*, ed. Susan R. Suleiman and Inge Crosman (Princeton: Princeton University Press, 1980), p. 375.

33 Bowering, *Flycatcher & Other Stories* (Ottawa: Oberon Press, 1974), *Protective Footwear: Stories and Fables* (Toronto: McClelland & Stewart, 1978), *A Place to Die* (Ottawa: Oberon Press, 1983). Hereafter cited as *F*, *PF* and *PD* respectively.

34 Naomi Schor, "Fiction as Interpretation / Interpretation as Fiction," in *The Reader in the Text*, p. 171.

REENTERING THE WASTELAND: ROBERT KROETSCH'S POSTMODERN FICTION

Karen Germundson

The landscape of Robert Kroetsch's world is sinister, littered with bones, stretching without ever reaching a reassuring horizon, under a sky that glows strangely. This glow is not perceived as the beauty of the northern lights, but as the sky consuming itself. The menaced inhabitants of this world are as bizarre as their environment; they spend their time hurling bones in the street, having punch-outs in the brothels and beer parlours, and, when they are not fighting among themselves, they are engaged in battle against nature, directing rifles, tank artillery, and cannons against the sky. Their other pastimes, equally as violent, include unusual sexual encounters and the grotesque act of dying. And, in the midst of this violence, they routinely sit down at the supper table with family and friends.

This is a postmodern vision of the world that Kroetsch gives us, grotesque, yet undeniably banal. Postmodern fiction is preoccupied with the more bizarre aspects of death, violence, and sex, yet insists all the while on the ordinariness of existence. Not many critics have been interested in the peculiar nature of this vision in Kroetsch's fiction, focussing instead on the purely technical aspects of his work, expressing a disappointment sometimes in what they misinterpret as a cynical, gratuitously bizarre, disgusting view of the world. They see his world as an unjustified distortion of the one we know.

But is the picture Kroetsch presents us with such an off-beat, warped view of reality? No more so than the world-view television presents us with daily. Catching the end of the eleven o'clock news the other night, I identified all the key elements of Kroetsch's world in the conglomeration of images on the television. First, an exile from Nigeria trekking across the desert facing a journey of many miles on foot, carrying, of all things, an elegant chintz loveseat on his head. Next were featured film clips of a farm as grotesque as any Kroetschian bachelor would run, sheds full of animal skulls and bones, bloated animal carcasses in the fields. Two commercials followed the newscast, completing the Kroetschian formula. The first was an advertisement for *Playboy Weekend*, featuring buxom young women dressed somewhat inappropriately for what appeared to be a sort of track meet.   An insistence on the mundane is part of Kroetsch's world, and it was the same with this zany television world.   An earnest farmer, looking somehow divine as he stood in the barn doorway flooded with white light, encouraged the practice of "good, honest eating," a decidedly Kroetschian prescription, proffering to his viewing audience his own bowl of shredded wheat which, for some reason, he had brought out to the barn with him.

What the eleven o'clock news tells us is that the violence, absurdity, and incongruity of Kroetsch's world are not a distortion but an accurate reflection of a world which is itself bizarre.   Our world *is* a juxtaposition of the brutal, the ludicrous, and the mundane;   this is not just a nightmarish fabrication of Kroetsch and other postmodern writers.   The bizarre *is* one aspect of reality, and our age is simply more aware of it than others have been.   In the past, values, systems of belief, and theories of universal order distracted attention away from the elements of reality not related to order.   Anything suggesting disorder or absurdity went unnoticed in the larger scheme of things.   Once these systems collapsed, however, the bizarre stood out starkly.

The postmodern mind is not only highly conscious of the bizarre, but is fascinated by it, obsessed with it.   Things which frighten always have a certain fascination, and it is this combination of fear and curiosity which draws the postmodern writer.   The response to a frightening object has two stages.   At first, we retreat, keeping a close watch.   This was the response to things unnatural, incongruous, unusual, and inexplicable at the beginning of the century, when belief in an ordered universe was gone for the most part, and the bizarre became highlighted.

The modern mind was repelled by the meaningless universe it beheld, and drew back defensively to view the absurdity of life from a distance.   This dismayed response is perhaps responsible in part for certain changes which took place in fiction in the early part of the twentieth century.   Authorial detachment became a prominent feature of the literature of this period, and the innovations that this detachment occasioned suggest a reluctance on the part of the modern sensibility to come into direct contact with an absurd world.   Irony, for example, a mode which allows the author to distance himself from his subject, became the dominant tone in literature.   The drastic change in narrative point of view, from omniscient to limited narrator, might also be related to this defensive reaction.   Taking in the cosmos from the vantage point of omniscience would naturally be appealing to a believer in universal order, but for one who saw only absurdity, such a viewpoint would hardly be attractive. The picture of a cosmos with all its elements functioning harmoniously is one thing — the vision of the universe as infinite absurdity is quite another. The eye becomes defensively myopic; omniscience is too painful and is exchanged for a truncated and anesthetized awareness of the world.

When the universe lost its ordered appearance, it also ceased to look beautiful. To the modern eye, it was sordid and squalid and sterile. For many modern writers, therefore, it held no interest, and the novel moved inside the head, and outside of time. Not that the dimension of objective, physical reality was left completely vacant: the school of naturalism flourished, exploring the squalor of the external world. But even naturalism is a form of detachment. The author is clinically distanced, not immersed in the milieu, but barricaded, as it were, behind the microscope through which he conducts his examination.

A retreat from something frightening is, then, the initial response, but viewing the source of alarm from a distance only creates further anxiety. As the suspense grows, there is a desire to stop that tension by confronting the source of fear head-on. The thing feared begins to hold a terrible fascination and must be approached. Hence the obsession of postmodern writers with the bizarre. What the moderns backed away from, the postmoderns feel compelled to confront. Samuel Beckett saw us as aliens unable to inhabit our own universe; apprehensive of venturing into an absurd landscape, his characters stand on the spot. Kroetsch's characters occupy the same sterile, bone-littered landscape, but they plunge obsessively into the very heart of their hostile surroundings, sailing recklessly and compulsively into the Badlands. T. S. Eliot's fisherman puts his back to the wasteland and faces the water, but Kroetsch's characters turn about and enter the wasteland in a determined effort to reclaim and reoccupy territory that used to be ours.

And we recover this territory by coming to terms with the absurd: hence the preoccupation of postmodern writers with the bizarre and the grotesque, their relentless focussing on the more repellent aspects of existence. Readers who dismiss postmodern literature as puerile, gratuitously obscene and perverse misunderstand its concerns. Postmodern literature deals with the more incomprehensible and disturbing aspects of life — cruelty, suffering, dying, unconscious impulses, especially the sexual drive — and they explore these aspects in their most extreme conditions because, as prominent features of our age, they demand confrontation.

Surveying Kroetsch's fiction, we can see a gradual willingness to face these questions. Johnnie Backstrom, the protagonist of *The Words of My Roaring*, published in 1966, and Peter Guy in *But We Are Exiles*, 1965, are haunted by dark impulses they cannot understand and would prefer not to acknowledge. They try to repress such impulses, regarding them as abnormal. Even thinking about them makes these characters feel guilty; they see such thoughts as unhealthy speculation. Inhibition paralyzes Peter and Johnnie: they are checkmated by events in their lives that demand from them that they learn to accept the bizarre nature of death and love.

Kroetsch's later characters are postmodern in their readiness to confront the bizarre. They do not regard their preoccupations as abnormal or perverse, and are liberated from the guilt frustrating Peter and Johnnie. They freely indulge in the most grotesque obsessions. Vera Lang in *What the Crow Said* is sexually aroused by bees, and by the bones and dehydrated remains of her husbands. Her husbands surrender to their morbid fascination with death, obeying a dark, unconscious impulse which makes one charge a bull, another swim away from the hole in the ice through which he has fallen, and another embrace death literally, spread-eagled on a windmill. Hazard Lepage in *The Studhorse Man*, despite his devotion to his fiancée, cannot overcome the fascination sex holds for him, and is sidetracked by the most unlikely women on his way home. In *Gone Indian* Jeremy Sadness indulges himself in a trip to northern Alberta to lose himself in the nothingness he is so terrified of, yet so obsessed with.

Focussing on issues that were previously avoided, or treated peripherally at most, postmodern writers have shown us a view of our world from a very new and startling vantage point. What looked like shapeless chaos to the moderns, from this vantage point now appears as a very patterned world. The universe remains absurd and inexplicable, but there is a design nonetheless. Prophesy, predestination, and foreknowledge are all important elements of the postmodern novel.

The modern writers have dispensed with plot, but for many postmodern writers, it is an element crucial to revealing the design shaping the world. For example, *The World According to Garp* has an extremely complex plot that links what seem to be the most unrelated events into a tightly woven design. Irving presents us with a world so crazy that we expect it to defy all order, but everything connects, and it turns out to be a world perfectly ordered. Beryl Bainbridge has given us another very bizarre world in which everything connects. Beginnings mirror endings in her novels, and what is prophesied at the opening of the novel comes to pass in a pattern scarcely perceptible to the reader, who is distracted by the outrageous and the incongruous.

But how can an absurd world have a design? The postmodernist envisions experience as a composite of opposite elements juxtaposed, the bizarre and the banal, the heroic and the antiheroic, the natural and the supernatural. This vision embodies Henri Bergson's definition of disorder, not as the lack of order, which is the modern concept, but as two orders operating at once. This is the design patterning the postmodern world.

Differing from the modern writer in his perception of disorder, the postmodernist cannot work within the conventions of modern literature. Realism has proven to be particularly inappropriate, and what we see instead in postmodern fiction are magic realism, high realism, and other interesting offshoots which are evidence of a very different kind of perception. Time is not perceived the same way by the moderns and the postmoderns. For the modern writer, existence in time is antiheroic. Only myth offers the possibility of heroic experience. For the postmodern writer, the antiheroic and the heroic are part of the same experience, and he has made use of forms such as the tall tale, which make the distinction between time and myth unnecessary. The difference between tragedy and comedy is another distinction the postmodern writer has rejected, presenting experience instead as tragicomic.

Kroetsch explains that behind his interest in postmodern fiction is a need to find truths unattainable in the province of realism.[1] In all his work, we sense an urgency to find those truths. Three very painful obsessions recur throughout his fiction, obsessions that must be mastered lest they overwhelm. The most overriding concern is with death, and for Kroetsch's characters, physical death is only one way of dying. A morbid fear of failure — the dismal possibility of losing an election, failing to make a significant archeological discovery, never finding the right mare to breed the perfect horse, never finishing one's

Ph.D. dissertation — all these translate themselves into an anticipated death. Likewise, falling in love, and, more perilous still, getting married, are viewed as an obliteration, a death. Comparing his approach to these three problems, the "terrors of human relationships," of failure, and of death, in his early and later works, we can see why realism frustrated Kroetsch.[2]

Death for Kroetsch is both tragic and absurd, and both aspects must be acknowledged. In his early works, which are predominantly realistic, he had difficulty presenting the absurd side of death. For example, in The Words of My Roaring, the suicide of Jonah is presented in a way that leaves the reader uneasy, confused, almost embarrassed. Kroetsch has no trouble incorporating the tragic nature of this death into the realistic mode he is using, but the other side of the vision, the grotesque, absurd view of death, cannot be accommodated by realism. We are disturbed by Backstrom's vision of his friend's corpse banging on the windshield while he cries inside his hearse. Even more disconcerting are Backstrom's speculations about the state of Jonah's corpse resting at the bottom of the lake:

> There it was, cool and light and safe on a hot day like this. A flower in full bloom, and the arms and legs like petals rising and moving and falling in the liquid air,the white of the plaster cast a conundrum to perch and pickerel alike. The hair on end.[3]

Also puzzling is the tone of the passage in which Backstrom overhears children swimming in the lake.

> They squealed at each other, "Guess what I stepped on?"
> "A foot," somebody said.
> "A thumb," somebody said.
> They'd shout and scramble for shore. They scared each other by naming parts of the human body, which was something I did not understand.
> "A kidney."
> "An eye." (pp. 137-38)

When they are pulled out of context, we can laugh at these passages, but when we encounter them in their framework of realism, this view of Jonah's death seems inappropriate. The eye of realism views the grotesque as disgusting, repelling, and horrible. It sees the absurd as ridiculous, degrading, and abnormal. Perceived this way, the grotesque both contradicts and undermines the tragic element of this episode, leaving us confused, unable to understand Kroetsch's view of death because his signals are interfering with each other. We receive a garbled message.

In his later novels, Kroetsch moves away from realism and has a new perspective, from which the grotesque and the absurd are normal, natural, human, rather than monstrous, and compatible with tragedy. If we compare the death of Jonah with the death of Tune in *Badlands*, published in 1975, we can see this. Tune is the beautiful and heroic character of this novel, and his death is tragic. It is, nevertheless, an extremely absurd death. Tune knows nothing about dynamite, and we have a picture of him absurdly singing while he tinkers with the detonator, oblivious to the danger. As well as the absurdity of the accident, Kroetsch insists on the grotesqueness of the death, focussing on Tune's corpse. He is concerned with morbid technicalities, showing us exactly what happens to the bodies. In Tune's case, not much is left. Dawe makes this macabre entry in his field notes: "I found one finger. I think. I. Kicked the dirt. Over —."[4] The buzzards which circle over the spot where Tune is buried heighten the grotesque nature of his death, as does Web's vision, as bizarre as Backstrom's vision of Jonah knocking on the windshield:

> Web went on driving the shovel into the clay, digging
> deeper, imagining that with one terrible stroke he would
> drive the blade into young Tune's face. Into his
> neck. The boy would sing out, mortally wounded, and
> Web would run screaming out of the coulee. (p. 222)

The difference between Web's vision and Backstrom's lies in the kind of response we have to each. We are disoriented and made uncomfortable by the grotesque in *The Words of My Roaring*, encountering an apparent contradiction in Kroetsch's otherwise tragic view of death, but in *Badlands*, the grotesque in no way conflicts with tragedy. We have a tragicomic vision, rather than a purely tragic one, so that it is possible for Tune's death to be both comic and tragic at once. Therefore, while Backstrom can only cry, and feel uneasy as we do about his inappropriate yet irrepressible thoughts on the absurdity of death, Anna Yellowbird laughs as well as cries, when she learns that Tune is dead.

A shift like this, from tragic to tragicomic vision, is achieved when the grotesque and the absurd cease to evoke a painful response from the reader, repelling and horrifying him, and cause him to laugh instead. We can see this difference by comparing another pair of deaths in Kroetsch's work, one from a very early work, *But We Are Exiles*, the other from his more recent novel, *What the Crow Said*. Both deaths are strange and gruesome. Mike Hornyak accidentally sets himself ablaze, while Vera's husband becomes trapped on the rotating windmill and dies of dehydration. But while both deaths are of a ghastly nature, we do not respond the same way to each. The description of Hornyak's death emphasizes the horrifying and the hideous. We are sickened and repelled:

> . . . Hornyak had crawled, had kept on crawling even after his clothes were burnt to ashes and his skin was fried and his hair set straight on end and singed almost to his skull. But he kept on climbing, with the skin hanging off his fingers and sticking to the steel rungs . . . . (p. 103)

The description of Vera's husband, however, seems comic, because of the narrator's ludicrous comparison:

> The tall gangling stranger from the road gang was hardly more than a bag of bones, he'd been so dehydrated, so perfectly dried. He was for a moment a kind of dried flower in Vera's arms.[5]

Again, the hideous is translated into the humourous when the corpse of Vera's second husband is brought home. His body is embedded in four blocks of ice which, absurdly, the searchers have not arranged in the proper order, so that he arrives like a misconstructed puzzle.

The reader can laugh at pain, mishaps, cruelty, and death, then, if he knows that he is not expected to take them seriously, and if he is not asked to sympathize or identify with those suffering. The reader of postmodern fiction is liberated in two ways from the painful identification with suffering that realism insists upon. He knows he is being presented with an absurd world which, like the world of nonsense rhyme, is one in which pain, suffering, and death have no consequences. And as reassurance that he should respond to this world as an absurd one, he has the tone of the narrator's voice to guide him.

The peculiar voice of postmodern fiction is one of its most fascinating elements. Philip Stevick has analyzed this unique voice as one of

> extraordinary innocence, either genuine or feigned, even
> a kind of common prose rhythm deriving from the un-
> willingness to subordinate and complicate that is an at-
> tribute of that innocence, a readiness to confront certain
> extremities in life, such as pain, accident, death, and
> mourning, but an investing of these extremities with an
> odd and terribly distant artifice, a playing off of a
> method of wit, tough, flip, and facile, that is reminiscent
> of the stand-up comic . . . against a personal fragility
> and vulnerability that is very different from the classic
> toughness, knowingness, and irony of the dominant
> modernists.[6]

This "extraordinary innocence" characterizes Kroetsch's narrators. They confront the most outrageous, gruesome, and horrifying spectacles without any reaction, too incredibly naive to
be disgusted, alarmed, or shocked. They make no distinction between the bizarre and the everyday, but record everything with
a steady matter-of-factness. Demeter Proudfoot, for example, is
completely oblivious to the elements in his description of the
woman who prophesies Hazard's death:

> A woman had prophesied that fate for him; an old
> woman on the battlefields of France during the Great
> War . . . Hazard found her sitting blue-eyed between
> two naked corpses in a flooded cellar . . . When he told
> me of the incident he recalled . . . the water lapping at
> the old woman's button shoes, the sea-glitter of an
> emerald ring, the soldier's helmet she wore on her ap-
> parently old and yet so beautiful head.[7]

Demeter describes the natural and the strange with equal detachment; the ring on the woman's finger, the helmet on her head,
are all the same to him. He is not the least horrified by the detail
of the naked corpses, nor does he wonder at the accuracy of her
foresight.

What would be an outright atrocity in a realistic story is
overlooked by the postmodern narrator, or even applauded. In
What the Crow Said, when Vera realizes that she is being over-
taken by wolves, she throws them her baby so that she can
escape. The narrator, far from being shocked, expresses his complete approval. He is just as oblivious to absurdity as he is to
horror. Describing the unusual wedding of Vera and her third
husband, he perceives nothing comic or bizarre about the
event. He presents his story as a purely factual account of an
entirely plausible event:

> He and Vera went into town on a D-8; the stranger
> drove the big yellow Caterpillar down Main Street, to
> the Church of the Final Virgin. Father Basil heard them
> coming and was ready when they arrived. It was
> rumoured that they were married right there on the dus-
> ty seat of the D-8, the engine idling while Father Basil
> intoned. At any rate, the stranger backed the big Cat
> away from the church steps and took his new bride on a
> honeymoon. Pulling a bunkhouse and a cookhouse —
> the entire road gang had quit — they went on a tour of
> all twenty-four of Vera's bee yards, preparing them for a
> shipment of bees from California. (p. 176)

The narrator's lack of response liberates the reader from attitudes that realism imposes. Kroetsch, unsatisfied with the view
realism takes of love, failure, and death, uses this narrative voice
to make the reader stop responding as he usually would to these
situations and perceive them in a new light.

If realism is too limited a vision, surrealism might seem like the
answer to the postmodern writer's frustration. If he must push
fiction to extremes to find answers, then surrealism would certainly give him that freedom. But for all its scope, surrealism fails
to embody the postmodern vision because it may include all possible alternatives to the reality we know, but it also ignores that
reality, unconcerned with the mundane and the
natural. Postmodern fiction, however, insists on existence as
bizarre as well as banal, and is firmly set in time. Surrealism
transcends time and therefore does not have the same kind of
reality. It is the reality of dreams, visions and hallucinations, but
cannot claim the reality of time.

We can appreciate the significance of this distinction when we
compare the surrealism of Kroetsch's *Gone Indian* with a very different treatment of the bizarre in *The Studhorse Man* and *What the
Crow Said*. In *Gone Indian*, Jeremy dreams that twelve thousand
buffalo invade Edmonton. In *The Studhorse Man* a thousand
horses really do invade the city. In *Gone Indian* Jeremy
hallucinates and believes that the people of Notikeewin have the
faces of muskrats. But in *What the Crow Said*, beings who are
animals with human attributes really exist. A pack of coyotes
raise Vera's boy, and a crow converses in the language of
men. Jeremy dreams of making love to a buffalo, but Vera is actually impregnated by a swarm of bees.

It is the same vision, then, in each novel, but in *Gone Indian*
that vision has a limited reality — it is only real to Jeremy. In

the other two novels, that same vision is not a dream, but objective, physical reality. The bizarre ceases to be a nightmare, and becomes an actuality.

What surrealism cannot do, magic realism does, because, as the name suggests, it includes both features of the postmodern world, the banal and the bizarre together. Magic realism puts the actual and the fantastic in the same plane by giving them equal validity. It insists on the reality of everything, and makes this assertion by presenting even the most fantastic elements with the clarity and precision of a photograph. By magnifying detail, magic realism in fact transcends reality. Its images are often described as being more real than real because their precision is uncanny. Magic realism renders the fantastic more real-looking than the real world itself.

This is a rigid application of the term "magic realism," and would only apply to a few postmodern writers — Michael Ondaatje, for example. Kroetsch is often called a magic realist by critics, but they seem to have a different concept in mind. Like a magic realist, Kroetsch is creating a world that looks deceptively like a world of realism, but which, disconcertingly enough, proves to operate very differently, denying logic, time and causality. But Kroetsch's world has none of the magnified detail and supernatural clarity of magic realism. His technique has nothing to do with photographic precision, but is similar, instead, to that of dramatists like Pinter and Albee, who give an absurd world a very banal, everyday surface so that it resembles, superficially, the world of realism. The settings of Pinter and Albee, so banal and naturalistic in their attention to detail, and their characters, so mundane in their outward appearance, persuade us that we are dealing with a world that will function according to the conventions of realism. But once the characters begin to interact, we realize our assumption was wrong. Kroetsch's world is much the same — it has the *look* of realism. On the surface, Kroetsch's small towns, Notikeewin and Big Indian, look like Margaret Laurence's Manawaka or Sinclair Ross's Horizon. The description in *Gone Indian* of a pancake breakfast in a church basement smacks of realism:

> city slickers in red woollen coats, businessmen in coon-
> skin, women in Gay Nineties bustles. Skiers who
> wouldn't part with their skis. Little girls in short skirts,
> carrying their figure skates. A gang of boys brandishing
> hockey sticks.[8]

In Kroetsch's zaniest novel, *What the Crow Said,* there is a description of people gathered for a wedding which could appear in *A Jest of God* or *Who Has Seen the Wind:*

> the women were upstairs in the church, gathered
> around the register in the center of the aisle, above the
> furnace. They let the hot air warm their legs while they
> chatted about the weather and asked after each other's
> health. They spoke of the early snow and hoped it
> wouldn't stay. Some of the farmers west of town hadn't
> finished threshing . . . .   (p. 103)

Along with magic realism, tragicomedy, and Pinter and Albee's brand of realistic absurdity, the tall tale is central to postmodern fiction. It is a form Kroetsch seems to favour particularly, employing it again and again in his novels, to relate the story of the horses invading downtown Edmonton, in *The Studhorse Man;* the strange adventures of Dawe's crew when they go ashore in Drumheller, in *Badlands,* as well as Web's weird experience escaping from the brothel, seeing dinosaurs hatching in a hailstorm, riding a tornado; the account in *What the Crow Said* of the famous card game that lasts 151 days.

Obviously, the tall tale suits the purposes of the postmodern writer because of its concern with the bizarre. But the vision it presents coincides even more closely with postmodern fiction than that. In the tall tale we have a world trying to be two things at once: natural, temporal, and mundane but also supernatural, eternal, and heroic. The world of the tall tale is set in time, but the events which happen there are of mythic quality. It is subject to natural law, but supernatural forces are also at work. Its inhabitants are decidedly human, but in their midst are heroes of god-like stature. Hyperbole, the hallmark of the tall tale, is a bridging of these two orders, the same kind of straddling that the postmodern writer is engaged in, trying to enclose two orders in a single world. The response to this world of juxtaposed opposites is common to the tall tale and postmodern fiction: we find a similar narrative voice in each, a voice that passively accepts what is outrageous and incongruous, recording the bizarre without wonder, as something entirely credible that can be documented factually.

Accepting everything as possible, the tall tale allows Kroetsch to create a particular kind of hero. For Kroetsch, the possibility of heroic accomplishment is a genuine one. He does not believe we are, by necessity, antiheroes. Realism, therefore, is an inappropriate mode because it does not believe in the hero. The protagonist in realistic fiction must be an antihero, who strives for nothing, or an absurd hero, who, in the act of striving, appears ridiculous, ludicrously enormous and god-like in a petty, mundane world.

In his depiction of the hero in *But We Are Exiles*, Kroetsch puts a strain on the realistic form he is working with. In the final episode, Peter Guy removes Hornyak's corpse from the reefer so that he can take shelter inside. His act is heroic on a symbolic level: Hornyak had stolen Guy's fiancée and now, Guy, in turn, usurps Hornyak's place. By throwing the body overboard, he also liberates himself from the guilt he has been suffering, feeling responsible for Hornyak's death. Reading this ending, we feel uncomfortable because unlike the other episodes in the novel, this one does not stay within the confines of realism, and, when we come to it, we must readjust our perspective. Kroetsch could not have ended the novel any other way, however; only such an exaggerated symbolic gesture could suggest the level of Guy's heroism.

A similar tension is at work in *The Words of My Roaring*. We are uneasy, even embarrassed, when the protagonist, Backstrom, transcends his mundane world at heroic moments. His plunging into the goldfish pond to be baptized into a new life, his taking a hammer to the fender of his hearse to uncreate a world he hates, his impulsive speech to the crowd at the rodeo, all are absurd because they are excessive in the world of realism. Kroetsch acknowledges and even emphasizes their ludicrous extravagance in an attempt to lessen the strain, but he wants us to appreciate these episodes as heroic breakthroughs for Backstrom nevertheless, and we have difficulty doing so.

In his later novels, Kroetsch finds a way to make the hero and the everyday world compatible by using the tall tale. While there are many literary forms that accommodate the hero by transcending the ordinary world, the tall tale reconciles the heroic and the everyday, letting the hero live in time without looking absurdly out of place. The postmodern hero, therefore, is banal and god-like at the same time. Joe Lightning is a small town pool player, and the hero who is borne up into the heavens by an eagle. His death is typically postmodern, being both heroic and absurd. Having exceeded the powers allowed to men, he plummets from the sky like Icarus, but unlike that mythical figure, Joe drowns when he lands, not in the sea, but in the outhouse pit. Web, like Joe, leads both the life of an ordinary man and of a hero. He is very human, afraid of spiders and lizards in his sleeping bag, queasy of stomach on the flatboat. Yet, he is the same man who also makes love to Anna Yellowbird while they are airborne, caught up in a tornado. Jeremy Sadness is at once inadequate lover, unsuccessful grad student and incompetent lecturer, but his death is that of a supernatural hero; he leaps off a bridge with the women he loves and never lands.

Part of the hero's experience is love and, for Kroetsch, love is too terrifying, beautiful, and mysterious to be conveyed by realism alone. He needs elements absurd, romantic, and realistic to express his vision of love, women, and sex as domestic, yet mystical, supernatural, utterly grotesque. The women in his novels have an attraction that is unnatural, even supernatural. Therefore, in his later works, Kroetsch depicts them as witches, Circes, and goddesses. Marie Eshpeter, a witch who uses black magic to keep Hazard prisoner on her farm, and Vera Lang, a woman whose perfect beauty drives Marvin Straw mad, a bee goddess who scorns the love of men and hides her unearthly beauty behind a bee veil, these two women are the most blatant examples. However, Vera's mother and sisters, along with Martha Proudfoot, Anna Yellowbird, America, and her sister, all are larger than life.

Kroetsch tests the limits of realism by portraying such a woman in *The Words of my Roaring*. Helen, like Backstrom, is out of place in a realistic novel, and Kroetsch has to transfer this pair of lovers into a romantic setting, the doctor's garden, a world apart. This shift from realism to romance puts a strain on the novel; in later works, Kroetsch has found a mode that allows for all possibilities. He can, and does, go to any extreme to depict the sexual act as a mystical, transcendental experience.

For the other woman in *The Words of My Roaring*, Elaine, Backstrom's wife, realism is a perfect fit. There is nothing extraordinary about her. But although she and her world are complements, we are unsatisfied, nevertheless. We feel the same way about the manipulative wife in Kroetsch's short story, ''That Yellow Prairie Sky.'' Kroetsch conveys the sense of a deep hostility between husband and wife in both works, yet at the same time, we understand there is some powerful attraction involved as well. This love-hate relationship somehow cannot be articulated, and in both the short story and the novel, Kroetsch resorts to ironic understatement to convey obliquely what cannot be expressed directly in a realistic mode. Once he rejects realism, and can move to extremes, this love-hate relationship can be formulated. It takes the shape, for example, of the perverse fantasy of the animalistic relationship between Hazard and Marie. Or it can take a very grotesque form, as in the case of Hazard's marathon in bed with the old, ugly, insatiable Widow Lank.

Backstrom's love for Helen, and Guy's for Kettle, have heroic dimensions that cannot be mapped by realism. Kroetsch creates a separate world outside realism for Helen and Backstrom, and for Guy and Kettle, when they go ashore on an island away from the crew and Hornyak's corpse. In this romantic setting, Kroetsch is able to express more fully the nature of this love, heroic in its intensity. But it is not until his later novels, where he can go to any length, that he can express the true dimensions of love. Jerry Lapanne and Marvin Straw are the ultimate expressions Kroetsch is aiming for.

But while love, for Kroetsch, is bizarre in its extremes it is still very natural and domestic, and for depicting this aspect of love he does not need forms that push to outrageous limits. The patterns of realism and romance are entirely adequate for expressing this half of the double vision. Like a novel by Jane Austen, *What the Crow Said* is very concerned with the marrying off of daughters. In most of Kroetsch's novels, there is a drive to complete the romantic pattern, to bring hero and heroine together. Usually, his novels end with a comic union of the lovers, or with a tragic death, the dramatic assertion of true love. *Badlands* is a notable exception, setting women at odds with men, ending with the two female characters not only rejecting, but denying the existence of the male world. But this is an exception; the general trend in Kroetsch's work is toward marriage and family life. Hazard, for example, gives up the quest Martha is so opposed to, and he goes home at last to his fiancee of thirteen years. Even Vera resigns herself to taking a husband — three, in fact.

In conclusion, then, by stating that realism is only a convention, Kroetsch rejects not only a way of writing, but a way of perceiving. The techniques of postmodern fiction — tragicomedy,

new types of realism, the tall tale, a unique narrative voice — are
not important in themselves. What matters is the new perspective they give us. Postmodern fiction reinterprets the absurdity
of our world. The moderns see existence as meaningless and antiheroic. Their vision of absurdity is bleak: man becomes a
grotesque, a clown, a misfit in his own world. Some modern
writers, such as Eliot and Faulkner, offer the possibility of a heroic
world, but it can only be entered by transcending everyday existence. Hence the concern of modern writers with myth,
memory, and the "internal" time of the mind.

But the postmodernist does not equate the absurd with the antiheroic. The moderns see man paralyzed by a meaningless
world, but for the postmodernist, far from reducing and limiting
the heroic potential of man, absurdity opens up endless
possibilities. In this kind of a world, man can be anything, a god,
a heroic lover, a supernatural being.

Postmodern fiction has given us a new kind of heroism. It lacks
the cynicism and irony that make the protagonist an antihero in
modern fiction, but it by no means gives us the ideal hero of myth
and romance. The postmodern protagonist is as absurd as his
modern counterpart, but can reach the same heights as the er-
rant knight and the mythical questor. Jeremy, who has never
succeeded at anything in his life, wins the snowshoe race. Web
rides a tornado, Hazard survives fire and water, Gus wins the
unattainable Tiddy. Clearly these triumphs are not taken as
seriously as the achievements in myth and romance, but they are
heroic nonetheless. They are not presented in the ironic, cynical
light of Backstrom's antiheroic feat, performing a false
miracle. Tune, Joe Lightning, Jeremy, and the cowboy skier who
may have transcended death in his spectacular fall, these
characters all end absurdly: they are definitely not conventional
tragic figures — their deaths are too comic — but in dying, they
are elevated to a heroic status. Their downfall is very different
from the ironic failure of Backstrom.

What keeps Backstrom a clown is his antiheroic world that
denies the possibility of heroic experience, of love, of achievement, of an encounter with the divine. Joe Lightning fares differently in his world. We appreciate the immense possibilities
of postmodern fiction in the unusual and yet consoling ending
of *What the Crow Said*. Kroetsch has reconciled man with his absurd world: Cathy, the "normal" one in the Lang family, is

crossing the fields barefoot, in perfect harmony with the grotesque landscape. She is not the widow of a man who has drowned in the outhouse, but a wife awaiting the return of a god who has left this world and entered the sky. Her love for Joe Lightning is eternal.

Notes

1   Donald Cameron, *Conversations with Canadian Novelists - I* (Toronto: Macmillan of Canada, 1973), p. 89.
2   Robert Kroetsch, *But We Are Exiles* (New York: St. Martin's Press, 1965), p. 19.   All further references appear parenthetically in the text.
3   Robert Kroetsch, *The Words of My Roaring* (London: Macmillan, 1966), p. 143.   All further references appear parenthetically in the text.
4   Robert Kroetsch, *Badlands* (Toronto: New Press, 1975), p. 239.   All further references appear parenthetically in the text.
5   Robert Kroetsch, *What the Crow Said* (Don Mills: General Publishing Co., 1978), p. 184.   All further references appear parenthetically in the text.
6   Philip Stevick, "'Scheherazade runs out of plots, goes on talking; the king, puzzled, listens: an essay on new fiction." *TriQuarterly* 26, 1973, p. 334.
7   Robert Kroetsch, *The Studhorse Man* (Markham: Paper Jacks, 1977), pp. 11-12.
8   Robert Kroetsch, *Gone Indian* (Nanaimo: Theytus Books, 1973), p. 65.

HIMMLER'S GOT THE KING:
AN ESSAY ON *BADLANDS* AND *BURNING WATER*
John Moss

Deighton, Len. *SS-GB*. St. Albans: Triad Panther, 1980.

"'Himmler's got the King locked up in the Tower of London,' said Harry Woods."

The opening sentence of Deighton's novel says everything he has to say. The rest is anti-climax; the explication of a premise. Yet many readers read the rest.

*　　　*　　　*

Len Deighton is closer to Ludwig Wittgenstein than quite possibly he knows. In the mode of existential realism adopted by most writers of male adventure from Dashiell Hammett to John Le Carré, by most novelists in fact of the twentieth century, Deighton exploits the actuality of language, the factuality of words. His writing is based on the assumption that he can say virtually anything he wants in print, so long as he says it with reasonable decorum. Words on the page are apparently more reliable, and even more real, than the time-tossed moment of our separate lives. Insofar as the reader reads, there is no reality but what is being read. That is the illusion, the fallacy and the largesse of literary realism.

*　　　*　　　*

"'Himmler's got the King locked up in the Tower of London,' said Harry Woods."

*　　　*　　　*

How is it possible not merely to arouse the willing suspension of disbelief, but to inspire reader complicity in the suppression of contrary knowledge. For Deighton's statement to work at all, the reader must be aware of the historical implications which render it absurd. However, in written narrative, words are the only facts, logic is the logic of grammatical structure, limits in all respects are determined by language. Within a declaration sanctioned by Harry's apparent disinterest, everything connects. Each naming word is a nexus of historical possibilities; the verbal phrase suggests plausible action among them. Harry, whose statement in the present tense contains the historical and therefore establishes his priority over it, speaks in the narrative past, *as the action is happening.* This then is the truth that counts, because it is immediate, past and irrefutable. The other, what we think we know, is only hearsay, an extra-textual rumour. History is re-made, as always, in order to make the present instance inevitable.

Why irrefutable? Because grammar is absolute. Even when it sustains enigma or anomaly, as is often the case in a poem, for instance, it is the precision by which the terms of the contraries are arranged that allows articulation beyond words, which is the genius of poetry. Verb tense and grammatical alliance in Deighton's sentence are open neither to ambiguity nor paradox. Meaning is no more irrelevant here than in poetry, but it follows the dictates of grammar — it does not determine them. Each part of speech relates to all the others in a relationship that ultimately is shaped into coherence as a clause subordinate to the fact-in-action, Harry Woods, speaking, or having spoken. There is nothing to refute. In the closed world of Deighton's opening sentence, and sustained throughout his novel, a separate reality prevails. Himmler's got the King.

*   *   *

Possibly because print occupies space in order to give language a temporal presence, it fosters the illusion that time and place are subject to the rules of grammar. Syntax, like gravity, apparently governs all. It has no substance and no duration, but time and the substantial world are utterly at its disposal. In ideogrammatic languages, syntax is relative, governed by proximity and implication: grammar is determined by meaning. But in phonetic print, the rules precede meaning. Perhaps the cumulative dynamics of syntax follow from alphabetical necessity (the word alphabet itself declares sequence.) Perhaps the exacting structure of syntax derives from a print form in which the letters bear no intrinsic relationship to the words they articulate. Without words, syntax has no relevance, like gravity in a vacuum. Yet paradoxically a phonetic word only exists as a potential of meaning, without syntax to place it in relation to time and space. The smallest self-contained phonetic unit is a sentence. The ideogram for chair is a spacial concept, a thing in itself. But the word "chair" in phonetic print awaits the linear context of a coherent grammatical construct to have meaning. Otherwise, it is simply a familiar arrangement of letters. Waiting.

*   *   *

Reading in a narrative world where the limits of consciousness and of knowledge and experience are established by the principles of grammar, the reader enlivens a reality more coherent and sound than his own — probably more exciting, since anything can happen there, if it is said right. We are apparently alive, reading realistic fiction, the way many of us never are in living life. God's word-whirled creation is no match it seems, for Len Deighton's world of words.

But of course the opposite is true. The success of such reading depends on the denial of self. The syntactically structured world only works at the expense of personality. A confrontation between reader and text or the critic and himself, a violation of absolute distance between the writer and text, threaten to collapse the illusion of narrative reality. If one approaches the fiction sufficiently informed, then nothing of matter will matter, least of all personal being. The highest achievement of such art, which is the essence of modernism, is to make life irrelevant: syntactical realism refines both the real world and the reader right out of existence.

*   *   *

Fiction in the realistic mode is the ultimate solipsism. There is no life beyond art. Therefore to be is to be fiction, a figure in the narrative ground, a word. As George Bowering's ironic conception of his namesake, George Vancouver, is described in *Burning Water*: "He wanted to be a famous story very much." And so, "he wrote all over the globe." His cartographical expedition was "a fact factory," writing the world down on maps to make it real. To make no-where into something, a text, and to place himself within it, Vancouver is obliged to name the world, and then become "the name they thought of first," to become, in short, a word.[1] Bowering's Vancouver is simultaneously an example and a parody of the ironic questing hero, in search of himself. Dawe, in Robert Kroetsch's *Badlands* likewise yearns to be a word, to have his name pinned to a rumple of bones, the

Daweosaurus. Not the man but his desire is what Kroetsch burlesques. William Dawe struggles towards immortality and when he discovers that it is not conditional on his personal presence, he lets himself die.

Both Kroetsch and Bowering confound heirs to the New Critics who take the illusions of realism for reality itself. The existential quest of the protagonist in these two fictions is conveyed in language and a context that insists such a venture is arbitrary and of dubious significance, either inside the narrative or without. The conventions of realism prove to be their own undoing. The more we doubt the verity of Bowering's ridiculous Vancouver, the more engaging he becomes. And Kroetsch's Dawe, his story told, is ultimately declared, like the view of life his life embodies, radically incomplete.

It seems more inevitable than peculiar that characters in modern fiction should quest for meaning to their lives through language, meaning which experience of the world increasingly denied. Even Sartre, ever suspicious of the word, called his autobiography *Words*; and Barthes wrote *Barthes par Barthes*. Both of them tried to make the phenomenon of personal being comprehensible; not to liberate or re-create it, but literally to make it real, the subject as object. But perhaps language all along has only been a metaphor. Perhaps it offers nothing more than illusory compensation for our bereaved conditions; or only a distraction from it.

In this sudden age of ours, which we sometimes call postmodern, it is equally as inevitable, perhaps, that the desire to be, through language, should be contained in a narrative design which not so much refutes or ridicules the existential quest as incorporates it into a more elastic and exacting vision. Kroetsch and Bowering often in quite different ways demand their readers be; but don't make being easy. Kroetsch reconstructs the deconstructed universe, with us inside. In Bowering, time and again, the word-world wobbles on its written axis, gravity for an instant dissipates, and we are flung back into reality for brief and disconcerting encounters with ourselves, reading.

Badlands does not insist there is reality beyond the text, except by implication; Bowering's world, sometimes quite aggressively, interpenetrates with our own. The differences between the closed world, re-conceived, and the defiantly open are evident in the different use of language to expose the arbitrary and limiting nature of conventional narrative. Bowering, for instance, delights in using proper syntax to convey the sheerest nonsense, in forcing the reader to accept as narrative reality what is patently absurd. He is adroit at deflating or violating expectations with a turn of phrase that makes the solemn suddenly obscene, or the bizarre tenderly affecting, or the outrageously fake for an instant real. One whole chapter, devoted in lurid detail to a sexual encounter, careens away from us when in the last line we discover the intimacies were experienced not by whom we had assumed but by another couple entirely, the incorporeal word-name Banks and his incorporeal wife. It is for the reader a jarring moment — stuck with trying to assimilate not only a retroactively extraneous response.

Kroetsch in a more subtle violation of expectations, consistent with the narrative illusion that must be sustained if he is in the end to declare it null, if not quite void, uses words to play response against meaning. The following allusion to a murder is effectively contrary:

> And Web's innocence would light the room. As it lit the dark that night, years before, when he burned his own father's shack to the ground. And used the light of that burning to make his way.[2]

Web's father was inside the shack at the time! One is exhilarated by the image, however, not horrified by the action. The word "innocence" is turned inside out and brilliantly illuminated. Kroetsch's language not only distracts from a conventional response to the event but evokes its nearly lyrical opposite.

Not that Kroetsch is always subtle in matters of language, especially where Web is concerned. Web probably swears better, with more verve and obscene affection, than most readers are likely to have encountered before, in print or on the street. But such innovative use of words, as with the shack fire and elsewhere, draws attention to elements within the narrative and not away from it. Essential to Kroetsch's novel, the illusion of narrative reality must remain intact. The quirks of language in *Burning Water* reach with frequency beyond the text — they intentionally violate narrative closure. Kroetsch's shore it up.

In the structure of *Badlands*, wherein Dawe makes field notes which through his daughter blossom into narrative, while Anna tells a story of herself, with another Anna, in which her father's notes are something of a talisman and ultimately as ephemeral, two distinctly separate versions of reality are held simultaneously present. They must be equally convincing if each is to prove the undoing of the other. As the novel draws towards completion, the woman's structural vision which contains the male linear quest, transformational reality nurturing the existential, proves as incomplete as the contrived experience of the man. But the closed system which contains and nurtures both, which is the novel itself, insists they are complementary and, together, form a whole. The two Annas at the end, resolutely free of time, walk off arm in arm singing a lusty song which commits them to its flow, in spite of themselves. We the readers walk between them.

The tremendous vitality Kroetsch gives to Dawe's and to his daughter Anna's, and the intriguing tension he sustains between them comes ironically in good part from the extent to which he taunts credulity. However, just as the misdirections and excesses of language lead not away from the fiction but deeper into it, so too with the plethora of ironies, conceits, motifs and thematic contrivances. The reader is repeatedly confronted in Dawe's narrative with such improbabilities as Grimlich's perpetual toiling beneath Drumheller, with such incongruities as Sinnott's car parked in the middle of the river, with such absurdities as Web's mid-air encounter with Anna Yellowbird and their subsequent discovery of the Daweosaurus. What is amazing is that the narrative sustains it all: it is all part of the story, episodes and adventures in the meaningful quest. Anna's world, though different, is no less a strain on the reader's tolerance. There are two Annas, many Billys, a lot of gin, a reversal of the river quest ending at the source, and a defacating bear suspended from the air, its genitals exposed. Yet the reader accedes without even realizing it. The patterns and transitions seem appropriate, even inevitable, in context.

Each version of reality works, yet they would seem to cancel each other out. If the male quest for meaning has narrative legitimacy, then the female remains Penelope on the sidelines. If the female transformation is convincing, then the male has properly been discarded. The reader, who has conspired to make both versions work, is caught in the middle, caught reading. The novel of course, subsumes both into a single version, one reality. The reader then is inside, looking out.

Bowering's *Burning Water* more directly involves the reader, not as a result of reading but in the process. In a brilliant series of deflations, Bowering uses the reader's vulnerability to the realist mode to highlight its fallacies. Many of his premises and postulations are more outlandish than anything Len Deighton could muster, but whereas Deighton's creation is deadly earnest, as realism essentially must be, even the gothic, romantic and comic varieties, Bowering demands that his readers have fun — extra-textually as well as within the narrative. He insists there is a world beyond the text as every turn, and adroitly makes it, too, a part of the fiction, as fiction is a part of it. And each time we, or one, or you and I, catch a glimpse of ourselves in the shards of interpenetrating realities that are strewn along the way, the possibility of the objective reader, the reliability of the dispassionate critic, both dissipate. There is no place for the bloodless, except in the boneyard of yesterday's prose (a macabre conceit, but one that Bowering makes plausible).

Bowering is as determined to expose the illusion of narrative reality as Kroetsch in *Badlands* is to maintain it — both for much the same ends, to break down the artificial and the arbitrary barriers between life and the printed word, to break through the walls of the labyrinth which language has built around us and in which we too readily find ourselves lost. Not surprisingly, Bowering's principal tool in the constructive demolition he undertakes is language itself. This he mercilessly deploys to flaunt our apparently obsessive will to accept the unacceptable. Words, phrases, clauses, sentences, paragraphs, in *Burning Water*, all fall into place according to grammatical convention. And if they baffle, mislead or confuse, if they amuse, infuriate or impress, so much the better. Instead of rejecting narrative reality when forced into confrontation with ourselves responding to it, we make allowances for its ideosyncracies. If a passage with Vancouver vomiting, after trying to quell his desire for a taste of the remnants of Captain Cook's flesh that have been retrieved from the cannibals, concludes on the entirely irrelevant note by Mr. Menzies that the sea is also a garden (p. 126), well why not. That is what happens to be on his mind. The breach of linearity makes him more real, not less. And if Vancouver occasionally contemplates the "reassembled body of his old teacher" (p. 189), that too is possible. Vancouver and Menzies are real inventions, after all, and if their behaviour is anachronistic or bizarre, or the focus on them is somewhat oblique, that in no way discredits their narrative validity. It only means that we must work at a more fren-

zied pace to suppress our disbelief, drawn to do so by the irresisti-
ble pull of imagination at the mercy of syntactical coherence.

On one occasion, with dazzling silly irony, syntax itself becomes
the joke. Captain Vancouver interrogates some Indians:

> "You have been a great distance inland?" asked the
> stout sailor of all the world's seas.
> "It is a relative question," said the first Indian . . . .
> Vancouver couldn't wait for the interpreter now. He
> leaned forward, his short wig slipping a little on his
> head. He addressed the young barbarian directly, in a
> rough estimation of the Nootka tongue.
> "How through forest it days with canoes many is?"
> Years later Benjamin Wharf would be built where this
> aching query was put. (p. 143)

Even here, Bowering cannot resist the historical follow-through
which, in context, is a jarring *non-sequitor*. To continue for a moment in Latin, however, *post hoc ergo propter hoc*. Everything connects; perhaps not always because print is a linear medium.

The foregoing aside, grammatical convention in *Burning Water*
sustains the illusions of narrative logic and progress, even when
the language itself, what it says, denies both. Consider the
following, in which the language struts and sprawls like a lexical
Mick Jagger — patently fake, ingenuous, aggressively trite. As
narrative it works — while simultaneously declaring itself absurd. The passage has to do with missing knives, table knives:

> . . . one evening, just when the orange and red sun
> was falling into the edge of the ocean like a polychrome
> postcard, an alarm went up from the galley, and a dark-
> visaged man raced by the guard and dived with less
> grace than dispatch into the darkening brine. He just
> missed two canoes on entry, and was halfway to shore
> on egress from the water.
> "That thief has five of ourd best *coltelli*," hollered Mr.
> Gransell, who was under the impression that he had ut-
> tered a French plural, and thought that the occasional
> such borrowing gave class to his galley.
> "Hang it, the Old Man will be hotter than last night's
> fireworks," said the watchman.
> "I am already heated fair to well," said Captain Van-
> couver, who had hied himself to the position upon first
> hearing the cook's shouts. He had been a bundle of
> nerves all day, and now he was glad that some action
> seemed called for.
> "You'll be wanting the cutter, sir?" suggested the
> sailor, anxious to deflect attention from his inevitable
> failure.

"Of course, we shall employ our one cutter to retrieve
our other five," said Vancouver, flushing with excitement and anger in the red light.
"Droll," said Menzies. (p. 68)

Droll, and much else besides.

*   *   *

It is interesting to speculate on the relationship between print and
time. To what extent does the predilection of our culture with
linear time and with causality derive from the sequential nature
of phonetic construction? One of a finite number of letters must
follow another, and they, another, in what may be infinite progression, as letters become words and the words, sentences, and
the pattern of sentences, a text. Could there be a determining
relationship between the linearity of phonetic print and our
various mythologies of origin and ultimate ends? Or between
the reduction of world to a sequence of letters and the abiding
cult of progress in Western civilization which presently goes by
the name of Science but has been in the past called Reason, Faith
and Destiny? Could the structure of the printed word itself bear
responsibility for our obsessive conception of history as a forward
flow or as the lengthening shadow at our feet? What is not
recorded as history, we call pre-history; that which happened
before the text. Perhaps time begins with the printed word; and
all else that we conceive as cultural absolutes are the consequence
of phonetic design.

*   *   *

While print was still the medium of an elite, perhaps myth, history
and religion were shaped by alphabetical construction. But
human consciousness must have remained essentially what it had
been since language first invaded and took dominion over
it. From Gutenberg to McLuhan, however (both are words, the
latter not without a web of irony surrounding it) print might be
seen to have increasingly determined not only what was thought
but how we thought about it. Possibly, the very nature of consciousness we have willingly, even wilfully, submitted to the
tyranny of syntax and the printed word. Bowering and Kroetsch
demand we wrestle free of print, the false and narrow dictates
of narrative reality. Their fiction means to jar us out of the
modernist fallacy (the fallacy of existential realism), wherein we
have come to accept words as facts and syntax as sense; where

we have come to think of reality as a text. Both Kroetsch and Bowering are determined, it would seem, to break us free of linear time and our obsession with the present moment as the culmination of an historical sequence, as if, again, reality were a text. Bowering's ambition in *Burning Water* obviously extends beyond a revisionist history of Captain George Vancouver — although it may well include a revision of what history is. To force the collapse of time as an ordered sequence in the reader's mind, Bowering does nothing so crude as to violate chronology — that would merely replace one questionable structure with another. Rather, through word-games of occasionally outrageous proportion but sometimes with the subtlety of needles, he makes the very notion of historical time both arbitrary and irrelevant. By fusing variants of a present-day idiom with blatant fakery of an idiom of the past, his prose insists that time has no dimension at all, that everything is now. So wary does the reader become of language which even hints at historicity that excerpts from the real Vancouver's journals seem a sham, a narrative trick (if indeed the note of acknowledgement can be trusted and they are Vancouver's words). It is as likely that Vancouver and Captain Quadra have interludes in one another's arms, as that Vancouver is shot by his Scots botanist, the one with the ''glittering eye'' who also bags an albatross which in this version skids into the deck on its chin, virtually at the same moment that Coleridge half way around the globe is envisioning his poem ''The Ancient Mariner'' on a like motif, and Blake is being put upon by philistines for confounding the linearity of print and carving picture poems, but of course is bound thereby even more to linearity as each line is painstakingly etched upon a copper plate, or that coastal Indians of the late eighteenth century debate middle-class values in the talk-show idiom of the educated modern masses (''There you go, speaking out of some habitual framework of guilt'' (p. 92), says one to another), or that Vancouver's men survive on sauerkraut (and perhaps they do: it is impossible to know where imagination has given way to fancy — but it is a curious culinary oddity that Bowering has them cook the sauerkraut and soak it down with vinegar rather than ferment it), or that Vancouver shares with Quadra, as well as tender moments, the occasional cup of Blue Mountain brand coffee. All this is as likely as not.

Historical linearity is an illusion which Bowering's zany sense of the absurd finds most accommodating. To be violated, conventions must be effectively present. The conventions of historical time, of sequence, coherence and causality, are so thoroughly ingrained in the reader's consciousness that nothing is too bizarre, if placed in the proper context; nothing is too silly, if surrounded by the pomp and circumstance of history. Language used against sense, words that violate authenticity, these do not impede the narrative flow. Events are related in the past tense, after they have happened, so no quirk of language, farce of words, will alter them — they exist prior to the immediacy of text, which is present experience in the reader's mind. History is what we make of it; whatever we will.

Kroetsch's demolition of historical time is not so much through ridicule as in *Burning Water*. Kroetsch does not play grammatical inevitability against absurd language and incidents. Consistent with the closed form of *Badlands*, time is not collapsed through reader response, but rather its nature is re-invented as an integral part of the narrative and the novel's structural form.

Irony. Kroetsch attacks conceptions of time in the Western world with an abundance of irony. The form of his novel is ironic. The journey in search of immortality, the quest to defeat time, become a word, is linear, a river journey. But the story comes to us through Anna — she does not so much tell it as mediates between it and our world outside the text. The words are not hers — they are a separate domain, the narrative world of existential reality. Anna's own story, which is not linear but transformational, as she moves through phases of drunken illumination towards an independent and separate self, contains her father's. The ironic tension between the two is sustained through the novel: historical time is merely the expression of one man's fear and desire; it is related courtesy of a woman's loneliness, which is its legacy. It is finally dismissed as irrelevant; but in letting her father's story snap like an elastic into another perspective, Anna implicitly acknowledges it as a source. She is not the son Dawe yearns for. With Tune's death even the chance for surrogate immortality expires (ironically, beneath the very clay that contains the bones on which Dawe rests his bid for fame). Anna is not his son: but he is her father (she being the result of one of his forays East). And she, in the end, displaces him.

Irony runs deep, through the Dawe narrative especially. The ironies of Anna's world are primarily in relation to what we know of her father's. But everything about Dawe is couched in irony. He is the questing hunchbacked shaman on a journey into dead land, in pursuit of immortality. While a World War rages in the distant background, he searches among bones for lasting life. He digs among pre-historic remnants, the detritus of an era discarded by time, for a place in history. His search to defeat the linear flow of his life is sequential, an exposodic narrative. Dawe is the ironic embodiment of Western man; he searches in death for meaning. He mounts history as if it were an aging whore, and rides it into oblivion. He dies of his own success.

*   *   *

In his important essay on Noam Chomsky's theories of generative and transformational grammar, originally published in *The New Yorker*, and reprinted in *Extraterritoriality* in 1971 with footnote responses by Chomsky, George Steiner argues that a universal grammar and innate deep structures as determinants of language acquisition and usage would lead to only one or a few languages whereas, he declares, there are over four thousand in current use and these are likely the remnants of an even larger number. Chomsky argues that multiplicity of language is the result of specific adjustments necessary for cooperative survival among separable groups. Steiner insists that such diversity is contrary to the Darwinian principles of competitive progress.

They are, of course, speaking of the spoken word — language as an oral medium. They are speaking of an epoch preceding rapid travel of the masses, when language was a garrison to protect the interests of an enclosed and participating segment of the species. Steiner is rhetorical and Chomsky, didactic; but both argue that language is the expression of a people, defines them, provides the limits of their consciousness, and is the repository of their collective experience with the world. Whatever the implications as to origin and evolution, the relationship between syntactical arrangements of the spoken word and man's enduring presence on the planet has undeniably been intimate. And the relationship between separate languages and sub-sections of the species seems in terms of anthropology an absolute, a magical or religious bond.

Perhaps print changed everything, but so subtly we hardly realized. The garrison became a weapon, the weapon a vehicle, the vehicle a prison; and the prison has become the labyrinth of our present lives.

*   *   *

In the beginning, before the word was written, reality could be conceived, perhaps, as female. Language and the consciousness it sustained occurred in the perpetual present, each word a timeless moment, each sentence an expression of the speaker's presence in the world. Continuity was through repetition, through re-birth, and language was magic. But after print, when the word became substance, language came to be the mediator between consciousness and the world, and reality became male. Magic gave way to reason; circles to lines; re-birth to renewal; timelessness to chronology; patterns to fact. History began.

Now we live among atomic particles and micro-chips, on the edge of an absolute night; and time means nothing again.

Perhaps language is only a metaphor. Perhaps another reality, integrated or even androgenous, is in the offing and history, finally and mercifully, has come to an end.

*   *   *

Kroetsch and Bowering both use language and the narrative text in efforts to effect a change between consciousness and the nature of reality. In their small immodest ways they aspire to alter not only how we perceive reality through print, but our conception of what it is. These are not mean ambitions, and if only partially realized it is perhaps because their objective is inseparable from the medium they are bound to use to achieve it.

Bowering's concern in *Burning Water* is primarily with perception; with how we read the world to be. With a lovely sense of paradox, the collapse of historical time is related through incidents which affirm the primacy of language to historical process. Languages that once held diverse peoples separate, at some point turned into the implement of collective aggrandizement. Captain George Vancouver sails "sixty-five thousand English miles" across the surface of the earth on behalf of the British Crown (p. 240). He uses language to turn the unknown world (from a British perspective) into historical and geographical facts, in the service of national interest. The blood red of an English tongue spreads over half the globe: Empire is founded and sustained on the written word.

But with even greater irony, George Vancouver inhabits a world written for him by a fictional George Bowering. The world he claims for England and for the sake of his immortal name, is just a fiction within another fiction. His story and all the facts that it contains are only the made-up project of a writer in search of himself in a story. Poor George. The poor Georges. One is merely an historical remnant, a word re-invented, and the other is an author who travels the globe in pursuit of the words that are already inside him. It is essential to note that the Vancouver written by the fictional George Bowering is intended as an authentic historical reconstruction. The benighted author of the dust-jacket copy apparently mistook this for the novel's intent. But the George outside the text, in control of the Georges within, of course insists that Vancouver is absurd, and history unreal, and insists that the quest of the textual Bowering for meaning and completion through narrative patterns is equally as absurd.

The two Georges are locked to a common destiny by patterns and affinities that derive in fact from accidents of language — Vancouver, a place and person; George, a word they both inhabit. The connections are not spacial (the fictional author flits about the globe with little reference to the subject at hand); and not temporal (the fictional author is convinced of the time that stands between them); and certainly not in deference to logic. Yet their lives eventually merge. When Vancouver at last weeps for himself "utterly and perfectly . . . alone" (p. 249), he transcends words to become a fiction inseparable from his fictional author. He dies, and that version of Bowering disappears into the words of his death.

The character, Bowering, has been the reader's persona as well, the reader inside of the text, for whom the narrative worked, likewise, as a real created world. But for the writer writing and the reader reading outside the text, that same reality is impossible, an illusion of words sustained by the most arbitrary of patterns, derived solely from language itself. *Burning Water* reduces the word-world to words, and restores to the reader a sense of the real beyond text, of reality as a *context* in which all time may be present, all places here, a context in which even books may be real.

In *Badlands* the conception of reality rather than its perception is the object of the narrative's implicit discourse. Kroetsch establishes within the text two distinct versions of reality: one is linear, an existential adventure, which Kroetsch associates with the male quest for continuity and significance, a quest for renewal

which is ultimately bound to failure; the other is transformational, a structuralist reality of patterned repetition, associated
with the female, with re-birth. Dawe's whole existence is contained within the story nurtured by his daughter into being,
transliterated from his field notes into narrative simply by virtue
of her being aware of them. But the female yearning for completion is no less illusory than the male's for continuity. Had
there been no Dawe, there would be no one to tell his story.

The triumph that Kroetsch allows the two Annas at the end
is not the destruction of linearity and the existential conception
of reality — merely its deflation. Reality, the text insists, is a story
told in two ways, each of which may deny the other, but which
are mutually dependent on the other's presence. The concept
of reality as a text has been reduced to metaphor.

In her novel, *Surfacing*, Margaret Atwood displaces the existential quest of the female narrator with transformational descent
into the primal source of human being. The image of her mother
guides the narrator back through all the selves that have preced-
ed her; but the image of her father snaps her into time again,
and leaves her there. In *Green Water, Green Sky*, Mavis Gallant
breaks narrative linearity by boxing a vapid central character
within four largely discontinuous accounts, and draws a sad and
squandered soul into substantial presence as the heir to familial
patterns that make her ultimate demise inevitable. This is a narrative world informed not by Heidegger and Sartre but Levi-
Strauss. In *Badlands*, Kroetsch insists: reality, despite the narrative flow, is not an existential treatise; nor, despite narrative
displacement, is it a structuralist design. It simply is; and
therefore so are we.

*   *   *

Criticism has long been the diversion of a colonized mind. For
consciousness governed by the printed word, the world of experience is derivative and ephemeral. But the conception of reality as a text, the conviction that text is reality, no longer
hold. Novels like *Badlands* and *Burning Water* challenge the logical
structures of conventional inquiry, which deny the uncertainties
born of the text or from prior knowledge. For myself, I would
choose at this point to be guided by Wittgenstein's fragmentary
and cumulative model or McLuhan's field approach, in which
the tension between antinomies might well convey more than

their resolution. How much that we mean, I wonder, has been lost in trying to be understood.

Notes

1   George Bowering, *Burning Water* (Don Mills: Musson, 1980), pp. 62, 63, 186, 100. All further references will be contained in parentheses in my text.
2   Robert Kroetsch, *Badlands* (Toronto: new press, 1975), p. 163. All further references will be contained in parentheses in my text.